Knowing and History

Also by Michael S. Roth
*Psycho-Analysis as History: Negation and Freedom
  in Freud*

Knowing and History

Appropriations of Hegel in
Twentieth-Century France

Michael S. Roth

Cornell University Press
Ithaca and London

First published 1988 by Cornell University Press.

International Standard Book Number 0-8014-2136-5
Library of Congress Catalog Card Number 87-47870
Printed in the United States of America
Librarians: Library of Congress cataloging information appears on the last page of the book.

The paper in this book is acid-free and meets the guidelines for permanence and durability of the Committee on Production Guidelines for Book Longevity of the Council on Library Resources.

For Laurence

Contents

Contents

Preface

From the 1930s through the postwar period in France, Hegelian philosophers such as Jean Hyppolite, Alexandre Kojève, and Eric Weil
turned to history as the source of truths and criteria of judgment.
They explored how a philosophy of history could serve as the foundation for understanding the modern world and for providing insight
into how that world might be changed for the better. They forged
connections between history and knowing as a means of confronting
key theoretical problems and of engaging contemporary political concerns. All three began publishing in the 1930s, and Hyppolite and
Weil taught philosophy in France after World War II. Kojève, leader
of a famous seminar on Hegel in the 1930s, continued to write philosophy after the war but spent much of his time working for the
French government on problems of economic development.

By the mid-1950s, however, all three thinkers had withdrawn from
the historical in search of a more secure, or more hopeful, subject for
reflection. Hegelian historicizing declined with the loss of faith in
the meaningfulness of history. Contemporary events seemed to undermine even the thought of heroic or radical political change, and
the development of sophisticated methodologies of the synchronic in
linguistics, anthropology, and cybernetics legitimated a retreat from
the historical.

I have chosen to study the Hegelians because their work illuminates
the power and the limitation of the philosophic approach to history.
In the development of their philosophies, moreover, we can see one
of the crucial transformations in modern intellectual history: the shift

from a concern with questions of significance to a concern with questions of use or function, from "What does our history mean?" or "How can we make sense of our past?" to "How does our history work?" or "How is our past put together?" This shift moves us away from interpretations of our past which generate stories that can guide and legitimate our actions, and toward analyses (or even deconstructions) that show how particular versions of our past serve specific interests, powers, or desires. The full implications of this transformation are still not clear, as they form part of our cultural present. My study of the French Hegelians is intended to clarify the significance of the contemporary retreat from questions of significance (especially, though not exclusively, in France), by providing some of the material necessary for situating our cultural moment in relation to its intellectual antecedents.

This book, then, is a re-collection of the Hegelian approach to history and of the transformation within the modern appropriation of Hegel. It should not be read as an expression of nostalgia for a mode of thought which has fallen by the wayside over the last twenty-five years as structuralism and poststructuralism have challenged the philosophy of history and even the usefulness of making meaning out of historical change. The questions that Hyppolite, Kojève, and Weil posed to personal and political history are not our questions, and my analysis of their work is not intended as an advertisement for their style of philosophizing. Yet I trust that what follows will be read as a history of the present insofar as an understanding of our connections with and differences from this style contributes to our ability to make sense of the questions we choose and refuse to pose in order to make meaning out of change over time.

The intellectual historian who turns to the history of philosophy is confronted immediately with difficult methodological and professional problems. Perhaps the most important of these are difficulties inherent in any study of the development of culture, most of which have to do with the relative autonomy of the object of study. One must always try to steer a course between the parallel pitfalls of isolation and reduction. If one treats the cultural object or field as fully autonomous, then the wider cultural—and contemporary—significance of the object or field can be lost. If one locates the significance of the object or field solely in its sociocultural relations, then its specific import or point dissolves as it is replaced by its role as an expression of something, or someone, else.

In the historiography of intellectual history, the problem has usually been seen in terms of the text/context relationship. Whether this relationship was never more than a mere presupposition of intellectual history, as Hayden White has asserted,[1] it seems clear that we can no longer simply appeal to a "balance" between text and context. Even the terms of such a compromise are now fully ambiguous: What is a context if not a more or less arbitrarily selected group of texts that refer to events or persons made relevant to the primary texts under consideration? My point in raising this question is not that "there is nothing outside the text," which has about the same claim on us as "there is nothing outside the void." Instead, the question points to the fact that in the study of history, the Real is always presented to us as mediated by texts.[2] What we want to find is the best way of reading these texts.

Much of the interesting theoretical writing on intellectual history in recent years has focused on ways of reading.[3] Hermeneutics and semiotics—with varying degrees of psychoanalysis and Marxism added to the mix—seem to be the techniques most favored in contemporary metahistorical discourse. Their respective foci on content and form have been enhanced by the cross-fertilizations of anthropology and linguistics, both of which have taught intellectual historians to look for meaning in places where otherwise they might not have strayed.

The form of the present work can best be characterized as "historical/internalist." This description does not mean that my analysis of the philosophers' texts excludes all consideration of referents "outside" their work, only that I have concentrated on the temporal and

1. Hayden White, "Method and Ideology in Intellectual History: The Case of Henry Adams," in *Modern European Intellectual History: Reappraisals and New Perspectives*, ed. Dominick LaCapra and Steven L. Kaplan (Ithaca, N.Y., 1982), 281.

2. See, for example, Fredric Jameson, *The Political Unconscious: Narrative as a Socially Symbolic Act* (Ithaca, N.Y., 1981), 82, 100–102.

3. See LaCapra and Kaplan, *Modern European Intellectual History*, and LaCapra, *Rethinking Intellectual History: Texts, Contexts, Language* (Ithaca, N.Y., 1983), and *History and Criticism* (Ithaca, N.Y., 1985); Robert Darnton, "Intellectual and Cultural History," in *The Past before Us*, ed. Michael Kammen (Ithaca, N.Y., 1980); and Hayden White, *Tropics of Discourse* (Baltimore, Md., 1978).

thematic development of the texts. It would be fair to say that I have aimed to explicate the "life of the work" in contradistinction to the "life of the philosopher." Intellectual historians have usually taken individual biography as the mediation between particular ideas and the culture in which they are produced. Although this approach has occasionally produced a brilliant picture of a cultural moment, it has often resulted in a trivialization of the problematics explored in the texts, or else in their excessive personalization. In this book I have tried to enter into a dialogue with the French Hegelians without the mediation provided by biography and have adopted a discourse that aims to speak with them at the same time as it addresses our own concerns. In so doing, I have on occasion reflected their concerns against the background of important changes in contemporary French culture, but only in order to illuminate the work of the Hegelians. If there is a "position" behind my own mode of discussion, it is that a historical/internalist approach to culture need not be an oxymoron.

Anyone who writes on modern French intellectual history does so in the shadow of the great wave of theoretical activity in the human sciences in France over the last thirty years. Indeed, I first chose this topic because the French Hegelian philosophers had developed a radical historicism that was in direct conflict with the succeeding generation's antihistoricist stance. Here, I thought, was the chance to understand, perhaps obliquely, structuralism and what follows by seeing what these movements were reacting against. Instead, I found that the move away from historicism had already begun with Hyppolite, Kojève, and Weil at the end of the 1940s. If there is a felt absence in this book, it may be the lack of any detailed exploration of the connection between Hegelianism and the development of structuralism and poststructuralism. Although not a systematic study of this connection, the last chapter attempts to explain how Nietzsche replaced Hegel as the locus of philosophic authority in France in the 1960s, and how this replacement was in part effected by Gilles Deleuze and informed the work of Michel Foucault. The use of Nietzsche against a so-called metaphysical history was an eventually unsuccessful attempt to avoid some of the crucial problems the Hegelians confronted, problems that remain relevant to the projects of both Foucault and Deleuze.

The retreat from—for some, the advance over—the humanist perspective essential for the Hegelians in the 1940s was a crucial condition for the evolution of structuralist modes of thought. Yet until the itinerary of these anti- and nonhumanist approaches becomes clearer, it seems to me unwise—except for programmatic purposes— to attempt to delineate their historical interrelations. I might add also that it seems to me unwise—except for the tactical purposes of certain individuals—to assume that these anti- and nonhumanist approaches have in any way been proved or legitimated by something called philosophy or theory. Certainly, the trope of sophistication makes it difficult to pretend otherwise, but a history of the academic importance of that trope lies beyond the bounds of this study.

That said, the reader may still find that the present work suffers from a nostalgia for the humanism that "deconstruction" has made *dépassé*. As far as I can tell, this book contains no implicit humanist agenda that would entail a return to earlier notions of the subject. Nevertheless, I trust it will become clear that I have re-collected the historicist/humanist problematic of French Hegelianism because I think it can speak to present concerns with how and why we make meaning out of change over time. That is, I believe that a faithful account of the development of the work of Hyppolite, Kojève, and Weil can enrich our historical understanding of the cultural present.

The other shadow thrown across my study of the French Hegelians is that of Hegel himself. I make no attempt to determine if the French "got Hegel right." I treat French Hegelianism as a mode of philosophizing and do not evaluate its interpretations and translations in relation to the German "original." For someone who retains the verificationist impulse that lies at the origins of professional historiography, such a project would not be a complete waste of time, but it is not mine. However, insofar as the Hegelian tradition has fed off the negation of a rigid distinction between history and philosophy, my work can be located within that tradition. In researching and writing this book, I have tried to be mindful of developments in both areas and of the exigencies of both disciplines. I hope that what follows will speak to the concerns of historians and philosophers; indeed, to all of us who have a stake in how we give meaning and direction to change over time.

Acknowledgments

I gratefully acknowledge the financial support of the Council for European Studies at Princeton University, the French Government Fellowship Program, the Social Science Research Council, and the Whiting Foundation, whose combined support enabled me to spend two years in France. More recently, Scripps College research fellowships have helped me return to France and have freed time for revisions. The American Council of Learned Societies Post-Doctoral Fellowship for the Study of Modern Society and Values supported the research for the final chapter of the book and gave me the time to put it in final form. Nancy Burson has shown remarkable patience, kindness, and competence in typing the manuscript.

Before going to Paris in 1981 I benefited from the intellectual stimulation and support of the history department at Princeton University. The freedom of intellectual inquiry which it preserves against the ever-rising tide of professional specialization is combined with a rigorous critical spirit to promote an openminded but fairly skeptical community of ideas. I am grateful for having had the opportunity to participate in it.

My work in France was made more fruitful and more enjoyable by amiable contact with French scholars. I express my debt to Raymond Aron and especially to Michel Foucault for reading drafts of this book and discussing them with me. The personal generosity and warmth of each man adds to the loss one feels in their deaths. I am most grateful to Claude Lefort for his help throughout my stay in France and for his criticisms and comments on all stages of this project. Eugène Fleischmann shared with me his detailed knowledge of Hegelian philosophy and opened new perspectives for me on philosophy and history. I am grateful to him for his encouragement and shall always value his friendship dearly.

The sections on Alexandre Kojève and Eric Weil would not be what they are without the help I received from Nina Ivanoff, the legatee of Kojève, and from Anne Weil and Catherine Mendelssohn, the wife and sister-in-law of Weil. Anne Weil gave generously of herself at the end of her life, and like so many others I keep a fond memory of her strong, sensitive spirit. The openness, intelligence, and generosity of these women have been equaled only by their kindness.

An earlier version of this book was read by Victor Gourevitch, Jerrold Seigel, and Sheldon Wolin, who gave me detailed comments on early drafts and talked with me at length and in depth about the interrelationship of politics, philosophy, and history. Professor Gourevitch first introduced me to Hegel and Kojève when I was an undergraduate at Wesleyan University, and he has responded with patience to my questions about history and philosophy ever since. At Princeton, Carl Schorske has also listened to these questions and suffered through my repeated attempts to work out answers to them. His criticism and support vastly improved my work, and his teaching remains for me a model of pedagogy.

By continuing to reveal to me some of the meanings of destiny, my wife, Laurence Roth, has contributed more than she realizes to my understanding of knowing and of history. Although these meanings are rarely very clear, they are never, I begin to see, unimportant.

MICHAEL S. ROTH

Claremont, California

Knowing and History

Introduction:
Between Crisis and Closure

One of the truisms of the history of French philosophy is that it was the importation of German philosophy, specifically of phenomenology, which loosened the rigid, academic orthodoxy of the neo-Kantians. This truism, like so many other philosophical myths, comes to us from existentialists, who early on began to think of themselves as historical figures. Perhaps the best story we have in this regard is about the young Sartre who, sitting in a café (where else?), listens to Raymond Aron's story about how in Germany (where else?) they can make philosophy out of a cocktail.[1] The human element will come back into French philosophy, so goes the moral of the story, when existentialism becomes the guardian of a radical humanism and keeps its philosophical lamp on everyday life.

When Sartre left for Germany in 1933, however, the French academic philosophical orthodoxy had already begun to change. Although the stimulus for some of these changes provided by Husserl and Heidegger was far from negligible, the impact of Hegelian philosophy in France was a crucial component of the new ground (or new groundlessness) of philosophy which emerged in the postwar period. The normal discourse of academic philosophy was changing, if not unraveling, by the 1930s, and the French reading of Hegel was a major force in that decomposition.[2] The protean character of He-

1. Given in Simone de Beauvoir, *The Prime of Life*, trans. P. Green (London, 1963), 112.
2. For useful summaries of Hegel interpretation in France from the nineteenth century through the mid-twentieth, see Iring Fetscher, "Hegel in Frankreich," *Antares* 3

gelianism added to the importance of the philosophy, because in France Hegelianism was aligned with critical intellectual movements, among them surrealism, Marxism, and existentialism. In most of its forms French Hegelianism was a vehicle for confronting the historical, for thinking about the connection between history and knowing.

The first work I examine in detail in this book was published in 1929, a fine symbol for the resurgence of Hegelianism. Jean Wahl's *Le malheur de la conscience dans la philosophie de Hegel* was in many ways a book about crisis, a book about history, even though the Great Depression would not reach France for some years after the stock market crashed in New York. Instead of focusing on the conditions of rationality or on the bases for the development of scientific knowledge, Wahl examined the centrality of alienation and longing to any form of historical progress. The crisis may be in one's personal life or in one's community, Wahl asserted, but the experience of crises is a necessary component of their progressive resolution.

The other forms of French Hegelianism I examine briefly in this chapter—those of Alexandre Koyré, surrealism, and Marxism—also stress crisis in one form or another. The surrealists, in many ways like Wahl, make history the object of philosophical reflection in order to show the irremediable element of alienation or diremption in psychological and social life. In contrast, Koyré and the Marxists have a different reason for focusing on these forms of crisis. Koyré is interested in the way in which Hegelianism passes from historical disjunction to philosophical closure as a system. The Marxists, of course, are also keenly concerned with historical disjunction. For them, the Hegelian notions of mediation and dialectical change are important not because they resolve crisis in a system but because they point to the closure that can occur through radical historical action.

Jean Wahl and Alexandre Koyré

Wahl's *Le malheur de la conscience* marked a beginning of the Hegel renaissance in France. Wahl aimed consciously to introduce Hegel to the French, and he did so from the perspective of the phi-

---

(1953), 3–15; Jacques d'Hondt, *Hegel et l'hégélianisme* (Paris, 1982); and Lawrence Pitkethly, "Hegel in Modern France" (Ph.D. diss., London School of Economics, 1975).

losopher's early works, which had been published in Germany in 1905 and 1907.[3] Because of this perspective, Wahl's book became a point of departure in the French reading of Hegel. To the extent that Hegel had been studied in France previously, he was read as the author of the *Logic* and of the *System* and represented at once the two great sins of philosophical pride and intellectual abstraction: "pride," because he rejected Kant's view that philosophy should *follow* the sciences and instead thought of philosophy as the supreme science to be followed by other disciplines; "abstraction," because to construct the grand machine of the System, Hegel seemed to omit all properly human elements. Wahl's book took a wholly different tack toward Hegel, for he wrote *Le malheur de la conscience* after having considered Kierkegaard's existentialist critique of the System.[4] In Hegel's early texts Wahl found a budding existentialist, a *copain* who would have identified with Kierkegaard's fear and trembling, and with the anxiety that many of Wahl's readers felt at the beginning of the 1930s.

Wahl's Hegel, then, is not the creator of a comprehensive philosophical method that can account for all entities in this world. On the contrary, the dialectic is first "an experience by which Hegel passed from one idea to another."[5] Wahl shows his reader the theologian behind the scientific philosopher and the romantic behind the rationalist.

Rather than summarize Wahl's book, I here point out only its major themes, those which played a role in French Hegelianism generally and in the work of Jean Hyppolite in particular. The first and most important of these themes is the idea of the "unhappy consciousness." Readers of the *Phenomenology* will recognize this concept as an important part of that work, but for Wahl the idea became emblematic of the Hegelian project and of modern personal and historical existence as a whole. Simply put, the unhappy consciousness is the awareness that all human development is a product of alienation; that is, personal growth and historical progress take place by virtue of a rad-

---

3. By Dilthey, in "Jugendgeschichte Hegel," *Abhandlung der königlichen preussichen Akademie der Wissenschaften* (1905), and H. Nohl, *Theologische Jugendschriften* (Berlin, 1907). Hegel's *Jena Realphilosophie* did not become available until 1931 and 1932.

4. As Wahl said in an interview with Pitkethly, "Hegel in Modern France," 382.

5. Jean Wahl, *Le malheur de la conscience dans la philosophie de Hegel* (Paris, 1929), 9. All translations of quotations are my own unless otherwise specified.

ical separation of the subject from what it desires. Human development bridges that separation, making the connection between the subject and its other. For the unhappy consciousness, though, the person is always divided and always longing for reconciliation.

Wahl thinks that the dialectic in all its forms can be understood best from this existential/romantic base. The contradiction between thesis and antithesis, and the mediation (or mediator) that brings about a synthesis, he understands as abstractions from the fundamental experiential basis of human alienation, despair and hope. The reconciliation or synthesis that does take place should produce neither a system nor a science; instead, it results in wisdom and *amor fati*. Wahl claims not that Hegel's early philosophy ends only with a romantic longing after a lost unity but that attempts at unification always begin from the *experience* of this longing. He does not deny the rationalist goal of Hegel's project, but he underlines the romantic inspiration at the core of that project.[6]

This emphasis on the unhappy consciousness leads Wahl to consider the role of a concept of history in Hegel's thought. History is at least the field upon which the quest for reconciliation takes place and at most the vehicle through which reconciliation is achieved. In either case, if we are to know anything about this reconciliation and how to achieve it, then we have to grasp change over time as triumph over alienation and separation. History is the story of moral or spiritual progress, and Wahl sets the structure of that story by giving prominence to the unhappy consciousness. Progress is therefore achieved at severe cost, for alienation and separation are the necessary conditions for history truly to continue—that is, for man not to sink into the oblivion of repetition.

Consolation for the unhappy consciousness is the belief that history *will* continue, the belief that the story of spiritual progress makes sense in the end because in the End, reconciliation will come. Change over time is configured as progress because reconciliation is figured as the goal of history. This is the guarantee that the unhappiness of separation will not be in vain, the Good News that the story of history is written in the language of eternity. The Hegelian "cross of the present" is only a sign of an ultimate homecoming in which the subject and its objects will be one.

6. For Wahl's interpretation of what he saw as the concept of a "sacred history" in Hegel, see especially *Le malheur*, 147, 186, 199n, 231, 248.

For Wahl's Hegel, then, history has a crucial role, though more a heuristic than a determining one.[7] As we come to understand the coherence and continuity in change over time, we gain insight into both the specific diremption of modern man and the necessary connection between all human development and a fundamental unhappiness. Yet structures of personal and collective experience exist that an understanding of history cannot account for and that make such an understanding possible in the first place. To apprehend change over time as progress, and to understand the price paid for our personal and collective advancement, Wahl's Hegel tells us we must look beyond the merely temporal. There we will find a guarantee that change over time has meaning and direction.

Wahl's writing on Hegel is part of what Wahl later referred to as the movement toward the concrete.[8] By viewing Hegel as a philosopher concerned deeply with history, not just with logic, Wahl was taking steps toward a philosophy that would not only concern itself with the conditions of possibility for a rational thinking based on experience but also focus on making sense of the stuff of experience as it changes. Wahl's Hegel helps the reader see that experience, when properly viewed, constitutes historical progress.

Wahl turned to history at a time when the contemporary world especially shook confidence in progress. France had emerged victorious from the Great War, but even a relatively simple notion such as "victory" seemed problematic by the end of the 1920s. The nation was having enormous difficulty with the path of progress marked out by modern industrial capitalism, and French thinkers were questioning how the nation could become fully modern without losing its identity. Wahl's Hegel provides an account of history that emphasizes conflict and alienation, elements familiar to Wahl's readers. He also offers reasons to hope that these elements of crisis, although the stuff of historical experience, are not definitive. The reasons Wahl provides are independent of historical change and allow us to affirm our confidence that history leads beyond crisis to a form of closure.

Like Wahl, Alexandre Koyré attempted to introduce Hegel to the French in large part by translating and commenting on Hegel's early texts.[9] For Koyré, however, these texts did not reveal a romantic or

7. Ibid., 173.
8. Jean Wahl, *Vers le concret* (Paris, 1932).
9. Koyré influenced Hegel studies in France largely through his courses on the Ger-

an existentialist thinker *as opposed to* the systematic philosopher of the *Logic* and the *Encyclopaedia*. On the contrary, Koyré saw the early texts as continuous with the mature work, as an indication of what needed to be systematized. Without the System, Koyré believed, Hegel's "experiences"—the term is Wahl's—would have no interest for us at all.[10]

This is not to say that Koyré denies the importance of the unhappy consciousness in Hegel's work. Koyré, too, emphasizes that philosophy grows out of alienation and the painful experience of separation. For him, philosophy enters a society when traditional avenues for unifying diverse beliefs and practices are blocked, when the meaning of the common language is becoming increasingly unclear. Philosophy is born of disintegration, but as a result of this heritage it seeks a totalization, a harmony in reason as a replacement for the lost coherence of faith. Thus the impulse toward totalization is not simply the effort to make the world conform to a principle that allows no heterogeneity. On the contrary, the experience of crisis, the felt absence of wholeness, is what gives rise to philosophy, "that which produces and realizes reason." The object of this production is closure in a significant—but not, and not to be confused with, a homogeneous—whole, the coherence of a system.[11]

Whereas Wahl's Hegel ultimately seeks reconciliation in the promise of divine mediation between subject and object, Koyré's Hegel looks to Reason for the coherence that is felt as a painful absence in the life of the individual or of the community. When Koyré's Hegel looks to Reason, he looks to humanity, to history. If Wahl's interpretation is existential and theological, then Koyré's Hegel is historical and anthropological. For Wahl, that is, the story of progress is written in the language of eternity, whereas for Koyré that story makes sense only if it is told in human—temporal or historical—

---

man tradition of speculative thought at the Ecole des Hautes Etudes, and also by three major articles published in the 1930s: "Rapport sur l'état des études hégéliennes en France" (1930), "Note sur la langue et la terminologie hégéliennes" (1931), and "Hegel à Iéna" (1934). All three articles are reprinted in Koyré's *Etudes d'histoire de la pensée philosophique* (Paris, 1961, 1971). Koyré is not a Hegelian philosopher but rather is stimulated by Hegel's Jena texts, which became available in the early 1930s. Some of the differences between his emphasis and Wahl's can be ascribed to the fact that these texts were not available when Wahl wrote his study.

10. Koyré, "Hegel à Iéna," *Etudes*, 151 and n. 1.

11. Ibid., 155.

discourse.[12] Koyré's reading is based on a detailed consideration of Hegel's conception of time. Hegel's great originality, Koyré tells us, is in developing a concept of time which gives primacy to the future. The meaning of a now is contained in its future and in the relation of that future to the past of the now. Hegel gives us, first and foremost, a conception of *human* time, because we humans are beings who determine our present by our orientation—hope, expectation, work— toward the future and by the connection we see between that future and our past. Thus Koyré's reading of Hegel, although it does not ignore the influence of religious thinkers on the philosopher's development, focuses on the secular, historical, and humanistic thrust of his work. Koyré concludes:

> Hegelian time is, above all, a human time, the time of man, himself this strange being who "is what he is not and is not what he is"; the being who denies himself in what he is in favor of what he is not, or is not yet; the being who, starting from the present, negates it, attempting to accomplish himself in the future, who lives for the future, finding there, or at least searching there, for his truth; the being who exists only in this constant transformation of the future into the "now," and who stops being the day when there is no longer a future . . . everything has already happened, when everything is already accomplished. And it is because Hegelian time is *human* that it is also dialectical, since because it is one and the other it is essentially a historical time.[13]

For Koyré's Hegel, history has more than a heuristic value. Knowledge of things human is a product of our ability to understand the connection of a present to its future and to its past. Indeed, knowledge of the human *means* understanding the place of the human in the closure provided by the total development of history.

---

12. Wahl and Koyré, like Hyppolite, Merleau-Ponty, Kojève, and Weil, at some point identify history and progress and give primacy to the future in their analysis of historical thinking. In my discussion of the Hegelians I follow them by using "history" to refer to future- or goal-oriented change over time. I do not here consider whether an idea of history independent of any notion of progress has been (or could be) coherently established, although my final chapter displays the difficulties that two postmodern writers encounter in leaving behind the problematic of progress.

13. Ibid., 177. Although Koyré was in no sense a Heideggerian philosopher, the concept of time that he found in Hegel had significant similarities to the analysis of time in *Sein und Zeit*. Heidegger himself saw in Hegel's philosophy a notion of temporality very much opposed to his own: see *Sein und Zeit*, sec. 82.

French Hegelianism attempted to steer a course between the positions that Wahl and Koyré developed. Hyppolite would pose to Wahl questions about the real value of history and of human action as such, given its dependence on an atemporal, nonhuman End. Although he privileged "history" in his own reading of Hegel, Hyppolite never fully accepted Koyré's anthropologism. The primacy of a future devoid of any suprahistorical dimension was, for Hyppolite, the primacy of uncertainty, a threatening uncertainty that history alone can neither guard against nor dissolve.

Kojève, on the other hand, would follow in the footsteps of Koyré, embracing Koyré's anthropologism, as well as his analysis of Hegelian time. For Kojève, however, the absence of a suprahistorical guarantee for a configuration of history as progress did not result in uncertainty. On the contrary, history itself offered a guarantee of universal significance once it became clear that nothing substantially new would occur. By the late 1940s Kojève was trying to articulate this clarity within an ironic discourse.

Weil, too, started with the radical anthropolization of Hegelian thought which is in accordance with Koyré's analysis of time. Unlike Kojève, however, Weil accepted the uncertainty that comes with giving primacy to the future. For Weil, this uncertainty was a crucial component of a culture that had renounced violence in favor of discourse. By the 1950s, though, Weil was looking for a framework for this uncertainty, a guarantee that the renunciation of violence was not in vain. Here we see shades of Wahl, although Weil's turn was specifically toward a neo-Kantian understanding of morality.

Although both Wahl and Koyré became important figures in French intellectual life, their early studies were far from the work being done in mainstream French academic philosophy. On the contrary, their writings were among the first breakthroughs against a general hostility toward Hegel that dated back to the philosopher's own time.[14] After World War I academic philosophy in France was dominated by a transcendental idealism, or neo-Kantianism, whose main proponent was Leon Brunschvicg. For Brunschvicg, all of traditional metaphysics worth saving could be reduced to a theory of knowledge, and history

14. d'Hondt, *Hegel et l'hégélianisme*, 49–54. The exceptions to the rule of hostility are underlined by Michael Kelly, "Hegel in France to 1940: A Bibliographical Essay," *Journal of European Studies* II (1981), 29–52.

was important for philosophy insofar as one could see scientific progress in it. Progress in science was the model for all forms of advancement. The chief obstacles to scientific and spiritual development, for Brunschvicg, were egocentric judgments or unfounded prejudices. By the 1930s, however, such obstacles, important though they might have been on an abstract level, hardly seemed the most threatening elements on the historical horizon.[15]

Many students in the 1930s agreed with Koyré and Wahl that the neo-Kantian approach to history through a study of the development of scientific thought missed the crucial components in the world. In the 1930s competing political forces were fighting to define progress, but the crucial arena of this fight had little to do with epistemology. Simone de Beauvoir complained that the neo-Kantian perspective ignored the "adventure of humanity," while Sartre and Merleau-Ponty agreed that the epistemological approach was a form of "high-altitude thinking" that failed to confront the concrete world.[16] It was in Germany they found a philosophic movement which seemed to be born of the desire to make sense of that world. The phenomenology of Husserl and its existentialist development by Heidegger attracted many young philosophers from France, most notably Sartre, Merleau-Ponty, and Aron. Koyré himself studied philosophy in Heidelberg before coming to Paris, and the discussion in Heidegger's *Sein und Zeit* of Hegel's understanding of temporality was a crucial aspect of the background for Koyré's article on the same subject. By the 1930s Koyré was coeditor of *Recherches philosophiques*, an annual journal whose central aim was to introduce German philosophy to the French.

In Germany, and later in France, the development of phenomenology and existentialism was a rebellion against the neo-Kantian reduction of philosophy to epistemology. Husserl's call to return to "things themselves" and Heidegger's ontological investigations of being-in-the-world were attempts to open philosophy to questions that the problems of scientific knowledge did not traditionally raise.[17]

---

15. See René Boirel, *Brunschvicg: Sa vie, son oeuvre* (Paris, 1964), 31.

16. Simone de Beauvoir, *Memoirs of a Dutiful Daughter*, trans. J. Kirkup (New York, 1959), 243, and Jean-Paul Sartre, *Situations*, trans. Benita Eisler (Greenwich, Conn., 1965), 158.

17. The debate between Cassirer and Heidegger at Davos in 1929 revealed the extreme differences between the style and substance of neo-Kantianism and existential phenomenology. I return in Chapter 2 to Heidegger's contribution at Davos.

The resurgence of Hegelianism in France was a facet of this opening of philosophy insofar as the French Hegelians saw scientific knowing as only one aspect of the development of Spirit, one way in which history was made by humanity. Whereas the neo-Kantians consigned most of history to the domain of the irrational, the Hegelians saw history as the development of Reason itself. Thus, for the Hegelians in France, history became important not only as the temporal container of scientific progress, but also as the fundamental dimension of our effort to make the world our own.

The French revival of interest in Hegelian philosophy was not confined to the academic world but had an important place in more overtly political domains. Surrealists and Marxists both turned to Hegel in order to redirect their political concerns.

Surrealism

The surrealist movement seems at first glance hardly a propitious place to look for the Hegelian interest in history as a forgotten domain of philosophy. The rejection of the historical in favor of the instinctual, of history in favor of automaticity, were crucial facets of the surrealist rebellion against the real in the 1920s. Breton's remark in the *Seconde manifeste du surrealisme* (1930) is emblematic: "I have more confidence in this moment, now, of my thought, than in everything that one would have declared a completed work, a human life having achieved its goal....In matters of revolt, none of us should need any ancestors."[18] Despite this effort at a radical break from the current of history, however, surrealists were led, by their desire to alter the course of the entire river, to a study of Hegel.

The surrealists came to Hegel after having immersed themselves in Freud. The study of Freud—or, perhaps more accurately, personal experiences with certain psychoanalytic texts—gave these artists a richer sense of the irrational and the daemonic, of what they took to be the underside of repressive, bourgeois cultural life. In a word, they thought they had discovered the reservoirs of desire untapped by mod-

18. André Breton, *Manifestes du surréalisme*, ed. Jean-Jacques Pauvert (Paris, 1972), 136.

ern capitalist society.[19] Freud and other depth psychologists must have known about these wells of instinct also, but they were too attached to the security of the surface or conscious life to permit any seepage—let alone the floods demanded by the surrealists—of the irrational into daily life. The surrealists did not have such attachments and so were ready to open the gates to the sources of energy and power.

By the late 1920s, however, surrealists were asking themselves how they were going to channel the waters of desire so as to change the forces that had managed to repress desire so well. Freud was content to point out the opposition between desire and reality and to identify the mechanism used to maintain that opposition, and he seemed less than helpful. But how to change social reality so as to bring the opposites together? How to break down what Freud seemed to think was a necessary, if not a natural, conflict?

For answers to these questions Breton turned to Hegel, whose *Logic* he read as an almost heroic attempt to think through the reconciliation of opposites. The dialectic for Breton was a technique for bringing together apparent irreconcilables.[20] Hegel seemed to offer an opportunity to escape the nihilism or narcissism that was the major legacy of "life in the depths." Breton hoped that the power of the Hegelian dialectic to overcome Freudian dualisms would allow the surrealists to reconnect to political life, to pump desire into a history-yet-to-be-made.

The story of the failure of this reconnection is well-known and need not be recounted here.[21] I emphasize only that Hegel seemed to offer the surrealists a bridge from the world of instinct to the world of politics. Hegel's promise was to connect psychology with history, to integrate the subjective realm of the individual with the objective realm of social action. Breton, moreover, did not think that Hegel himself had fulfilled his promise in his mature work. Like Wahl, and unlike Koyré, Breton claimed that the experience of the dialectic had

19. See Anna Balakian, *Surrealism: The Road to the Absolute* (New York, 1959), 100–101; Maurice Nadeau, *Histoire du surréalisme* (Paris, 1964), 20, 76, 157, 186; and Breton, *Manifestes*, 28, 48, 146–147, 165.

20. See Balakian, *Surrealism*, 108, and Ferdinand Alquié, "Humanisme surréaliste et humanisme existentialiste," in *L'homme, le monde, l'histoire* (Paris, 1948), 153.

21. See Nadeau, *Histoire du surréalisme*, and Robert S. Short, "The Politics of Surrealism, 1920–1936," *Journal of Contemporary History* 1, no. 2 (1966), 3–25.

to be isolated from the *avortement colossal* of the System in order to grasp Hegel's most important contributions.[22] Breton, like young French Marxists, saw the dialectic as a technique for thinking about the possibilities of revolutionary change, while he condemned the System as a reactionary attempt at totalization or closure. Such a critique of totalization had begun shortly after Hegel's death, and it has been repeated many times since 1945.[23]

Marxism

The surrealists were, of course, only a small group within the fragmented French political scene of the 1920s and 1930s. The deep disappointment with the fruits of the victory of 1918, and the quest for some form of national identity in the face of rapid international industrialization helped push French political life away from a consensus of the center. On the one hand, the international socioeconomic order built after the war and against the Russians was culturally repulsive to both leftists and rightists, for whom it was a form of modernization that meant Americanization. On the other hand, a refusal to participate in this order could mean the further decline of France on the world scene, so that the nation would lose not only its power but its respectability. Political radicalism feeds on such times, and there appeared a plethora of Marxist groups devoted at least as much to theoretical speculation as to political action.

French Marxism was, of course, stimulated greatly by the revolution in Russia. For many intellectuals, the revolution represented a great experiment, but it was not at all clear how the results of this experiment were to be relevant to French politics. The Russian revolution aroused at once hope and fear; hope, because it pointed to the possibility of radical, even heroic, change; fear, because even a revolutionary movement could become slavish in its repetition of

22. Breton, *Manifestes*, 148–149.
23. On the connection between surrealism, Marxism, and Hegelianism in France, see Martin Jay, *Marxism and Totality: The Adventures of a Concept from Lukács to Habermas* (Berkeley, Calif., 1984), 276–299. Jay focuses on Henri Lefebvre. For a more detailed account of Lefebvre and his context, see Fred Burkhard, "Priests and Jesters: Henri Lefebvre, the 'Philosophies' Gang, and French Marxism between the Wars" (Ph.D. diss., University of Wisconsin, Madison, 1986).

formulas inappropriate to the particular conditions of French political life.[24]

During the twenties and thirties, new translations of Marx's work, as well as the discovery of some of his early manuscripts, further stimulated theoretical work in French Marxism. Between 1925 and 1940 the complete works of Marx and Engels were published in French in an inexpensive, popular form. More important for our purposes, the 1844 manuscripts were published, piecemeal, between 1929 and 1937. These texts highlight the connection between Hegel and Marx, showing both Marx's debt to Hegel and the struggle of the later thinker to free himself from the burden of influence. One cannot, however, describe these early works of Marx as well known, and there is some truth to Mark Poster's assertion that "no real reading of Marx was possible in France until after the Second World War."[25] Here I merely point out that the question of the relation between Marx and Hegel, though even among communists it can hardly be described as a mainstream concern, was indeed raised and discussed in France before 1939.[26]

The point is important, because in the Marxist treatment of Hegel we can see some of the same themes as in the interpretations of Wahl, Koyré, and Breton. The *Revue marxiste*, which was dedicated to introducing Marx and Marxist themes into French intellectual life, published a series of articles on Marx's "method" in which Hegel had a prominent place. The author, Charles Rappoport, followed an orthodox communist line in separating what he called Hegel's method—the dialectic—from his System. The latter, he affirmed, is reactionary insofar as it reifies a particular stage in the development of the Idea and subordinates social reality to the supposedly universal rationality of that stage. Thus the Idea was used to justify the status quo of the society of the philosopher who produced the System. Nevertheless, Rappoport emphasized, with the dialectic Hegel introduced a "rev-

---

24. This is one of the major themes of David Caute, *Communism and the French Intellectuals* (New York, 1964).

25. Mark Poster, *Existential Marxism in Post-War France* (Princeton, N.J., 1975), 42. For Poster, a "real reading" is one that is compatible with existentialism. Compare with Jay, *Marxism and Totality*, 276–299.

26. Indeed, Jay's *Marxism and Totality* shows that the relation between Marx and Hegel has been an issue for Western Marxism across Europe at least since Georg Lukács's *History and Class Consciousness* was published in 1923.

olutionary principle of change and transformation" into philosophy, a principal that, when wed to materialism by Marx, has progressive implications for social change. Hegel introduced the idea of movement in the *Logic*, and this notion was the foundation of a scientific socialism that would put the social world into movement.[27] Marx, the reader is told, subordinated the idea of any status quo to the exigencies of social reality itself. If these demands were in contradiction with the status quo, then society would have to change, eventually becoming a fully developed, socialist reality.

A second noteworthy connection was made between Hegel and Marx during the interwar period by means of the concept of alienation. The publication of some of the 1844 manuscripts in 1933 and 1937 seemed to clarify the importance of the idea of alienation in Marx's thinking. The scientificity of the dialectical materialism of *Capital* was undercut by the straightforwardly humanist concerns of these early texts. (It was the discovery of Hegel's early texts that had allowed Wahl to highlight alienation in his *Le malheur de la conscience*, and in Marx, too, the alienation discussed in early work seemed to make the thinker more "concrete" and historical—even "relevant.") Marxist commentators emphasized that Marx's idea of alienation was even *more* historical—or less spiritual, less abstract—than Hegel's. The emphasis was their way of, so to speak, keeping John the Baptist from becoming more important than Jesus.

Rather than divide neatly along political lines, or even along a theological versus secular axis, some of the major readings of Hegel underlined particular aspects of his project to show their importance for contemporary concerns. As with most readers of Hegel (and Marx) during this period, Wahl, the surrealists, and the Marxists saw the early texts as representing the good Hegel, whereas they viewed with suspicion or condemnation his mature work, which was less easily applied to the concerns of the 1930s. Koyré was the exception in this regard, not because he denied the importance of the early works, but because he—in good Hegelian fashion—attempted to integrate them with the philosopher's project as a whole. This is not to say that Koyré's reading was less "presentistic" than that of other commentators. Alexandre Kojève would bring out the contemporary thrust of

27. Charles Rappaport, "La méthode marxiste," *Revue marxiste* 1 (1929), no. 1, 54–63; no. 2, 154–163; no. 3, 317–324; no. 5, 552–561; quotation from 156.

Koyré's reading with originality and force. Indeed, one striking aspect of all these interpretations of a German philosopher dead more than a hundred years was their noisily presentistic character. They had some real interest in Hegel's thought, of course, but it is hardly a matter of these philosophers, artists, and militants suddenly becoming passionately interested in the *real* connection between a philosophy of history and a philosophy of life. Nor was their latent philologic curiosity deeply stirred at this time by the difference between the course Hegel had given one semester and the one he had presented the following year. Instead, for a brief period—roughly from 1935 to 1955—French intellectuals adopted the language of Hegelianism in order to engage in some of the crucial political, religious, and socioeconomic, as well as philosophical, battles of the day. These battles stirred passions and sometimes even led to action, and Hegelian discourse offered one style of containing them, of making them the object of reflection and discussion.

Part One

From Humanism to Being:
Jean Hyppolite

Chapter One

Heroic Hegelianism

> One cannot deny here the revolutionary character, perceived by Marx, of the Hegelian dialectic. If the consequences of the system are conservative, the march of the dialectic is revolutionary....
> It is human history... which confers on action its consistency and its reality.
>
> *Jean Hyppolite, 1946*

When Jean Hyppolite published his first article on Hegel in 1935, the clearing in which French Hegelianism would grow had already been made. Though philosophical orthodoxy was still strong—and from the neo-Kantian perspective of this orthodoxy Hegel was at best an aberration in the history of philosophy—the mighty Hegelian dialectic was not the one skeleton key necessary to open the gates of the institutional love of wisdom to the flood of new ideas, fashions, and movements, which we have seen in France since World War II. By 1935, however, the normal discourse of academic philosophy was breaking down, and the French reading of Hegel was already having an impact on intellectual life. Jean Hyppolite contributed decisively to this reading and, perhaps more important, to the ever greater capacity of Hegelianism to be aligned with diverse intellectual movements.

Hyppolite's Hegelianism, however, did not function as simply a vehicle for liberating the road to wisdom from neo-Kantianism. Hyppolite used Hegelianism to try to renormalize French philosophic discourse after World War II. The key to this attempt was the philosophy of historical development which can be taken from the *Phe-*

nomenology, read back into Hegel's early writings, and projected into his later work. The problems of philosophy and of politics could be fully apprehended by emplotting them in a larger story of development. The interrelatedness of the various issues confronting French cultural life after 1945 could be demonstrated through a philosophic approach to history. Given the logic of progress, perhaps the issues could be resolved.

By the mid-1950s Hyppolite had abandoned this approach to history; indeed, he retreated from the humanist notion of the historical as that field in which we make meaning out of, or give direction to, our experience. He continued to work to show the interrelatedness of apparently diverse problems; he made the connections no longer through history, however, but through a conception of Being which is logically prior to the temporal.

What was the road Hyppolite traveled from humanism to Being? In the first part of this chapter I examine his discovery of the early Hegel in the context of efforts to introduce Hegel into the French philosophical scene. The second part deals with some of the major themes of French Hegelianism, and especially with Hyppolite's ambivalent consideration of the historicist humanism of that philosophy. In the third part I show how this historicism is qualified by a conception of forgiveness which comes to terms with the past by erasing it. In the next chapter, I examine Merleau-Ponty's radical formulation of historicism in *Humanisme et terreur* and Hyppolite's uneasy response to a philosophy that did not contain any suprahistorical dimension. I also consider Heidegger's radical challenge to both humanism and historicism insofar as that challenge is relevant to French Hegelianism. In chapter 3 we see how Hyppolite abandoned exploration of the Hegelian approach to history in favor of a study of philosophy as an expression of the poem of Being.

In Part 1 of this book, therefore, I do not concentrate exclusively on Hyppolite's work but discuss some of the most important developments in European philosophy to which he responded. These discussions break the continuity of my presentation of the evolution of Hyppolite's thought. That they do so is not an accident of style or of organization but points to the reactive, discontinuous quality of his intellectual evolution. The discussions are not intended as complete historical or philosophical evaluations but as vehicles for understanding the significance and transformation of Hyppolite's thought.

Hyppolite's Early Studies

In his first published articles Hyppolite was concerned with many of the themes that were important for Wahl, Koyré, the surrealists, and the Marxists. He also concentrated on the interconnections between Hegel and other philosophers of his time and on the effect of historical events on the development of Hegel's thought. Indeed, "history" became Hyppolite's chief focus in these essays, as he examined Hegel's own attempt to carve out an independent field for philosophical reflection.

It is in the contrast between Hegel and Schelling that Hyppolite sees most clearly the development of what will become the Hegelian philosophy of history. Schelling, we are shown, strives to develop a "philosophy of life," which will be part of a philosophy of nature as a whole. Hegel, on the other hand, is preoccupied with the problems of the human. Although the two projects are not incompatible, Hyppolite underlines Hegel's effort to find the structure of spiritual life in contradistinction to Schelling's attempt to derive an ontological structure from his study of nature. Most important, he notes, Hegel tries to show the evolution of this structure in the concrete, historical world.[1]

The discovery of Hegel's early texts made the philosopher's connection with Schelling a more pressing historical problem than it otherwise would have been. The question, for Hyppolite, was when the Hegelian Hegel made his first appearance, when he broke original ground in the already overplanted soil of German idealistic philosophy.

But what was at stake in this question? First, writing an article on Hegel's early work might help one move from a lycée in the provinces to one in Paris—as Hyppolite himself did in the 1930s. The early texts were fashionable then, perhaps comparable to a later philosopher's studying ordinary language with the latest techniques, or to a historian's counting births and deaths in the musty records of some obscure parish in southern France. Why, though, did this particular topic have more than academic marketability in the mid-thirties?

---

1. Hyppolite, "Les travaux de jeunesse de Hegel d'après des ouvrages récents," *Revue de métaphysique et de morale* (hereafter *RMM*) 42, nos. 3–4 (1935), 550.

After distinguishing between *la vie spirituelle* and nature, Hyppolite points out that Hegel always considers the former from an anthropological perspective. Whereas Schelling is concerned with something called "life itself," Hegel concentrates on the consciousness of life. Abandoning the attempt to find the meaning of freedom, development, or community *in itself*, the early Hegel instead thought that the philosopher's task was to uncover the significance of such ideas *for us*.

This distinction between *for us* and *in itself* leads Hyppolite to perhaps the major theme of French Hegelianism; namely, that the domain of the *for us* is the domain of history. One of Hegel's earliest philosophic problems, according to Hyppolite, was how our experiences became our history, how the status or quality of experience changed as it became part of our past. Hegel, Hyppolite says, "does not want to sacrifice historical existence to the exigencies of pure reason. He respects empirical data too much to dissolve it in a universal concept. If 'positivity' implied a real presence in history, a lived experience, it also implied a radical separation between thought and its object. History brings about a transformation the necessity of which Hegel will understand still more deeply; it transforms that which was living for consciousness into a dead residue, into an objective fact."[2] In much of his work Hyppolite focuses on the nature of this transformation. He is concerned to understand the ways in which we keep a past alive—the ways in which we attach a significance, a *sens*, to our past—as he also tries to grasp the way a past preserves a form of life, giving it a *sens*.[3]

We can now begin to see why the question of when Hegel became Hegelian has more than an academic importance. With this question Hyppolite examined the moment when philosophy turned to history as a distinctive field for understanding the human. With Hegel, to understand the human means to apprehend the historical. The philosopher should concentrate, then, on charting how the collective experience of our culture becomes part of the world around us and hence that which molds our future experience. Hegel becomes Hegelian when he turns the light of philosophy on the process through

---

2. Ibid., 412.

3. I use the French word *sens* throughout this book because the English word "sense" does not capture its connotations accurately.

which we make *sens* out of personal and collective experience; French Hegelianism acquires extraordinary cultural importance because it focuses upon this process in a moment of crisis for the modern capacity to make *sens* out of historical development caught in a spiral of intense violence.

Hyppolite, reading Hegel's early texts, sees the transition from experience to consciousness as parallel to the transition from nature to history. The Hegelian dialectic, we are told, was "invented in order to understand history"—a *Geisteswissenschaft*, to use Windelband's term, that Hyppolite surely meant to evoke here—and understanding history is itself a primary task of human consciousness. Consciousness is viewed by Hyppolite as the source and the End of history in its largest sense; it is the "absolute subject" of history.[4] Historical development is inseparable from the development of consciousness, and the story of their mutual progress is what Hegel calls Spirit.

Here one can see themes that were dear to much of nineteenth-century thought about history. "The story of history as the story of liberty," Benedetto Croce's gloss on these themes, clearly had a strong appeal to European intellectuals trying to come to terms with a past becoming more distant because of accelerating change.[5] The appeal endured even the radical critique of the connection of progress and history by Nietzsche and Burckhardt; as we shall see throughout this book, the ideal of progress is not buried easily. Hyppolite, in returning to the early works of Hegel, was not, however, merely trying to refloat this buoy in the troubled waters of the 1930s. On the contrary, he was trying to draw from Hegel a post-Nietzschean conception of progress.

The motor of progress for Hyppolite's Hegel is the human effort at self-conscious understanding. It is through the dynamic of consciousness that the story of Spirit unfolds, and Hyppolite's reading emphasizes two crucial facets of this dynamic. First, the effort at

4. Hyppolite, "Vie et prise de conscience de la vie dans la philosophie hégélienne d'Iéna," *RMM* 45, no. 1 (1938), 61, 56.

5. Croce had an important impact on Hegel studies in France. Translations of his work appeared regularly in the *Revue de métaphysique et de morale*. See, for example, "Antihistoricisme," *RMM* 38, no. 1 (1931), 1–12; "Un cercle vicieux dans la critique de la philosophie hégélienne," *RMM* 38, no. 3 (1931), 277–284; and "La naissance de l'historisme" *RMM* 44, no. 3 (1937), 603–621.

comprehension necessitates an acknowledgment of difference, of separateness. Consciousness, that is to say, has to recognize significant others—those things and persons whose existence is linked with but independent of its will—as separate, if not distant or threatening, before it can begin the process of reconciliation through understanding. Second, the act of *understanding* itself introduces a new modality of separateness and otherness into history.[6] The process of comprehension increases the desire for knowing as it deepens the awareness of separation.

Here again is the theme that one discovers negativity, suffering, and alienation in the heart of progress. The "story of liberty" is also the "slaughterbench of history," and, if one cannot understand and say "Yes!" to the latter, then the former is a fairy tale for those who choose to be innocent by accepting blindness. Innocence was hard to find in 1935, when Hyppolite began publishing his interpretations. The promise of progress, however, was made across the entire political spectrum, with energy and often with violence. It was no longer a matter of the smooth and easy development offered by a Whiggish liberalism. The Great War had destroyed the credibility of that offering in international political relations, just as the Depression had undermined its power on the economic level. In the political appeals to history made in the 1930s, the key term was struggle: there were battles to be fought, whether against fascism or against the decadence of modernity, if the course of history was to be steered in the direction one favored.

Hegel's theory of history recognized, and often even seemed to celebrate, the importance of violent confrontation as a necessary component of progress and as a preface to contemplation and understanding. Lenin had invoked the importance of reading Hegel to understand dialectical materialism fully as Hegel, according to Lenin, helped make clear through his *Logic* that any new stage in world history could be born only after the most terrible agony of labor. In claiming the legacy of Hegel, Lenin's heirs joined ranks with some of their most extreme enemies on the right, who also saw in this agony a potential for renewal.

A philosophy of history is also a philosophy of power, a legitimation

6. Hyppolite, "Vie et prise," 58.

of political action, and often a high-minded worshiping of success.[7] A philosophy of history that does not address the problem of loss and suffering, however, even for the successful, is merely a call for heroism at the expense of thought. Hegelian philosophy of history is very much concerned with the contributions of losers to the development of history and with the ways in which even the winners have to acknowledge the necessity of their losses (what Hegel calls the "problem of negativity"). Hyppolite addresses this issue in the context of Hegel's discussion of the Christian redemption of suffering, a discussion that prefigures the integration of "loss" into the later Hegelian philosophy of history.

From the perspective of the young Hegel, as we have seen, suffering is an integral part of historical development. The pre-Christian Hebraic tradition found consolation for this unhappiness in the Law. The Law explained suffering as punishment, as the price paid for failure to live in accordance with the Universal. The very existence of the Law was a sign of human separation from the Universal. Christianity, according to Hegel, replaced the Law with love. The love preached and given by Jesus was the promise of redemption, the promise that the sufferer would find relief from suffering.

With the replacement of Hebraic law by Christian love, a new explanation for human pain had to be found. Hegel advances the concept of destiny to do so. All people suffer, despite the love announced by Christ, but this love can help us live at peace with our destiny by promising reconciliation *through* suffering. Jesus himself is the emblem for this reconciliation, for the saving power of his love as God is actualized through his crucifixion as a human.

Hyppolite sees Hegel's consideration of the forgiveness of sin as a particular example of his view of "the dialectical structure of all life."[8] This structure points to the necessary existence of suffering and separation—of alienation in its widest sense—but it also provides some final consolation for the pain of negativity. This final consolation is connected with the historical world but is not part of it. Although in Hegel's *Life of Jesus* the function of the promise of redemption is

7. This was pointed out early on by Georges Canguilhem, in "Hegel en France," *Revue d'histoire et de philosophie religieuses* 28–29, no. 4 (1948–1949), 282–297.

8. Hyppolite, "Les travaux de jeunesse," 563.

fairly straightforward, in the *Phenomenology* and in the Hegelian philosophy of history generally, as we shall see, this promise takes diverse ethical and political forms. Hyppolite underlined the place of this promise in the structure of Hegel's dialectic in his first articles, and it remained one of his chief concerns after World War II, as he wrestled with the function of this promise in the Hegelian conception of history adopted by Marxism.

Hyppolite did turn to more obviously political questions of Hegel interpretation in the preface he wrote for a French translation of the *Philosophy of Right* (1940). In this preface he restated the two major themes of his interpretation of the early texts, and, for us, his essay serves to bridge the concerns of French Hegelianism before and after World War II.

Hyppolite addressed the traditional reading of Hegel as an absolute idealist, a thinker who swallowed up all of human history in a "pan-logicism" that attained systematic coherence only by paying the important price of abstraction from the real. Hyppolite emphasized, on the contrary, the pan-tragedism in the heart of the pan-logicism. He insisted that the Hegelian Absolute contained within it the all-too-human force of negativity. Even this total reconciliation, the End of history as work and struggle, should not be viewed as a final resting place, however, or as an annulment of any trace of difference. Hyppolite insisted on the essential role of negativity in every facet of the Hegelian system, and he understood negativity as history. Thus one apprehends Absolute Spirit only in its movement or development, in contradistinction to one's understanding of nature in its sameness.[9]

Hyppolite showed how the Hegelian idea of freedom is always an outgrowth of history, and he contrasted this Hegelian notion with what he took to be the Cartesian attempt to ground freedom in an individual's ahistorical, subjective certainty of self.[10] In this regard Hyppolite joined those who complained that the established neo-Kantianism "refused history" insofar as it maintained the Cartesian view that the goal of philosophy is the creation of a clean, internal mirror which reflects the world as opposed to an understanding of

---

9. Hyppolite, "Préface aux *Principes de la philosophie du droit*" (1940), reprinted in *Figures de la pensée philosophique*, 2 (Paris, 1971), 78–79, hereafter *Figures*.

10. Ibid., 80. Hyppolite refers specifically to Paul Valéry's complaint against historical thinking in the latter's *Regards sur le monde actuel* (Paris, 1931).

our concepts and prejudices accumulated in the course of our attempts to cope with the world.

The preface did not conclude, however, that for Hegel there was nothing outside of history. The State that the philosopher celebrates at the end of the *Philosophy of Right*, although a product of historical development, somehow transcends this development. Its rationality is not merely temporal. Like the promise of Jesus, given in history but pointing beyond it, the State appears in—even dominates—the historical scene but does so as the incarnation of something (Reason/Spirit) that does not wholly belong within that temporal theater. This form of divine reconciliation sublimated into a political redemption was to become increasingly important in the postwar debate over the meaning of history for politics.

Clearly Hegel represented a turn to history for a French philosophy that many thought was dominated by epistemological concerns. Still, an epistemological question remains central for this turn to history: How do we rank the importance of diverse historical events? Ranking is not a matter of pure speculation, for it conditions how one will act in the future. If the realization of the final stage of history is the goal of one's action (for Hegel, the State; for Marx, the Realm of Freedom), then that stage clearly is more important than other moments in historical development. The eschatology is in some sense programmatic, and its final chapter gives meaning to all the preceding chapters. But how can one *know* that a chapter is the final one? How can one know *this* is the messiah, or the revolution, not just a necessary (and regrettable) stage? Is the crisis we are passing through in some sense good, because though it involves mass killing of the most staggering proportions, it is setting the conditions for a fuller form of progress? Or is it a dead end, a digression? How can one be sure?

At stake in Hegel's sublimation of divine reconciliation into political redemption is whether the meaning and value of human action are determined solely from the action's place within historical development, or whether they are to be judged against criteria independent of change over time. Hyppolite, as we have seen, emphasized the historical dimension in his early writings on Hegel, but he remained suspicious about a humanism that closed off the possibility of any suprahistorical criterion. Hyppolite's work always expressed an ambivalence about specific forms of political and personal transcendence, but it retained a space for the promise of redemption, and in his late work Hyppolite turned to a Heideggerian understanding of Being in order to find some content for that space.

Heroic Hegelianism

Hyppolite's philosophic career is a sign of the academic acceptance of Hegelian philosophy by the beginning of World War II. He taught at the prestigious lycées Henri IV and Louis-le-Grand during the Occupation and prepared his first thesis, what was regarded as a magisterial translation of Hegel's *Phenomenology of Spirit*.[11] His massive academic commentary on the book earned him his *doctorat ès lettres* and was published in 1946. Three years later he was called back from Strasbourg to teach at the Sorbonne. In 1954 Hyppolite returned to the *Ecole Normale Supérieure*, where he was a student in philosophy, as director of that prestigious institution. He left the post only when appointed to the *Collège de France* in 1962.

Many of the themes from his first articles appeared in sublimated forms in Hyppolite's voluminous scholarly output after the war, as the philosopher's concerns shifted in focus if not in substance. There are three major periods in Hyppolite's postwar work, each corresponding in important ways to trends on the French intellectual scene as a whole. This is not to say that Hyppolite's work caused these wider developments in French cultural life; rather, his writings help illuminate them and can contribute to our understanding of the dynamics behind them. Similarly, these developments help us understand the genesis of Hyppolite's thought.

From the years of the Occupation to the end of the 1940s Hyppolite's philosophic labors evince what I call a "heroic Hegelianism." Although Hyppolite retained his emphasis on tragic negativity, he concentrated on showing how we work in and with this negativity for freedom, and on how the Hegelian understanding of history can help us see our goal and the price we pay for it more clearly. The

---

11. See, for example, Canguilhem, "Hegel en France," 285; Mikel Dufrenne, "A propos de la thèse de Jean Hyppolite," *Fontaine* n. 61 (1947), 461–470; and Iring Fetscher, "Hegel in Frankreich," *Antares* 3 (1953), 6.

1940s were the heyday of Hegelianism in France, and Hyppolite was a leader of this turn in philosophy. By 1949, however, doubts about the strength of Hegelian philosophizing were appearing with more urgency in Hyppolite's work. These doubts were typically expressed as a reaction against historicism, and through 1952 Hyppolite became more sharply critical of Hegel's philosophy of history, using the history of philosophy as a vehicle for this criticism. In reacting against humanist historicism, Hyppolite was rejecting a philosophy that he saw as offering no firm criterion allowing us to make rational choices about change. In denying the possibility of the suprahistorical, the humanist/historicist reading of Hegel apparently leaves us at the mercy of forces not only beyond our control but beyond our capacity for judgment. Hyppolite's criticisms of this reading expressed his doubts as to whether history could fulfill the "promise of redemption" and his belief that philosophy, and people, require some form of this promise. After 1952 Hyppolite entered what I call a "hopeful Heideggerian" perspective on the role of philosophy in modernity, in which he replaced making sense of history with a reflection on (and of) Being. In the rest of this section I trace the brightest markers on this road from the Hegelian to the Heideggerian, from heroism to hope.

The change in Hyppolite's work from a Hegelian to a Heideggerian perspective parallels a more general transformation in French intellectual life from a concern with questions of significance to a concern with questions of use or function: from "what does my (our) history mean?" to "how is the past (and language) put together?" The development of Hegelianism in the context of this transformation is the major link between Hyppolite's writings and those of Kojève and Weil.

The two most important intellectual influences on the interpretation of Hegel which Hyppolite began formulating in the mid-1930s were existentialism and Marxism. His own reading was neither existentialist nor Marxist, however. Rather than try to synthesize these influences into a modernized neo-Hegelianism, Hyppolite strove to create the grounds for a mutual dialogue. Both existentialism and Marxism took on a new force in France after the war, in large part because of the work of Sartre and Merleau-Ponty, on the one hand, and because of the prominent place of communists in the struggle against the Nazis, on the other. Hyppolite was influenced by this force, but he also felt compelled to use Hegel to define it, and its dangers.

Hyppolite's early concern (1945–48) with existentialism centered on the concept of historicity. As defined by Karl Jaspers, historicity encompasses an individual's connection to his or her past as that which enables—gives meaning and force to—him or her to choose a future.[12] The freedom to create or choose a future entails willing a particular *sens* to a past, connecting project and history in a meaningful present. It is this insistence that an individual's freedom is always already connected to a past which Hyppolite underlined in his presentation of Jaspers's work. The idea of historicity emphasizes that the past is not an empirical field "out there," separate from us, but that it is the temporal dimension of our existence which we make our own when we confront the future as possibility. We give meaning and direction to our past as we decide to act on specific possibilities. Historicity is the connection we can *remake* with our past as we attempt to make our future, giving a *sens* to our temporal continuity.[13] We are not, as individuals, trapped by the burden of our pasts but find our freedom in acknowledging our existence over time.

The concept of historicity clearly has important connections with the Hegelian idea of history. Hyppolite, however, stressed a crucial difference between the Hegelian and existentialist appropriations of the past. Hegel's concept of the past is crucially linked with reconciliation, with the promise that in the end *the sens* of history is unequivocal. In Jaspers's existentialism, however, the individual has a past that is necessarily bound to *particular* experiences and projects. Historicity cannot be separated from this particularity, and it does not anticipate the integration of the individual past into anything like the universal march of Spirit. On the contrary, the reconciliation promised by Hegelianism is, in existentialist terms, a flight from the fact of our essential finitude. The idea that the dissonance of particularity will be transformed into the harmony of the Absolute is to the existentialist a contradiction rather than the highest form of di-

---

12. Throughout this book I have avoided the use of masculine pronouns to stand for men and women. None of the writers discussed in this book, however, had any qualms about doing so.

13. Hyppolite, "Jaspers," *Dieu vivant* no. 3 (1945), and *Figures*, 570.

alectical synthesis.[14] The radical finitude at the core of the existentialist view of the human condition precludes either a final redemption of the suffering of history or the totalization of this history in a systematic philosophy.

Hyppolite did not fully embrace this view of a person as locked into the particularity of a past and of purely personal projects for a future. The freedom of an individual who can acknowledge particularity and finitude, although a crucial moment in the human situation, remained for Hyppolite only one moment of that situation. Indeed, the chief contribution of existentialism was for Hyppolite its recognition of radical finitude and freedom within the limits of an individual's experience, but this contribution led to what he saw as the central problem of French philosophy in the 1940s: how to create a freedom that neither degenerates into the solipsism of an isolated existant nor collapses from the pressure of an anonymous and powerful collectivity. In searching for a way to speak to this problematic, Hyppolite came close to the language of Hegel: "The historicity of each existence should be able to lead to the historicity of the human drama as a whole; to the history which is ours and which is common to us. It would be necessary to pass from historicity to history... without falling back into the banality of philosophic idealism or of positivism; that is, while conserving that which is authentic in existentialism."[15] This expression of philosophy's central problem in the language of Hegel may obscure some of its basic importance. Hyppolite here is focusing on a fundamental dilemma of political thinking that takes freedom as an important value. How can one be free if one is alone? How can one retain one's authentic freedom by giving oneself to a community? Echoes of Rousseau's dilemma can be heard here. Hegel built upon Rousseau by historicizing the connection between the individual and the community; the connection is achieved over time. Existentialism, however, provides a radical

14. Ibid., 579. Hyppolite did discuss Jaspers's concept of horizontal transcendence, but this is not relevant to our concerns here.

15. Ibid., 585. The gap that Hyppolite sees between historicity and history is important for Judith Butler's interpretation of the philosopher's rejection of teleological closure. See her "Geist ist Zeit: French Interpretations of Hegel's Absolute," *Berkshire Review* 21 (1985), 66–80. In her forthcoming book on desire in contemporary French philosophy, a draft of which the author kindly showed me, she expands on this interpretation. Here I stress Hyppolite's ambivalence about closure if not teleology, which is less than a rejection of it.

version of the discontinuity between the realm of the individual and the realm of the community.

Hyppolite, like so many other intellectuals of his generation, felt the powerful impact of existentialism's analysis of our condition, and it is not necessary to interpret this force as an expression of some more fundamental European malaise or French decadence in order to understand its appeal. Clearly existentialism was, among other things, a response to particular historical conditions. The most important of these for our purposes was the historical failure of the ideas of progress and community. One of the most important legacies of Hegel's philosophy—although it is a legacy not only of his philosophy—is a faith in history as progress. To the question of where we find our freedom, Hegelian philosophy responds, "In history." And history is identified with progress. The individual is always already embedded in a narrative that is not only a particular story but also the Story of humanity as a whole. Faith in the coherence of this tale is both a comfort and an inspiration to us as individuals, for it connects our own perhaps less than satisfying lives with the great tasks of humanity and can motivate further efforts in the service of the whole.

Existentialism exposes the dynamic of this negation of the individual by undermining faith in the coherence of the Story of humanity; it emplots the tale of participation in this story not as a quest for the true self but as its loss.[16] The individual does not find freedom in the idea of progress but flees from it. The Big Story is the Big Lie. The lie may function quite well as comfort and inspiration—that is, it may be a "noble lie"—but its nobility depends on one's evaluation of the society whose stability depends on it and on the ability of that society to keep hidden its own foundations.

Various events can serve as evidence of the historical failure of the idea of progress. It is easy enough to find thinkers in the nineteenth century (and earlier) who understood that the long march of the West is maintained because the goal of that march is shrouded in darkness, if not in mystery. Certainly, the senseless slaughter of World War I deeply undermined confidence in the ability to determine which roads

16. See, for example, Sartre, *L'être et le néant* (Paris, 1943), 280–291, and Heidegger, *Sein und Zeit* (Tübingen, 1927), Division 2, sec. VI. Richard Rorty has recently pointed out that Heidegger here repeats Nietzsche's criticism. See Rorty, "Heidegger against the Pragmatists," in his *Consequences of Pragmatism: Essays, 1972–1980* (Minneapolis, Minn., 1982).

were continuations of human self-improvement and which were perilous detours if not outright regressions. The rejection of the historical by diverse forms of modernism has been a symptom and an annunciation that the Big Lie has been uncovered and, further, that its abandonment can liberate artistic expression.[17] The plunge into the depths of the instinctual by psychoanalysis and surrealism explicates the subplot of the story of progress and, for the latter, results in the claim that this hidden tale is the *real* story. Existentialism grew out of these cultural critiques of the idea of history as progress and also out of the experience of the failure of this idea after the bloodletting of Europe's twentieth-century Thirty Years' War.[18]

In our own time, when many claim to have put away the idea of progress with the ease they put away other intellectual fashions, it is worth recalling the felt difficulty of giving up the notion. In some ways the existentialists' rejection of progress is only a projection to the collective level of their emphasis on finitude. But not only is history, too, finite, its End does not make the rest of the process meaningful. In other terms, history has no narrative structure, and so historical action does not take its significance from a future goal. The difficulty in accepting this lack of structure arises, at least, for anyone whose actions are not immediately successful. There is no appeal, and so there seems to be no judgment. Rather than reveal progress, history reveals only our irremediable alienation and the futility of our projects in common.

If existentialism grew out of and extended the critique of history as progress, it did not, at least in its most important French forms, entirely abandon the idea of community. "Community" has been the bad conscience of French existentialism, for though philosophers have thought they have found the ground of freedom in our radical and individual finitude, they have not been content to remain on this ground. Hyppolite spoke to this conscience when he defined the contemporary intellectual task as finding the passage from historicity to history, from individuality to community.

After the war the major influence on existentialism, and perhaps on French intellectual life as a whole, was Marxism. Marxists gained

17. See on this theme Carl E. Schorske, *Fin-de-siècle Vienna: Politics and Culture* (New York, 1980).

18. I borrow the phrase "Europe's twentieth-century Thirty Years' War" from Arno Mayer.

33

an increasingly prominent role in French cultural life because they developed more eclectic theories in the 1930s—in and alongside the Parti communiste français—and, more important, because of the part played by communists in the Resistance. Like Hegel for the surrealists, Marx for the existentialists seems to offer a way to integrate an understanding of the individual's life with a theory and practice in which that life finds its place in a collectivity without giving up its grasp of particularity and finitude.

Hyppolite, too, turned to Marxism as a possible bridge between historicity and history, a way to escape the failures of idealist Hegelianism through a hard-headed materialism. In 1946 he published an account of Marx's critique of Hegel which showed both Marx's debt and the progress Marx made through intelligent use of what he borrowed. Hegel might have been the last philosopher, but Marx teaches us that philosophy is not enough and must itself be negated.[19]

Hyppolite was not, however, fully satisfied with the advance that Marx made over Hegel, nor with Marxism's ability to solve the historicity/history dilemma only indicated by existentialism. In a second article, on Marx's critique of Hegel's idea of the State, Hyppolite stated clearly what he thought was lost in the Marxist solution. The problem of historicity versus history was parallel to that of liberalism versus socialism, of how the freedom of the individual was to be merged into the unity of the general will.[20] Hyppolite recognized that Marx and Hegel themselves saw this as *the* problem of modern political life and that both saw integration of the individual into the whole as necessary and good.

According to Hyppolite, Marx's conception of the effective realization of this integration—in contradistinction to Hegel's so-called philosophical or spiritual realization—fails to underline the loss that coincides with progress. That Hegel left this merger at the philosophical level, Hyppolite tells us, pointed to the ongoing necessity of realizing it, to the necessity of continually *re*integrating the individual into the general, and to the costs that this process always exacted. Here again, we see Hyppolite's strong sympathy with a Hegelian conception of history which takes seriously the necessity of suffering. Marx meant to remove that necessity, but he meant to do so neither

19. Hyppolite, "Marxisme et philosophie," *Revue socialiste* no. 5 (1946), 543.
20. Hyppolite, "La conception hégéliennae de l'état et sa critique par Karl Marx," *Cahiers internationaux de sociologie* 2 (1946), 146.

by looking somewhere beyond time for consolation through transcendence nor by simply understanding history itself more fully. For Marx, rather, history has to be changed if the dynamic of suffering is to be broken. Hyppolite states the contrast between the two thinkers:

> The Hegelian dialectic always maintains the tension of opposition within the heart of mediation, whereas the real dialectic of Marx works for the complete suppression of this tension. The latter pretends to run its course *in the real* itself. But if we considered the objection that Hegel would make to this [Marx's] critique, we would see that he would reject the possible disappearance of the "tragedy of the human situation."...In other words, it is in the *existential tragedy* of history that Hegel apprehended the Idea, and, on the contrary, in the suppression of this historic tragedy—in effective reconciliation, or *effective synthesis*—that Marx discovered the real equivalent of the Hegelian idea.[21]

Hyppolite's doubts as to whether we can in fact change this tragic deep structure of our history—doubts, that is, as to whether the promise of redemption can be fulfilled in (and by) history—preserved his distance from Marxism, just as his continued concern with the dynamic of collective change within this history left him dissatisfied with the existentialist vision of historicity.

The themes of history versus historicity, alienation, and pan-tragedism and the problem of individualism are all highlighted in Hyppolite's *Genèse et structure de la Phénoménologie de l'esprit de Hegel*. The commentary follows the original text closely, offering an explication of each section, often paragraph by paragraph. Reviewers generally praised the book for its thoroughness, attention to detail, and prudence. At the same time they noted that the thesis was unambitious insofar as Hyppolite subordinated his own perspective on Hegel to the wealth of textual presentation and explored the problems that arose from the *Phenomenology* as immutable dilemmas, making no real attempt to propose solutions to them.[22] The *Phenomenology* was for Hyppolite an authoritative text, because it dealt with what the French philosopher considered to be the most pressing theoretical

21. Ibid., 152–153.
22. See, for example, Rolland Caillois's review in *Les temps modernes* no. 31 (1948), 1898–1904; Mikel Dufrenne, "A propos de la thèse de Jean Hyppolite," and Dufrenne, "Actualité de Hegel," *Esprit* 17, no. 9 (1948), 396–408; and Henri Niel, "L'interprétation de Hegel," *Critique* no. 18 (1947), 426–437.

problems, and it dealt with them within a coherent narrative but with no attempt at rigorous systematization.

In contradistinction to Kojève, who, we shall see, appropriated Hegel for specific purposes, Hyppolite made a conscientious effort to find inside the *Phenomenology* a language with which to speak to what he saw as the major problems facing French philosophy in the forties. Hegel's texts did not contain solutions to these problems, but they expanded one's ability to speak to them. Hyppolite's was the ambition of any serious commentator: by creating dialogue with a text he aimed to raise that text to a more general and richer level of conversation. Hyppolite also wanted to enrich normal philosophic discourse by confronting it with the language of Hegel. Hegel might facilitate this discourse, as his work could bring together many of the increasingly isolated language games within the contemporary conversation of philosophy.

The central problem of Hegelianism, Hyppolite tells us, is the problem of individuality. The *Phenomenology* can be read as a *Bildungsroman*, as a tale of the individual's formation in the larger story of the development of culture, and as the development of culture through the progressive formation of individuals. The dynamic of this development drives the "I" to become a "we," to carry, that is to say, the isolated world of private experience into the historical community. The *Phenomenology*, by Hyppolite's reading, re-collects the itinerary of this development; it describes how the isolated ego raises itself to the level of the "absolute ego" through the stages of world history immanent in individual development. The story of this development explicates how the individual becomes conscious of immanence, and, finally, the *Phenomenology* serves to bring consciousness to its highest form.[23]

What Hyppolite called the central problem of Hegelianism (what he saw as the fundamental problem of the *Phenomenology*) was what he saw as the legacy of existentialism and the same theme highlighted by its confrontation with Marxism. The task he identified as most pressing in his article on Jaspers—for example, to pass from historicity to history—is for him the substance of the *Phenomenology*.

How, then, on Hyppolite's reading, does the individual raise herself

---

23. Hyppolite, *Genèse et structure de la Phénoménologie de l'esprit de Hegel* (Paris, 1946), 53n, 44.

or himself out of private existence toward the universal level of History, of Spirit? The turning point in this regard, the point at which consciousness turns away from its exclusive preoccupation with itself, is the *unhappy consciousness*. For Hyppolite, this turning point marks the redirection of the individual toward the social and is a figure for all further development of the individual within the social.[24] With the unhappy consciousness the full strength of alienation—the "pain of negativity"—is disclosed and its necessity acknowledged. Hyppolite describes the turn: "Self-consciousness is subjectivity constituted as truth, and this subjectivity must discover its own inadequacy and experience the pain of the Self that fails to reach unity with itself. . . . Consciousness of life is a separation from life, an opposing reflection: to become conscious of life is to know that true life is absent, and to find oneself thrown back into nothingness."[25] The unhappy consciousness is the recognition that subjectivity is not enough, the acknowledgment that one's own life cannot provide the basis of freedom or reason because, as particularity, it remains lost in a sea of contingency.

The unhappy consciousness section of the *Phenomenology* is important for Hyppolite because of its connection to what he terms Hegel's pan-tragedism and pan-logicism. Pan-tragedism is manifested in the description of of the pain of consciousness when faced with its own inadequacy. Pan-logicism will be developed out of this pain *qua* contradiction. The experience of contradiction leads to change and specifically to work and struggle, which make up the heart of Hegel's conception of the dialectic. Contradiction is the soul of development, whether that development be personal, historical, or conceptual. The goal of development is universality—the incorporation of the personal into the historical and the historical into a systematic understanding of the whole. The unhappy consciousness is the hinge upon which development turns. For Hyppolite's Hegel, this turning is the dialectical integration of subjectivity into objectivity.[26]

24. Although Jean Wahl also highlighted this section of the *Phenomenology*, as we have seen, such emphasis was an interpretative choice and was by no means self-evident. We shall see in Chapter 5 that Kojève similarly privileged the master/slave section and that this determined much of his reading of Hegel.

25. Hyppolite, *Genèse et structure*, 184. I have used, with small changes, the translation by Samuel Cherniak and John Heckman, *Genesis and Structure of Hegel's Phenomenology of Spirit* (Evanston, Ill., 1974), 190–191.

26. *Genèse et structure*, 187–188, 197.

With the unhappy consciousness, then, we make the dialectical transition from historicity to history or, to recall the language of surrealism, we begin to integrate the depths and the surface. Hyppolite uses the idea to show that the painful and necessary conflicts of subjective life can lead to— perhaps even be worked through at—the level of historical development. We have noted that this transition from historicity to history is made through the painful contradiction of alienation, but this is still to speak at a very general level. After all, our experience, as individuals, of alienation need not force us a priori out of the private realm; the antiheroes of existentialism are supreme sufferers of alienation even as they wallow in the quicksand of their own subjectivity. Why does Hyppolite's Hegel think that the alienation of the unhappy consciousness presents us with a way out of this threatening, but no doubt also seductive, embrace of narcissistic repetition in a preoccupation with the conflicts of the self?

The dialectic of the unhappy consciousness tells of the progressive loss of the self through the tormented descent into subjectivity. In their turn inward, that is to say, individuals become conscious only of their own nothingness; the depths are empty. The model for Hegel in this regard is what he takes to be the religious sensibility of medieval Christianity: I am nothing and God is all. The Church mediates between the individual and God, both as the connection between the two and as the vehicle of God's consolation.[27] The Church stands as a figure of the Universal vis-à-vis the specificity of consciousness, and it is through participation in the Church that individuals begin to escape from the prison of subjectivity.

For Hegel, the universality of the Church prefigures the universality of Reason. The unhappy consciousness begins to participate in the collectivity (the Church) despairing of its own nothingness, but through that participation it gains the recognition of the other members and a connection to the whole, that is, to God. It is the desire for recognition which impels individuals to participate, and through the dialectic of that desire they grasp that dependence on the whole is an interdependence. In other words, we grasp that as we depend on the Whole for our existence as individuals, so the Whole depends on our recognizing it as Universality: even as I am nothing and God all, so God would not be all without my nothingness.

27. Ibid., 206–207.

38

Thus the unhappy consciousness is led from simple self-abnegation to ever greater levels of participation and finally to history as the development of Reason. The desire for recognition is the motor of this history; individuals seek through participation to bridge the gap that connects but also stands between them and the Universal. Eventually the recognition that comes from participation itself—from the community in the form of the State—creates the self-consciousness that the individual is always within the Universal as a moment of its history, of Spirit.

By seeing history through the lens of the unhappy consciousness, Hyppolite structures change over time. He identifies progress as the self-conscious integration of the individual into the community, and he underlines the suffering that is an irremediable component of this integration. The experience of loss is a permanent part of the experience of progress. The final, that is to say, total embodiment of community is the modern state; by emphasizing the unhappy consciousness as a crucial fact of historicity and history, however, Hyppolite expresses his doubts as to whether any community can dispense with the painful reintegration and reconciliation of individuals. The state will not be the cure for, let alone the redemption of, the painful process of historical integration; changes in social relations will situate the unhappy consciousness in different contexts, but they can not remove the "existential tragedy of history." Thus Hyppolite uses his understanding of the permanence of the unhappy consciousness against Hegel's tendency to elevate the state beyond the dynamic of history in much the same way as he uses it against the Marxist idea that revolution can solve the problem of alienation. In both cases Hyppolite underlines the "labor and suffering of the negative," discouraging any attempt to break away fully from the dialectic of history.

Hyppolite meant his emphasis on the unhappy consciousness to keep the Hegelian dialectic open, to undermine the totalizing aspects of Hegelian systematization. Hyppolite, like Wahl, was attracted to Hegel's pan-tragedism, not to his effort to consider history as a totality that could be fully apprehended. For Hyppolite, history could be raised to the level of eternity by neither knowledge nor wisdom.

Insofar as Hyppolite seemed to figure the unhappy consciousness as an eternal aspect of human existence, however, there is an important ambiguity here. He used the concept to undercut any projection of a suprahistorical dimension on to the modern state or postrevolutionary society, but in so doing he elevated the concept itself to suprahistorical status. How, we must ask, is the existential tragedy embodied in the unhappy consciousness connected with change over time?

History and Forgiveness

The problem with which we are concerned is how to understand the passage from historicity to history, from the individual to the community. Hegel's solution seems to be simply to call that passage itself "history." There is no larger story behind the story of individual development. The big story is the account of individual discoveries that people are not merely individuals, and that they are always already a part of the development of history as Reason. What kind of history are we talking about here? What is included, and what left out? How can this history be the development of Reason if it is also the eternal unfolding of the unhappy consciousness, if everyone does not escape from the prisons of subjectivity, to say nothing of other prisons?

Hyppolite addressed these questions within a context provided by the *Phenomenology's* discussion of forgiveness. The dialectic of the remission of sins had had a substantial importance in Hyppolite's analysis of Hegel's early texts, where the issue was the promise of redemption in the love of Jesus. In the *Phenomenology*, forgiveness is given not by God but by humanity. If in the early texts Hegel was concerned with divine redemption, in the *Phenomenology* he examines historical redemption.[28]

Historical redemption is presented in the *Phenomenology* through the dialectic of the judging consciousness. The poles of this dialectic— or, if one prefers, the characters in this story—are the persons of action and of morality. The actor is a hero, a historical individual whose deeds, though they are successful, bring with them much pain and misery. The moral individual views the hero with disdain, because

28. See Hegel, *Phenomenology of Mind,* trans. A. V. Miller (Oxford, 1977), 383–409 ("The Beautiful Soul" and "Evil and Forgiveness"). Hyppolite's commentary is *Genèse et structure,* 475–510. Hyppolite cites the relevant texts from Hegel's early writings on sin and forgiveness in *Genèse et structure,* 506–510.

heroic action, although it may in the long run create conditions for obedience to the Universal Law, is not likely to have followed it.[29] In Hegel's account the hero realizes his own failings in regard to the Moral Law, realizes how his passion to be successful, to win, has displaced his desire to act in accordance with duty. This realization opens the historical actor to reconciliation with the moral. The moral individual turns his back on this opening, however, and by so doing reveals the moment of the isolation of the Universal, the moment of the moral stance. By turning his back on the confession of the hero, in other words, the moral person wants to disconnect the pure idea of the Good from contamination by history. This separation cannot be maintained, and finally the historical actor and the moral individual recognize themselves in each other. For Hegel, this ultimate reconciliation of the moral and the historical marks the appearance of Absolute Spirit in the world.[30]

This reconciliation is, however, of an order different from the previous coming together of opposites in the Hegelian schema. It is far more than mutual acknowledgment and acceptance—as in the dialectic through which the unhappy consciousness comes to participate in the Church—because it introduces a concept of forgiveness that cannot be reduced to recognition. Forgiveness comes in the form of a confession, and in the act and acceptance of confession the past is not integrated and preserved but *transcended*.[31] It is the failure to understand this power of forgiveness which first leads the moral individual to refuse the hero's offer of reconciliation—the moral person, paradoxically, takes history *too* seriously, not realizing that the power of forgiveness is the power to "wipe the slate clean." In this first refusal the moral consciousness shows itself to be alien to the process by which history as the development of Reason is reconstructed. It shows itself to be alien, Hegel said, to the ways of Spirit: "It thereby reveals itself as a consciousness which is forsaken by and which itself

---

29. *Genèse et structure*, 504–505. I have retained Hegel's use of male characters ("he") in this story, although the dialectic of morality and action is clearly as relevant to women as it is to men.

30. Ibid., 505–506; and Hegel, *Phenomenology*, 409.

31. In the following pages I emphasize an aspect of this reconciliation which Hyppolite did not stress. I do so not to provide an alternative reading of the *Phenomenology* but to illuminate a facet of the problematic of suffering in history and its suprahistorical redemption which preoccupied Hyppolite during most of his career.

denies Spirit; for it does not know that Spirit, in the absolute certainty of itself, is lord and master over every deed and actuality, and can cast them off, and make them as if they had never happened." Thus the dialectic of forgiveness is a historical redemption in the sense that another offers forgiveness in time and also in the sense that through this forgiveness, history is denied. The human power to forgive is thus inseparable from the power to forget. Hegel describes the result of this process with one of the most powerful metaphors in the *Phenomenology*: "The wounds of the Spirit heal, and leave no scars behind. The deed is not imperishable; it is taken back by Spirit into itself, and the aspect of individuality present in it, whether as intention or as an existent negativity and limitation, straightway vanishes."[32] Whereas in the dialectic of the unhappy consciousness we saw the integration of individuality into the whole that is Spirit, here this aspect "straightway vanishes"; the wound leaves no scar, no trace.[33] In this crucial moment of the appearance of Absolute Spirit, struggle becomes confession, recognition becomes forgiveness, and history becomes an illusion that can be dispelled in the reconstruction of History as Reason. We do awake from the nightmare, and we can know we were only dreaming. Hyppolite quotes Hegel's succinct formulation of this point from the *Philosophy of Religion*: "Spirit can manage things so that what has happened has not happened."[34]

The great force of the Hegelian emplotment of history should now be apparent. It is a configuration that takes conflict in history very seriously. That is, a Hegelian writing during World War II, when Hyppolite himself was writing his commentary, could preserve his faith in the reasonableness of historical change by remembering that all progress has come through painful conflict. For Hegel, indeed, history is conflict, conflict whose results make for progress in the consciousness of freedom. We can preserve our confidence in the meaningful-ness of our action in the world despite the suffering that action engenders. Suffering, for the philosopher who knows how to look at history, is not senseless, it makes sense within a totality. With the notion of forgiveness, however, we also come to see that even for

32. Hegel, *Phenomenology*, 406, 407.

33. Hyppolite emphasized here that Hegel was not reaching toward mysticism but that he wanted to show the immanence of the Infinite in history.

34. Hegel, *Philosophie der Religion*, ed. Lasson, XIV, 172; the quotation is from Hyppolite, *Genèse et structure*, 509.

Hegel the totality cannot include everything. Some wounds cut too deeply, and we cannot point to scars and tell how we learned from the injury. Some scars must simply vanish if we are to go on believing in the meaning and direction of our action.[35]

Hyppolite's commentary on the "evil and forgiveness" section of the *Phenomenology* led him to a consideration of the place of religion in Hegel's philosophy—or, as he put it, whether Hegelianism was finally a mysticism or a humanism. With this question he was able to address the problem of whether a coherent historicism can have a connection with a suprahistorical dimension. Characteristically, he rejects an either/or response to this question, seeing greater value in its opening to philosophical reflection.

The split between interpretations of the religious implications of Hegel's philosophy is as old as that philosophy itself. Religion plays a crucial role in Hegel's understanding of history in the early texts, as we have seen, whereas in the *Phenomenology* the development of Christianity and the steady advance of philosophy are the most important facets of historical change. In any interpretation of Hegel, difficulties arise in regard to the possible inadequacy of religion vis-à-vis the progressive, self-conscious integration of the individual and the Universal. On the one hand are readings that view history as the revelation of the Infinite and the confirmation of religion, thereby giving importance to man's work over time but also emphasizing that the truth, the *sens*, of this work is found only in the Divine.[36] On the other hand are secular readings that view Hegel's major accomplishment as having been to show that what had been called the Divine is nothing more than history, that God is a product of man's work.[37]

Hyppolite tried to split the difference between these two schools

---

35. On this theme in Hegel and the dialectical notion of freedom in Freud, see my *Psycho-Analysis as History: Negation and Freedom in Freud* (Ithaca, N.Y., 1987), 125–133.

36. Originally known as the interpretation of the Right or Old Hegelians, this perspective was shared in some form by the following authors in France: Jean Wahl, Gaston Fessard, Henri Niel, Mikel Dufrenne, and Marcel Regnier.

37. Originally known as the interpretation of the Left or Young Hegelians, this perspective was shared in some form by the following authors in France: Koyré, Kojève, and Rolland Caillois. On the varieties of Hegelianism in the nineteenth century see John Edward Toews, *Hegelianism: The Path toward Dialectical Humanism, 1805–1841* (Cambridge, 1980).

of interpretation. He emphasized that history in some sense replaces God in the Hegelian schema, but he would not, as it were, collapse Hegel into Feuerbach. Hegel, Hyppolite tells us, did lean toward the humanism found later in Feuerbach and Marx, but he was not satisfied with it. He looked for some form of transcendence (*dépassement*) which would escape a traditional God/human dualism.[38] In this regard, Hyppolite went on to say, Hegel turned to history: "That which appears to us as essentially characteristic of Hegelian thought is its effort to overcome the major Christian dualism, that of the *beyond* [*au-delà*] and the *here and now* [*en-deçà*]. Is not...the aim of the dialectic of religion to arrive at a complete reconciliation of *spirit in the world* with absolute spirit? But then there is no longer any transcendence aside from historical development. In this regard, Hegelian thought...appears to us quite distant from religion."[39] Can "historical development" bear the weight of the philosophical baggage that Hyppolite, in his consideration of Hegel, loads onto it? How can change over time replace the separation of the human and the divine, and how can progress be the bridge that unifies them?

The answer from Hyppolite's Hegel is that history is not merely change over time, it is the comprehension of the *sens* of that change. History can bear the philosophic weight only when it has been understood by us, only after we have acknowledged it, *grasped* it as Reason. Religious consciousness is inadequate precisely because it rejects the responsibility of this understanding in its "fervent longing" that salvation will be *given* from the Beyond.[40] With the replacement of religious consciousness by philosophy, people give up this longing and live with the knowledge that if we are to find salvation, it will be the product of our own work. But we have to live also with the knowledge that this work—this struggle—often has results that have little relation to a potential salvation.

It may well seem that we have departed further from concrete considerations of "what counts as history." Indeed, the explication of Hegel's idea of the "wounds of Spirit," and the issue of the role of religion in his philosophy, give hard-headed questions even more ur-

---

38. Hyppolite, *Genèse et structure*, 509–510, 524.
39. Ibid., 525n.
40. Ibid., 548.

gency: Why did philosophers care about this Hegelian understanding of forgiveness in and of history in the 1940s? How was this understanding relevant to the question of what would be included, and what left out, in the story of history as the development of Reason? Most important for our purposes, what was at stake in the interpretation of the *Phenomenology*?

Hyppolite came to the question of history because he was considering the possibility of making action in common meaningful. Once we give up the expectation that freedom is something that a benevolent god, one who guarantees the meaningfulness of the universe, will give to us, how can we act in such ways as to ensure the creation of freedom? All action entails inevitable loss, but the pain of negativity may be enough to instigate action. This is understandable enough. But how can one know that the chosen action will lead away from the unhappy consciousness toward some form of meaningful totality? To make the same point in the language of this chapter, how can one be sure that any action will facilitate the connection of historicity and history instead of merely connecting personal conflicts with false, even more painful, personal pseudo-solutions? What counts as history for the Hegelian will be all actions that *do* connect historicity and history, the individual and the whole. Establishing the connection *for us*, however, will be a task laden with great moral and political risks for the philosopher writing in the 1940s.

Chapter Two

Logic in History and the Problematic of Humanism

> There is a progress of the dead and this is our history.
> Being is the only concern of the German philosopher [Heidegger]. And in spite of a philosophy which they at times share, Merleau's principal concern remained man.
>
> *Jean-Paul Sartre, 1961*

Hegelianism was introduced into France as a vehicle for thinking about the connection between knowing and history and, most generally, for making sense of historical change. Questions of systemization, redemption, religion, and politics were all raised by philosophers and artists who turned to Hegel for keys to integrate the individual and the general, the personal and the political. Jean Hyppolite found in Hegel a language with which to consider what he thought of as the most pressing philosophical problem of the day: how to connect personal authenticity with collective freedom, how to differentiate autonomy from narcissism and participation from subservience to society.

The language of Hegel tends to a certain abstraction, however, and at times leads to euphemism. In France just after World War II, the question of forgiveness for those who acted "incorrectly" because they misunderstood the direction of history was simply academic. And the issue of meaning and direction in history despite the "pain of negativity" took on an especially powerful dimension if one substituted the name Auschwitz (as Theodor Adorno did) for the Hegelian words. Within the Hegelian questioning of history and our relation to it lay some of the crucial issues of the postwar world.

46

The significance of these questions becomes clearer as we examine Merleau-Ponty's attempt to think through an answer to them in *Humanisme et terreur* (1946–47). This work explores in detail the problem of evil or suffering as a necessary component of progressive historical development, and it underlines the transhistorical (if not suprahistorical) function of the idea of a goal of history. The importance of these issues for the creation of a Marxist theory of historical change is made clear. *Humanisme et terreur* advances a radical historicism that aims at the realization of humanism through revolutionary political action. Political action is legitimated by its function within a logic of history. The book reveals the general significance of the issues raised in Hyppolite's interpretation of Hegel, as well as some of the philosophical problems behind Hyppolite's unanswered question as to whether Hegelianism was a humanism or a mysticism.

At the end of the 1940s Heidegger presented a strikingly different account of the possibilities for the realization of our highest ends. He portrays history no longer as the story of progress but as the repetition of the essential. The important human task is the cultivation of that which makes all things possible, Being. Perhaps even cultivation is too strong a word for Heidegger, who sees the best people as those who care for, are the shepherds of, the expressions of the truth of Being in language. By the 1950s the Heideggerian version of humanism was playing an increasingly important role in French intellectual life and, as we shall see in the next chapter, in Jean Hyppolite's later work.

Logic in History

The ways in which persons make their own history, justify it, and understand it were at the forefront of intellectual debate in France after the war. Clearly, history weighed heavily on this period, both as the burden of the world war and as the potential for giving a *sens* to this past by creating a viable future out of the ruins. Hegel, who addressed the dilemma of this double burden, spoke to many attempting to think through their relation to the past and the relevance of that relation to action in the future.

Merleau-Ponty was deeply influenced by his reading of Hegel. After attending Kojève's seminar on the *Phenomenology*, he continued to

47

reflect on Hegelian philosophy and began a lasting dialogue with Hyppolite that would end only with his death.[1] As Merleau-Ponty said in 1948: "Hegel is at the origin of everything great that has been done in philosophy during the last century. . . . He initiated the attempt to explicate the irrational and to integrate it into an enlarged reason; this remains the task of our century. . . . One could say without paradox that to give an interpretation of Hegel is to take a position on all the philosophic, political and religious problems of our century."[2] For Merleau-Ponty, as for Hyppolite, Hegel seemed to offer the possibility of escaping the narrow individualism of existentialism and of moving to an understanding of history. In accepting that offer, Merleau-Ponty sought first and foremost to understand political history.

It is with understanding history and its connection with politics that *Humanisme et terreur* is concerned.[3] The book brings many of the Hegelian themes we have discussed to bear on Marxist theories of historical change and on the specific path that communism has taken in the Soviet Union. In this text we see more clearly what is at stake in the interpretation of Hegel's rather abstract (in the sense of highfalutin) formulations and begin to understand why questions about such things as the "appearance of absolute Spirit" or the "role of negativity" could stir up passionate debate among people who otherwise seem to have been quite reasonable.

1. Some doubt exists as to who actually attended Kojève's seminar, in part because of the rather informal structure of the Ecole Pratique des Hautes Etudes. Merleau-Ponty's name does appear, however, in the official register of students for Kojève's class for 1937–1938 (see Appendix). I am grateful to the librarians at the Ecole Pratique des Hautes Etudes for making this and other archival material available to me.

2. Maurice Merleau-Ponty, "L'existentialisme chez Hegel," in *Sens et non-sens* (Paris, 1948), 125–126. This essay took as its starting point a public lecture given by Hyppolite in 1947.

3. The following discussion of Merleau-Ponty's work is limited to *Humanisme et terreur*. In his later writings, however, the philosopher, not satisfied with the mode of analysis he employed in this work, explicitly rejected the political position it contained. See Claude Lefort, "Introduction" to Maurice Merleau-Ponty, *Humanisme et Terreur: Essai sur le problème communiste* (Paris, 1980), 11–38. General accounts of Merleau-Ponty's political thought can be found in Sonia Kruks, *The Political Philosophy of Merleau-Ponty* (Atlantic Highlands, N.J., 1981); James Miller, *History and Human Existence: From Marx to Merleau-Ponty* (Berkeley, Calif., 1979), 197–230; James Schmidt, *Maurice Merleau-Ponty: Between Phenomenology and Structuralism* (New York, 1985); and Scott Warren, *The Emergence of Dialectical Theory: Philosophy and Political Inquiry* (Chicago, 1984), 102–143.

Humanisme et terreur can be read as a detailed reflection on the dialogue between the hero and the moral individual. The specific problem with which Merleau-Ponty is concerned is the significance of the purge trials—most important, Bukharin's—for the history of communism. The more general problem that the text confronts is that of violence in history. How can one make sense of a history so full of pain and suffering? In 1946 this question was clear and immediate.

One of the first points established in *Humanisme et terreur* is that the choice offered between violence and nonviolence, between the chaos of revolution and the orderly rule of law, is fundamentally dishonest. It is, we can say, the choice offered by the moral person to the hero: achievement through great deeds motivated by passion, or obedience to the moral law. Merleau-Ponty asked, Who today can offer this choice? The purity of the moral individual, the pristine life of nonviolence, does not exist in our history. The liberal who contraposes the rule of law against the dangers of revolutionary retribution is a hypocrite, we are told, because that rule is founded upon and maintained by violence.[4] Assuming the role of morality, the liberal pretends to speak from outside history, from the suprahistorical realm of principle untainted by the exigencies of successful action. It is this pose, and not the violence of modern capitalist society as such, which Merleau-Ponty attacks.

The historical development of liberalism in the West and its export as colonialism and imperialism reveals liberalism's own use of violence. Once established, however, liberalism is legitimated as a natural, rather than a historical, fact, and its violent foundations are repressed from discussion. The results of the struggle for liberal democracy have been reified as *Raison impersonelle*, which is then used to condemn socialist revolutions.[5] The true choice is not between violence and nonviolence, however, but among the diverse implications of historical action.

How can such a choice be made if we cannot take as a standard *Raison impersonnelle* or some form of natural right that is valid transhistorically? Clearly, to say that politics is violent is not enough, unless we are content to rest with the nihilistic relativism of the

4. Merleau-Ponty, *Humanisme et terreur*, 39, 213.
5. Ibid., 123n.

ironic spectator or to recommend the unquenchable desire of the would-be tyrant. Merleau-Ponty argues instead that we must situate violence "in the logic of a situation, in the dynamic of a regime, in the historic totality to which it pertains."[6] For him, *the* question is where a form of violence fits in the *sens* of history, and whether it carries with it the promise of the negation of future violence.

History, then, will give us the final word as to the *legitimacy* of a particular instance of violence. This does not mean that our task is to watch the flow of events so as to discover their hidden secret. A deification of History as the inevitable and esoteric process of change is, according to Merleau-Ponty, a caricature of the Marxist position, which holds that it is *we* who make our own history.[7] History is not the new god who will one day reveal the answer; it is the sum of our efforts to create a world in which we can live in mutual recognition.[8] For the Marxist, though, the question remains— indeed, it acquires a new urgency—as to how we can know the *sens* of history. How can we know if political violence is progressive or if it is merely gratuitous suffering for a historical community that had learned to live with the necessity of struggle?

Merleau-Ponty's response to this question, unsatisfactory to both his communist and his noncommunist readers, is that we *cannot know* the answer to this question unless history is over, in which case it is not clear why we even want to pose it.[9] The dynamic of historical change contains an irreducible element of contingency. The decision to be a revolutionary or, more accurately, the effect of living within a revolutionary historical period implies a will to create a radically new future on the basis of present action, but there is no guarantee either of the success of this action or of its legitimacy.

---

6. Ibid., 84.

7. This is the position that Raymond Aron criticized as Merleau-Ponty's in *L'opium des intellectuels* (Paris, 1955), 155–277. See also Aron, *Mémoires: 50 ans de réflexion politique* (Paris, 1983), 312–316. For a general perspective on Merleau-Ponty's critique of Aron's understanding of history, see Kerry Whiteside, "Perspectivism and Historical Objectivity: Maurice Merleau-Ponty's Covert Debate with Raymnd Aron," *History and Theory* 25, no. 2 (1986), 132–151.

8. Merleau-Ponty criticized Koestler for having his characters deify history and hence separate it from human will: *Humanisme et terreur*, 102–104.

9. Merleau-Ponty, *Humanisme et terreur*, 191–192, 162. For reactions to his response, see Jean-Paul Sartre, "Merleau-Ponty," in *Situations*, trans. Benita Eisler (New York, 1965), 174. The idea of an End of history was taken as far as it probably can go by Kojève, and it is discussed in detail below in Chapters 4–6.

Merleau-Ponty characterizes the justice of the purge trials as revolutionary *"because they deal with facts still open toward the future,
whose significance is still not clear, and which will assume criminal
characteristics only when seen from the perspective of future men
in power.* In a word, these are political, not cognitive, acts. To say
the same thing differently: the Moscow trials have a revolutionary
form and style, because to be revolutionary is to judge what is in the
name of what is not, taking the latter as more real than the real."[10]
This attitude seems to leave us with no ability to evaluate actions
that are intended as revolutionary. Is to stamp an action or a context
"revolutionary" to stamp it "exempt from judgment"?

Merleau-Ponty turns to the theory of the proletariat in order to
avoid an affirmative response to this last question. He does so to
uncover within the Marxist reading of history its logic of development
and the function of revolutionary violence within that logic. This
logic separates Marxism from forms of "vulgar relativism" and simple
"authoritarian politics."[11] It enables the Marxist reader of history to
have a sense of the end of the story—not knowledge about how it all
worked out in the end (for then there would be no reason to keep
reading), but at least an understanding of who the main character is
and what its major tasks will be. This character is the proletariat. It
is set apart from everyone else in the story by its potential universality, by the fact that all other figures in the story revolve around
it. The plot of this story— and it is a *Bildungsroman* we are reading—
is a familiar tale of progress from isolated individuality to integrated
universality. The story, then, is Hegel's, with the improvement that
in Marx's characterization one has a more miserable unhappy consciousness and therefore a more impressive triumph of dialectical
negation in the climactic achievement of wholeness. Hegel's universality is not universal enough, if only because it is philosophical and
hence inaccessible to humanity as a whole. The values of liberalism
will not be destroyed by the triumph of the universal class, but they
will be *dépassés* as values insofar as they become the lived experience
of the proletariat.[12] The humanism that underlies the revolutionary

10. Merleau-Ponty, *Humanisme et terreur*, 114.
11. Ibid., 226, 210.
12. Ibid., 232. The influence of Lukács on Merleau-Ponty's understanding of the role
of the proletariat is important. On the connection between the two thinkers see Martin

violence of communism is the justification the triumph of the proletariat will provide by *actualizing* the ideals of liberalism. The violence that leads to this triumph will be vindicated by a way of life in
which violence will no longer be necessary.

The logic of history that grows out of the theory of the proletariat,
then, allows for the evaluation of a historical (even revolutionary)
action on the basis of whether that action contributes to the triumph
of the proletariat *qua* universal class. History is ordered, given a *sens*,
in this way. Even if the history of the communist movement is fraught
with mistakes and horrors, and even if many of its concrete analyses
of capitalist development prove to be false, this will to order history
remains decisive. Without it, the burden of the slaughterbench is too
much to bear. Merleau-Ponty sees this will to order history as the
crucial contribution of Marxism:

> It is the simple expression of conditions without which there would be
> no humanity in the sense of a reciprocal relation between men, nor any
> rationality in history. In this sense, it is not a philosophy of history, it
> is *the* philosophy of history, and to renounce it would be to give up
> historical Reason. After that, there would be nothing more than dreams
> or adventures....
>
> History has a meaning and direction only if there is something like a
> logic of human coexistence, which does not make adventure impossible
> but which at least, as in natural selection, eliminates in the long run the
> diversions in relation to man's permanent necessities.[13]

Marxism's claim on us, then, is its serious attempt to think history
as the evolution of Reason or, more important, to make history
reasonable.

In Merleau-Ponty's essay *"sur le problème communiste"* we can
see the contemporary relevance, if not the urgency, of many Hegelian
themes in the forties. It was not only the question of the value of
communism which thrust these themes to center stage. The general
problem that *Humanisme et terreur* raised—the meaning of violence
in history—had implications for the entire spectrum of politics in

---

Jay, *Marxism and Totality: The Adventures of a Concept from Lukács to Habermas*
(Berkeley, Calif., 1984), 367–373.

13. Merleau-Ponty, *Humanisme et terreur*, 266–267.

1947. The concept of a logic of history which Merleau-Ponty used, for instance, was important for one of the major political questions of postwar France: the status of collaborators. How did one determine the responsibility of a collaborator after the defeat of the Germans? Merleau-Ponty's answer should not surprise us: "Look at history." In this regard he meant to meet an argument used to defend those who collaborated: namely, that in 1940 it was reasonable to think Germany would win the war, and so some accommodation with the Nazis had to be made. The judgment of German victory was not, however, based on a neutral assessment of the conditions of the time; more important, *action* on the basis of this judgment helped determine whether in fact it would be true. In the last analysis, Merleau-Ponty argued, the victory of the Allied forces demonstrated that the judgment was false, that collaboration was not necessary. Victory transformed accommodation into treason, regardless, he emphasized, of the intentions of those involved.[14]

Political and moral responsibility, then, is determined only through a history that is ordered—that has meaning and direction. The power of Marxism, for Merleau-Ponty, is its will to order history and thus to make sense of our actions in the world. The logic of history that Marxism provides enables us to understand, and to judge, collaboration, revolution, and any action that significantly affects our lives by locating them within the context of meaningful change over time.

The philosophical baggage that Hyppolite piled onto History is at least equaled by the political weight Merleau-Ponty is prepared to strap on. Not only is History to provide us with the metaphysical consolation we once expected from religion or transcendental philosophy, it is also to be our guide for making secular political judgments and planning our tactics. Armed with the mighty weapon of the "logic of history," the intellectual can "remind the Marxists of their humanistic inspiration, and the democracies of their fundamental hypocrisy."[15] With a firm grasp of the *sens* of history, nihilism and totalitarianism can both be avoided.

Alas, confidence in this philosophical-political weapon cannot be total or at least cannot stand up to sustained reflection. The great gap

14. Ibid., 138–139. For a recent account of this period in French history see Herbert R. Lottman, *The Purge* (New York, 1986).

15. Merleau-Ponty, *Humanisme et terreur*, 298. The reversibility of this proposition did not seem to disturb Merleau-Ponty.

in *Humanisme et terreur*, the unasked question whose absence is at the center of the book, is where this logic of history is to be found or derived. As a *logic* of history, is it historical or is it a structure that enables us to understand any series of change over time, any epoch? In order to "read history well," to use the metaphor repeated throughout the book, does one simply approach the text and take a stab at it? This seemed to be Merleau-Ponty's response, following Trotsky, but it is not satisfactory.[16] We want to know how we will be able to choose between different readings, how we will know what is a good reading, what a misreading. The stakes are high.

Humanisme et terreur is in many ways characteristic of the Hegelian influence on existential Marxism. In it we see the extraordinary faith in history used to justify extreme violence against potential domestic enemies. The legitimacy of a political act can be judged only by virtue of its contribution to historical progress. Revolutionary acts, which by definition create the ground for surges of progress, can be judged only long after they are completed. Merleau-Ponty is not, of course, saying that intellectuals can do nothing in the meanwhile, that they cannot judge because the time has not come for judgment. On the contrary, he is emphasizing that one must judge, and that one must act, before full knowledge is available.

It is difficult to read *Humanisme et terreur* today without thinking that this is what all that historicism comes to: justifying Stalinism's mass murders. One thinks immediately of recent warnings about teleology and the violence inherent in a thinking that places itself between an origin and an end. Merleau-Ponty's book seems to add weight to complaints that a certain style of totalizing history leads to a totalitarian political philosophy.

But the problematic in which Merleau-Ponty worked is not all that different from that in which the antiteleological thinker Michel Foucault finds himself at the end of his life. Both writers take history seriously enough to recount what seem to them to be crucial moments in our past in order to enhance a political stance in the present. If Merleau-Ponty offers us a narrative of continuity where Foucault emphasizes gaps between historical epochs, this difference should not

---

16. Ibid., 188. See also "La querelle de l'existentialisme," in which Merleau-Ponty compared Marx and Hegel on history. One of Marxism's chief tasks, he writes, is to "make the logic of history prevail over its contingency, without any metaphysical guarantee" (*Sens et non-sens*, 164).

obscure the fact that both thinkers look for elements within history to help them make critical judgments about the present. Without the option of suprahistorical values, they have nowhere else to look. Foucault's own project is to hasten a shift in the structures of our experience, and his books are to be judged on their contribution to this task.[17] However, Foucault—and here he is quite different from his predecessor at the Collège de France—could not say why the structures of experience yet to come should be in any way preferable to our own. Both thinkers legitimated action in relation to their reading of history, but only Merleau-Ponty's reading contained a criterion for making sense of the whole story. As this criterion—which, as we shall see, Kojève called the End of history—was in the future, how could it be known? Without such a standard of judgment, however, how could a reading of history justify anything at all?

In a short book on Hegel's philosophy of history published in 1948, Hyppolite addressed some of the same questions as Merleau-Ponty did in *Humanisme et terreur*, though in a less overtly political form. Hyppolite was concerned to situate Hegel in the history of philosophy generally and in relation to the history of French philosophy specifically. Hyppolite's Hegel embodies the eighteenth-century Enlightenment faith in Reason while at the same time plunging into the nineteenth century's romantic turn to History; he is the "hinge of two epochs."[18] Hegel confidently charts the development of Reason, but he emphasizes that this development is immanent in historical progress itself and defines freedom as our acknowledgment and reconciliation with this progress.

Hyppolite stressed that the Hegelian notion of freedom as a reconciliation with history is foreign to the French philosophical tradition. The reconciliation with history is also a reconciliation with the state, and Hyppolite had reservations about this. According to him, in modern terms Hegel's call for the complete development of

17. See Michael S. Roth, "Foucault's 'History of the Present,'" *History and Theory* 20, no. 1 (1981), 32–46.

18. Hyppolite contrasted Hegel's idea of a historical freedom with French philosophy as follows: "From Descartes to Bergson, our philosophy seems to resist history; it is more dualist and looks for freedom in a reflection of the subject on itself. It is not that our philosophy lacks a wealth of rationalist or mystical conceptions, but that it resists seeing in the State the realization of the divine on earth; it resists also this unity of exterior and interior which is expressed in Schiller's famous phrase: "Weltgeschichte ist Weltgerichte."

the individual *within* the state is an attempt to synthesize liberalism and totalitarianism.[19] For Hyppolite such a synthesis was the political form of the attempt to negate the opposition between subjectivity and objectivity. It seems that although the French philosopher did not want to see these two spheres as separate from each other, he did not think they could be fully integrated without loss.

Hyppolite ends his study by posing this problem: If the goal of historical development for Hegel is the modern state, what is its status in modern and contemporary history? If the state is the revelation of Absolute Reason, how will we make sense of conflicts between the state and religion, art, or philosophy, to say nothing of the apparently irremediable conflict between the state and civil society and the battles among states? If the logic of history is completed and manifested in the state, he was asking, does the state have some claim to a suprahistorical status in relation to action in the modern world?

Hyppolite's short study echoes many of the problems raised by Merleau-Ponty. If the goal of history, be it Hegel's state or the existential Marxist's idea of a triumphant universal class, has a transhistorical status that enables it to legitimate, if not promise redemption for, suffering in the past, then the meaning and direction of change over time seems to be relegated to some suprahistorical dimension (whence the Hegelian talk about the End of history and the Marxist idea of prehistory ending with the revolution). If history has no goal, on the other hand, then we seem to be left with a historical relativism, which Merleau-Ponty identified with liberalism because he thought it invariably served the status quo.

With this issue we approach what Hyppolite called "the entire problem of Hegelianism," the connection between the *Logic* and the *Phenomenology*. The last chapter of *Genèse et structure* explicated this dilemma without proposing an answer to it: the *Logic* presented the structure of Being, what Hegel following Spinoza compared with the "mind of God before the creation," whereas the *Phenomenology* "re-collected" the ongoing development of the creation. *Humanisme et terreur* clarifies the importance of the relative weight given to each of these texts: if we are able to understand our past by virtue of a

---

19. Jean Hyppolite, *Introduction à la philosophie de l'histoire de Hegel* (Paris, 1948), 94.

logic (some structure that this past necessarily fits into), our major philosophical problems will be concerned not with the content of the historical but with the form and the power of this structure.

Let us translate this Hegelian problem into a political issue in France at the end of World War II. After the Liberation the Communist party was at the apex of its political influence in the country. Since 1942 it had played a crucial role in the organization of the Resistance and to a large extent had cooperated with other groups working to defeat the Nazis. With the end of the war the Party was faced with a dramatic choice: Should it cooperate with other political forces, especially General Charles de Gaulle, in the reestablishment of the state, or should it throw its power behind a revolutionary movement?

In fact, the choice was made fairly easily. With the war continuing, and the strong presence of American soldiers in the country, there was little real chance for a communist revolution. The PCF therefore adopted a short-term policy of rebuilding the country: republicanism not bolshevism. But this policy should be seen not as an abandonment of a revolutionary strategy, merely as its postponement. The postponement was possible because the Party is armed with a logic of history that enables it to see its tactical conservatism as serving the long-term interests of the Revolution. This was not merely a rhetorical ploy. The PCF confidently pursued alliances with its "class enemies" because its actions were legitimated by a logic of history which concluded in revolution. In France the power of that logic to convince militants was certainly a comfort during times when the political power to convert or destroy enemies was not yet available. Of course, *Humanisme et terreur* shows us how that same logic could be extraordinarily vicious when the power was available.

Problematic of Humanism

In an article published shortly after *Genèse et structure*, Hyppolite formulated what I call the "humanistic problematic" as follows: "For him [Hegel], man is *spirit*, that is, history and collective becoming; the truth which man can claim appears in and by this history. How to *found* this history, and a possible truth, a *reason* in the becoming of this history? In our view, this is the problem Hegel has posed."[20] The reason upon which history is founded in the *Phenomenology* is the human itself. Our truth will be our satisfaction, the product of our efforts to mold the world to fit our needs and desires. Truth is created in the course of history through the human struggle for recognition and final reconciliation. Hyppolite here gives us Hegel as a radical humanist/historicist. Hyppolite's Hegel is not, however, content to terminate the story with the human. Instead, he raises questions that point beyond what he thought of as the "merely human." Is an all-too-human truth firm enough to stand as a philosophical foundation? Does not history lead us beyond its own contingency toward some guarantee against the uncertainties of the temporal?[21]

These questions are further examples of Hyppolite's ambivalence toward the humanist/historicist reading of Hegel, an ambivalence that we have seen throughout his work. The poles of this ambivalence will be fully developed in a seminal debate in postwar Continental philosophy on the meaning and value of humanism. This debate enables us to understand the context of Hyppolite's own final response to the problematic of humanism.

In 1946 Sartre published a brief essay, "L'existentialisme est un humanisme," which declared that the idea of a "human nature" is a fiction and that individuals *are* what they *do*. In the language we have been using, Sartre chose history and the *Phenomenology* as opposed to an atemporal structure and the *Logic*. The choice of engagement in history is the sign and the burden of human freedom, a freedom that for Sartre was rooted in individual subjectivity and historicity. Sartre's essay was, in large part, formed by and directed at the debates surrounding French communism after the war. His piece triggered angry responses from intellectuals who had made what they saw as a total commitment to the PCF and who bitterly resented Sartre's construction of a freedom so rooted in individual subjectivity as to make collective, disciplined action impossible.[22] The communist in-

20. Jean Hyppolite, "Situation de l'homme dans la phénoménologie hégélienne," *Les temps modernes* no. 19 (1947), and *Figures*, 106.

21. *Figures*, 105–106, 121. See also Hyppolite, "Humanisme et hégélianisme," in *Umanesimo e scienza politica: Atti del congresso internazionale di studi umanisti* (Milan, 1951), 217–228. The congress took place in 1949.

22. See Mark Poster, *Existential Marxism in Post-War France* (Princeton, N.J., 1975), chap. 4. See also Poster, *Sartre's Marxism* (Cambridge, 1982), and Ronald Aronson,

tellectual, we might say, chose the discipline of the *Logic* over the adventure of the *Phenomenology*. Communists know their place in the logic of history and regard Sartre's subjectively based freedom as the petty individualism of the petite bourgeoisie.

Sartre's humanism, however—at least in the 1940s—could not be assimilated to the *Phenomenology* or to Hegelianism generally, because it divorced itself from historicism. Even though Sartre stressed the primacy of action over nature, of existence over essence, his "freedom" is founded on a Cartesian notion of subjectivity: freedom, while being historical or "in-situation," was based on the idea of a self that precedes historical development. Sartre, as Mark Poster has put it, "was convinced of the primacy of acting in the world only with the undertone that the world was still a Fall, albeit a necessary one, from the purity of the Self."[23] In the *Phenomenology* the purity of the Self is achieved fully only at the end of the story, whereas for Sartre it is the condition of a story that may not have any end.

The debate over the individual's place in the logic of history was of primary importance in the politico-philosophical scene of postwar France. A basic question for philosophy in the 1930s, to be or not to be *engagé*, was *dépassé* into the question of the late 1940s: *How* are you *engagé*? In essence, which side are you on? In the context of the developing Cold War, Sartre's attacks on communist rigidity could be dismissed or accepted because, *qua* critique of the PCF, they were ostensibly ("objectively") pro-American. Once the concept of intellectual detachment was given up, and after the militant role that intellectuals had played (or seemed to play) during the Occupation, one could ask for the "political implications" or "practical point" of almost any intellectual position.[24] The Hegelian historicism that was creeping into various forms of intellectual discourse during these years added to the politicization and polarization of cultural life.

Jean-Paul Sartre: Philosophy in the World (London, 1980), 164–175, 214–226. The literature on Sartre is, of course, enormous, but these works offer helpful insights on Sartre's relations with the French Communist party. For a recent general account of the PCF's connection with intellectuals, see Jeannine Verdes-Leroux, *Au service du parti: Le parti communiste, les intellectuels et le culture (1944–1956)* (Paris, 1983).

23. Poster, *Existential Marxism*, 127.

24. For a discussion of this feature of French intellectual life see Pierre Bordieu and Jean-Claude Passeron, "Sociology and Philosophy in France since 1945: Death and Resurrection of a Philosophy without Subject," *Social Research* 34, no. 1 (1967), 162–212.

It is against the deep structure of this debate that Heidegger addressed his *Letter on Humanism* (1947). He was not concerned with whether the communists or Sartre attained the *real* humanism; he was not about to become *engagé* on behalf of any political group. He had tried that path at least in 1933–34 and had seen that, for him, it led nowhere. The failure of this attempt formed part of the background to the *Letter*. Heidegger's essay was a critique of humanism as such, and it is no exaggeration to say that it changed irrevocably the way the issue would be discussed. Indeed, one can justifiably say that this brief text marked the beginning of the end of Hegelianism in France.

Heidegger's influence on French philosophy can scarcely be over-estimated. *Sein und Zeit* (1927) was a decisive, though not a final, blow against both neo-Kantian orthodoxy and the scientific pretensions of Husserlian phenomenology. A text of critical power and rich suggestion, it helped break down the stability of normal philosophic discourse in the 1930s. Young French philosophers such as Aron and Sartre returned from Germany with parts of the message Heidegger seemed to be delivering, and establishment philosophers heard the angry force of this message at an international congress of philosophy at Davos in 1929. The congress had as its theme the question "What is Man?" and was the occasion for an important debate between Ernst Cassirer and Heidegger on the latter's book on Kant. This debate led to the question of the role of philosophy vis-à-vis the human and of whether Heidegger's existentialism could be reduced to a philosophical anthropology.

Heidegger took great pains to separate his own style of inquiry from any kind of anthropological investigation. The latter assumed the object of investigation, whereas Heidegger claimed to be exploring the conditions of possibility for the very existence of the human. The point, for Heidegger, was not to liberate a person so that he or she can do more or better things. Instead one must learn to think what it is in a person that is *really* human; that is, to know those moments when we exist at the limits of our own possibilities. Heidegger defined the task of philosophy vis-à-vis the human as follows:

> It is both the task and idea of a philosophical anthropology to be concerned with man, not as an empirically given entity, but rooted in the basic problematic of philosophy itself, to turn him beyond himself and back to being in its wholeness; thus revealing to him, despite his freedom,

the nothingness [*Nichtigkeit*] of his existence. This "nothingness" is no cause for pessimism or sadness. It only helps to realize that there can be real productivity only where there is resistance, and that it is up to philosophy to turn man around, from the passive [*faulen*] preoccupation with the products of the spirit back to the hard severity of his destiny.[25]

Note how much hangs on the meaning given to the phrase "the hard severity of his destiny." Heidegger here can be assimilated without difficulty to the humanistic Hegelianism—even Marxism—we have discussed in this chapter, if one reads "destiny" as "history" and understands the possessive pronoun to connote that we are responsible for this possession because we create it (it is *our* destiny). On the other hand, one can also read this passage as calling us away from the merely human and giving to philosophy the task of pointing to the facets of *Dasein* too fundamental for any anthropological vision to apprehend.

Heidegger's later work followed the line of thought traced by this second interpretation, and his *Letter* took important steps in that direction. The *Letter* is a response to a question of Jean Beaufret as to how we can restore meaning to the word "humanism," and Heidegger devotes an important part of the essay to discussing the relation of the human to words, meaning, and language generally. He is concerned primarily to dissolve the idea that we *use* language as one uses a tool. This "technical" understanding of the human and of language covers over a much more fundamental truth. For Heidegger, we are not primarily creators, we are *revealers*, and our thinking—in the strongest sense—accomplishes this revelation in language.[26] In the following passage we can see clearly the difference between Heidegger's understanding of "unfolding something into the fullness of its essence" and the Hegelian understanding of historical action that we have discussed:

> Language is the house of Being. In its home man dwells. Those who think and those who create with words are the guardians of this home. Their guardianship accomplishes the manifestation of Being insofar as they

25. Carl H. Hamburg, "A Cassirer-Heidegger Seminar," *Philosophy and Phenomenological Research* 25 (1964), 218–219, 220.

26. Heidegger, "Letter on Humanism," in *Basic Writings*, ed. F. Krell (New York, 1977), 193.

bring the manifestation to language and maintain it in language through speech. Thinking does not become action only because some effect issues from it or because it is applied. Thinking acts insofar as it thinks. Such action is presumably the simplest and at the same time the highest, because it concerns the relation of Being to man. But all working or effecting lies in Being and is directed toward beings. Thinking, in contrast, lets itself be claimed by Being so that it can say the truth of Being. Thinking accomplishes this letting.[27]

We do not use language to achieve satisfaction, we live within it. We are not the authors of our language; above all, we do not control it or create it. To care for language is one of our highest tasks, because in this caring we think the relation of all that can be (Being) to the human and not just the relation of particular things (beings) to persons. Thinking is not connected to action as theory is to practice but is itself the highest form of accomplishment. When thinking, in other words, we are existing at the limits of our own possibility.

Noteworthy is the specific nature of thinking as accomplishment. As the highest and simplest form of action, thinking is *passive*: it "lets itself be claimed" and "accomplishes this letting." The contrast with the Hegelian understanding of historical action could not be more pronounced.[28] For the Hegelian, action is negative; that is, it alters or manipulates something in the world so that this something becomes what it is not yet. Action is a product of human desire; we change the world—work on it—to achieve greater satisfaction. Heidegger, in contrast, proposes an understanding of action as a "letting be" or "preserving something in its essence, to maintain it is its element."[29]

What, then, does the Heideggerian understanding of action and thinking have to do with humanism? For Heidegger, all humanisms have been metaphysical, because they have "presupposed an interpretation of being without asking about the truth of Being." In other

---

27. Ibid., 193–194.

28. As Heidegger conceived of thinking as the highest form of action, it is appropriate to compare his concept with Hegel's understanding of action. Obviously, a comparison of Heidegger and Hegel on thinking would highlight different aspects of the two philosophers and would have to underline the ways in which Hegelian thinking—the owl of Minerva, and the *Logic*—does not aim to change the world but to be reconciled with it.

29. Heidegger, "Letter," 197, 202, 208, 209, 210, 221.

words, the Marxists, Sartre, and Christian thinkers all assume a definition of what the human really or naturally is in relation to other things in the world, but they do not ask what the relation is between the human and the possible existence of everything. Sartre, in reversing an old metaphysical proposition, says existence precedes essence, but to reverse a metaphysical proposition is not, Heidegger points out, to cease being metaphysical. Heidegger left open the possibility that Sartre's existentialism, or the "preparatory" work of his own *Sein und Zeit,* might lead to more thinking about the "truth of Being," but Heidegger made it clear that such progress has little to do with the Hegelian understanding of history which we have discussed. If one day we will live at the limits of human possibility and think the truth of Being, we will discover that this accomplishment (like all others) is not our own but that of Being. The goal of philosophical thinking is not the vindication of our civilization and culture; for Heidegger this conception of philosophy (and history) depends on a notion of the person as the "Subject of beings" or even the "tyrant of Being." Heidegger meant to elevate our *humanitas* beyond this notion, to shift it away from what he considers to be merely the objective comprehension of beings. Rather than the "lord of beings," Heidegger's person is the "shepherd of Being," and he or she has to learn the "essential poverty of the shepherd."

Heidegger's understanding of "freeing the essence of man for his destiny" is strongly opposed to Sartre's notion of grounding human freedom in a Cartesian subjectivity. Indeed, one of the major effects of Heidegger's work is to contribute to the dissolution of the notion of the person as subject. The Heideggerian hero has learned not to be *engagé* and instead knows how to let be, to dwell within the light of Being which shines through our language.

What effect did Heidegger's conception of our highest tasks or possibilities have on his understanding of history? Clearly, the Hegelian schema of historical change is heavily dependent on the person as subject. History is the progress (through action) toward the coincidence of the *in itself* and the *for us.* In Heidegger's work, history is important not as progress but as the series of attempts by the "essential thinkers" constantly to "think the Same." Humanity does not *have* a history; Being "gives itself and refuses itself simultaneously."[30]

30. Ibid., 215.

When we turn to the past—that is, to the work of great thinkers—we see Being revealing itself and hiding itself through language. The language of the greatest thinkers is of particular importance because in it is best revealed the "concealment and unconcealment of Being."[31] History has significance for us *qua* shepherds of Being because it contains expressions that we should always remember as part of our flock—texts to be kept alive and cared for because, in their creative language, a clearing is made in which the light of Being can shine forth.

Legitimation and Letting Be

In the next chapter we shall see in what ways Hyppolite was attracted to Heidegger's notion of Being, but in conclusion here I note how this notion is related to the logic in history we explicated in the context of *Humanisme et terreur*. Merleau-Ponty was concerned with the elaboration of a philosophy of history which legitimated political action. A political strategy is legitimate if it conforms to the logic of development revealed by the philosophy of history. Violence is not redeemed, but it can be justified if it aims at the creation of a world in which violence will no longer be necessary.

For Heidegger, the whole notion of a person as a creator of a world is faulty. People do not make their own history, they live within a history that is the revelation of Being. The human task within this history—the destiny that a person can assume—is to care for clearings in which this revelation can take place. There is a special human place in history, but for Heidegger it is not the place of action or of politics but the place of watching over and letting be. Thinking from this perspective is not tied to a praxis whose legitimacy will be judged by the success of its effects. Thinking, rather, is yet another form of the unveiling of the truth of Being which can be seen through our language.

The philosophy of history of *Humanisme et terreur* is the conversion of the Hegelian slaughterbench into the development of Reason and Freedom through the legitimation of a particular form of political action. The Heideggerian shepherd of Being does not want to sort out

31. Heidegger, "The Question Concerning Technology," in *Basic Writings*, 315.

the intricate relationship between the moral individual and the hero;
instead, he or she wants to preserve a place *away* from these conflicts,
a place where the light of Being can shine for those who know how
to let be.

Chapter Three

From Humanism to Being

It is not I who created this vocabulary, this lexicon whose terms
are all interrelated. I did not create those nuances which change
meaning, nor this syntax which determines the possible connections. When I speak, I still must inquire and ask: Who
speaks in me?

Jean Hyppolite, 1966

Heidegger claimed that in looking at either individual subjectivity
or the progress of world history one was missing the essential question. Despite his admonition, the debates over humanism and historicism continued throughout the 1940s. Hyppolite's participation
in these debates, and his studies in the history of philosophy, reveal
his growing doubts about a humanism, such as Hegelianism, that
relies heavily on history. These doubts can be seen plainly in the
context of the problematic he formulated toward the end of *Genèse
et structure*: whether Hegelianism is a mysticism or a humanism.
The significance of this question is clear: if Hegelianism is a humanism, it sees all truths as the product of human action, or of history;
if Hegelianism is a mysticism, it allows for a criterion or criteria that
are not dependent on our action and that can still be used to make
sense out of or to judge our actions.

By the early 1950s, however, Hyppolite's concerns shifted from
making sense of human change over time to conserving and repeating
the essential expressions of Being. This turn allowed him to deal more
explicitly with the suprahistorical dimension that had been left in
his studies of Hegelianism as the open possibility of mysticism. But
whereas in the Hegelian perspective he discussed this dimension in
terms of some final social/political organization, after his Heideggerian turn Hyppolite addressed the ways in which this dimension is

revealed in language. He replaced problems of power with problems of poetry and logic, which was part of a larger replacement of questions of meanings with questions of use or function. This may seem a curious formulation, but the turn toward language is a partner with a turn toward logic, a partner with syntax rather than semantics. The implications of this turn I shall make clear in the final chapters of this book.

Seeing Hyppolite's work as a turning toward Heidegger allows us to understand Hyppolite in relation to an important intellectual development in France. True, one can also understand his work as moving from one pole of Hegelianism (the *Phenomenology*) to another (the *Logic*), or even, as Hyppolite said, as moving closer to Fichte's perspective. In this chapter, however, I show how the Heideggerian critique of humanism illuminates Hyppolite's abandonment of historicism. The path of his retreat would become well traveled by the 1960s, and Heidegger was the guide.

In 1949 Hyppolite published an article on Alain which featured the recent French philosopher as an antidote to the historicist Hegel. Alain, we are told, refused to dissolve the necessary separation of values and power and, in further contrast with Hegel, rejected the integration of the individual into the grand process of a theodicy.[1] The trouble with seeing values as only the product of history—the trouble that is, with historicism—is that more often than not people who struggle for power in the name of humanist values or ideas are less than humane. Their struggles do not exemplify the ends that are attached to them only post hoc. Alain did not leave a system that allows us to solve this problem, nor even with a logic of history to explain it away, but, according to Hyppolite, he left us with the hope that individuals can retain their values in the face of historical forces that seem to deny them. Hyppolite, however, offered no clues as to what a suprahistorical legitimation of these values consists in.

The hope that Hyppolite found in Alain at the end of the 1940s might not itself have been based on history, but it was certainly illuminated in relation to history. Alain underlined that even when history offered no basis for one's values (that is, when one did not have the power to actualize one's values), still a person could rightly

---

1. Hyppolite, "L'existence, l'imaginaire et la valeur chez Alain" (1949), in *Figures de la pensée philosophique* (Paris, 1971), 2:530–532.

retain those values. This position probably did not seem extraordinary—even the Merleau-Ponty of *Humanisme et terreur* would agree, though he would do so because the logic he found in history justified struggling for values that *for the moment* could not be actualized. For Alain, the imagination was the support of values in *defiance* of history, and, as Hyppolite said, "this defiance in regard to history and the great ideologies that dominate man is, and will always be, necessary."[2]

Defiance in regard to history and ideology comes from a loss of faith in the ability of collective action to change the world for the better. A decade earlier Hyppolite had seen the most important problem in philosophy as the connection of historicity and history, the matter of individual fulfillment within a reasonable community. He had thought of this as a philosophical problem in part because it was a political and historical problem. By the end of the 1940s things had changed, or rather, the possibilities for change were greatly diminished. No longer was there talk of a Third Force growing out of the spirit of the Resistance which would place the French polity on a radically new basis. The defeat of fascism was not to inaugurate a revolution, or a time of peace and freedom, but instead a time of reconstruction and of international tension. History was not going in any clear, hopeful direction, and Hyppolite saw in Alain a philosopher who did not make values dependent on any form of progress. Individual imagination, not social change, was the key for Hyppolite's Alain.

In the same year as the article on Alain, Hyppolite also returned explicitly to the problem of humanism and Hegelianism, showing again that he had grown more suspicious than he had been of the Hegelian schema of historical change and its connection to reason and freedom. The supervaluation of the historical was dangerous for the individual who had no appeal beyond the judgment of the victors. Hyppolite was less than confident of the ultimate justice of history: if history was the "court of world judgment," it might base its judgments on the rights and needs of the State, perhaps ignoring the requirements of the individual not fully integrated into the collectivity.[3] The judgment of history was the ruling of those with power;

2. Ibid., 2:532.
3. Hyppolite, "Humanisme et hégélianisme," in *Figures*, 1:224.

to what, Hyppolite asked, can the individual without power appeal? His question would be increasingly important in postwar France.

If Hegel did not, like Feuerbach and Marx, reduce God to the human, Hyppolite worried that he might have reduced God to History. The point was one for concern, it seems, because Hyppolite's own faith in history as the finally happy result of our efforts to improve and understand our existence had been undermined. Loss of power and, more important, loss of the hope for power coincided with the retreat from the philosophy of history. A philosophy of history can be a useful tool in the critique of those in power only if the philosophy has a logic that shows how the critique will be legitimated at some point by the acquisition of power; that is, by success. When there is little or no hope for success, a philosophy of history is useless as a form of critique. But the modern period, when doubts are great about anything with suprahistorical status, poses an extraordinary problem for the legitimation of any positive or critical values that are divorced from a philosophy of history. For Hyppolite, Weil, Deleuze, and Foucault, the turn away from the Hegelian philosophy of history leaves a vacuum of legitimation. For Kojève, who remained committed to the Hegelian philosophy of history, legitimation became an ironic gesture at the End of history.

It was probably not only these doubts about history as reason which led Hyppolite to a more detailed study of Hegel's *Logic* in the 1950s. Clearly, his study of Hegel would have been incomplete had he not at some point turned from the philosophy of culture and history of the *Phenomenology* to the structure of absolute knowledge developed in the *Logic*. If the 1940s was the epoch for studying—indeed, professing—the former, the first half of the 1950s provided the occasion for Hyppolite to propose a reading of the latter. This reading borrowed heavily from Heidegger, who provided the language that made a retreat from historicism legitimate if not downright fashionable.

Hyppolite's 1952 essay on the *Logic* makes clear the link between the concern with the System of Hegel and the abandonment of the radical humanism of the 1940s. Heidegger's understanding of the role of philosophy vis-à-vis the human, of the person as vehicle of Being and not as subject, provided the bridge over which this retreat could be made. From this perspective, the *Phenomenology* now appeared as *merely* historical, all too human because it did not describe (name, recite the poem of) Being and presented only a story of beings. Humanism, Hyppolite now said unequivocally, was not enough:

> While remaining with the *Phenomenology*, we study the development of essences, goal of artists and philosophers, but we distinguish these essences from Being itself. They remain human interpretations, more or less subjective, more or less recognized, but we do not ground them ontologically, we do not show their intrinsic necessity. The result of a *Phenomenology* which refuses to become *absolute knowledge*, Hegelian logic, is a sort of philosophy of culture. This philosophy certainly enumerates all the richness of experience, and the ways of expressing this experience, but it does not overcome humanism—the interpretation of Being by man. With that, the phantom of the thing-itself always arises and returns humanism to a faith beyond all knowledge.[4]

Here are the new rules of the game: when Hyppolite says "interpretation of Being by man," we are supposed to realize, following Heidegger, that this is a bad, or at least an inadequate, form of thinking. To the now naive question "Who *else* should interpret Being?" one receives the following reply: "It is not man who interprets Being, it is Being which is spoken in man; and this unfolding of Being, this absolute logic, substituted for a metaphysics...passes through man."[5] Humanity is no longer the hero of a story it is writing itself, it is instead the voice of Being. We do not create the language we speak but protect it through repetition. Our roles have changed from heroes to prophets, from political actors to shepherds.

In 1953 Hyppolite wrote a brief introduction to a French translation of Heidegger's *What Is Called Thinking?* Heidegger provided a way out for a thinker who felt trapped by history, for a thinker like Hyppolite who had deep reservations about the creation of a transhistorical standard of judgment through human work and struggle but who continued to feel the need for a suprahistorical set of criteria or values. The story in which humanity is hero and author had lost its plausibility, even its power to charm. But where is one to look for consolation and for legitimation? In the development of Hegelian humanism the old gods had been killed off; recourse to transcendental philosophy had become *passé*. What was needed was a new exit from

---

4. Hyppolite, "Essai sur la *Logique* de Hegel" (1952), in *Figures*, 164.
5. Hyppolite, "Ruse de la raison et histoire chez Hegel" (1952), in *Figures*, 1:157.

the temporal. For Hyppolite, Heidegger carried the conceptual keys that would unlock the prison of the historical:

> Heidegger has once again given us hope, that which all philosophers need in order to believe in the validity of philosophy when confronted with science and the world's technologies of domination. The first priority is given to ontology, to the relation above all of being and sense; the sense of all sense, we can say. . . . The minor philosophers who have been lost while painfully searching for a way out of the forest are indebted more than we can say to the appearance of a great philosopher. The air suddenly becomes more pure; it is the air of the summits. The reading of the philosophers of the past takes back all its contemporary relevance.[6]

It is with this new hope that Hyppolite wrote *Logique et existence* and, indeed, with which he continued the rest of his work in the history of philosophy, now legitimated as a re-collection of the poem of Being. This re-collection would serve what Heidegger called the repetition of the Same. The history of philosophy no longer needed to be concerned with the problems of progress, nor even with change. Perhaps more important, it no longer needed to be concerned with what happens outside the realm of the philosophical.

It is not necessary to discuss *Logique et existence* in any detail. The book had little impact on the philosophical scene when it was published, and it has little of interest for contemporary philosophy. For our purposes, the work is important only insofar as it completes the circle of Hyppolite's studies on Hegel and as it points to the Heideggerian turn taken by French philosophy in the 1950s.

Logique et existence is not a simple renunciation of Hyppolite's earlier works on Hegel. The book is a turn within the problematic we have seen throughout Hyppolite's work. Whereas in the thirties and forties Hyppolite read forward to the *Logic* from Hegel's early texts and the *Phenomenology*, in *Logique et existence* he was reading back on those works from a Heideggerian approach to the *Logic*. Even in his early works Hyppolite had been concerned that humanism/historicism was not a sufficiently secure foundation upon which to build a coherent philosophical project, concerned that there be more than a human basis for a vision of history. In *Logique et existence*

6. Hyppolite, "Note en maniére d'introduction à 'Que signifie penser?'" (1953), in *Figures*, 2:610.

he thought, following Heidegger, to have discovered that foundation in Being and its language.[7] One can read Hyppolite as changing within the Hegelian tradition rather than as having been turned by Heidegger. To do so, however, reduces the significance of his work and obscures its place in French intellectual history. For the Hyppolite of the 1950s, humanity stands now on firm, if not always visible, ground; we are the carrier of the *Logos*, we do not have to construct it over time. The philosopher has the all-important task of revealing this ground and of repeating or recollecting the revelations made through the great thinkers of the past. The task of legitimating action, of situating struggle and work within a logic of history, fades away in favor of (re)-expressing the poem of Being. The grand importance of this task can scarcely be overestimated: Hyppolite went as far as to say that man exists fully because he is a philosopher. Note his new confidence: "The *Logic* is opposed to experience as ontology to anthropology. The Hegelian ambition is not to do without experience, but to reduce... the anthropological, and to show that in the very heart of the ontological 'philosophy must alienate itself.' Thus, philosophy alone is the element of the truth and of every truth.'"[8] It is, to be sure, Hegelian confidence, not Heideggerian hope, that is being expressed in this passage. Here I stress only that it is Heidegger that allowed Hyppolite to understand Hegel with sympathy.

For Hyppolite, the connection between logic and existence is language. His book is concerned not with how we use language but with how language contains meaning and makes claims to truth internally. His operating assumption is that language refers only to itself,[9] and it permits him to isolate the question "How does language work?" His earlier concern with how we make sense of our past reappears only in the form of his interest in the linguistic possibilities for organizing experience.

Many of Hyppolite's favorite themes do reappear in *Logique et existence*, though they are modified to fit the antianthropological perspective of the book. Hyppolite tries to integrate his understanding of Hegelian pan-tragedism into his study of the *Logic*, but he no longer talks about human suffering and sacrifice, nor about the forgiveness

7. I emphasize that Heidegger himself did not seem to think that he had discovered a new *foundation* for philosophy.

8. Hyppolite, *Logique et existence: Essai sur la logique de Hegel* (Paris, 1953), 216.

9. Ibid., 38.

of sins and the redemption of historical action. No longer is negativity first and foremost a facet of humanity, a result of work and struggle; it is now a moment of Being. There is still an important place for the tragic in Hyppolite's interpretation of Hegel. The tragedy, however, is no longer ours; it is Being's.[10]

Logique et existence says that Hegel has advanced beyond humanism in having progressed beyond the perspective of Kant. The Kantian, we are told, is concerned with the categories of our thought/language or with the possibilities of our experience. The Hegelian, in contrast, is concerned with the categories of thought/language as the possibilities of Being. Hegel's *Logic* details the structure of this eternal self-consciousness, thus transcending every "moral and human vision of the world" by revealing the ontological basis of the very possibility of humanism.[11]

Change over time is discussed in *Logique et existence*, not as human history but as the "absolute genesis of Being in its total self-comprehension." This genesis can be seen in the history of philosophy, but the perspective of Hegel's *Logic* rigorously accounts for it by tracing the progressive (systematic) development of language. Hegel's perspective is crucial, Hyppolite says, because Hegel sees language only in terms of its internal relations, its immanent development, and does away with unfounded, extra-linguistic grounds of explanation such as the subject as self or the object as thing-in-itself. The systematic relations of logic are those of language, and, because of Hyppolite's presupposition that language is the self-consciousness of Being, these relations are the foundations of ontology.

In the perspective of *Logique et existence*, persons are still regarded as free, but the human relation to that freedom is completely different from what we have seen thus far: "The freedom which permits man to wander from determinations to determinations, or to be dissolved into abstract nothingness, it is not man who possesses this freedom, but this freedom which possesses man.... Man, then, *exists* as the natural being-there [*être-là*] in whom the universal self-consciousness of Being appears. He is the trace of this self-consciousness, but an indispensable trace without which it would not exist." We have transcended, or retreated from, the dilemma of the hero and

10. Ibid., Part II, chap. 4.
11. Ibid., Part III, chap. 2, and pp. 244–245, 246.

the moral individual and have arrived at humanity as the trace of Being, essential not so much for what it does as for what is spoken through it or even what it unconsciously signifies as an element in the language of Being.[12]

It is tempting to search for arguments, or even a vague process of reasoning, that led Hyppolite and many other philosophers in the early 1950s away from heroic Hegelianism toward this hopeful Heideggerian perspective. The history of this development might make more sense to us if we could see how the project of uncovering a "logic of history" was exposed as unreasonable, or how its assumptions were somehow refuted. But although Heidegger's *Letter* was certainly a decisive text, it did not attempt to join argument or even dialogue with Sartre's brand of existentialism. Instead it offered a competing way of making sense of the world. The same can be said of the early texts of structuralism or of the "new social history," neither of which, in sharp contrast with what I have called heroic Hegelianism, viewed persons as the subjects of the stories they recount.

The question that we must address, then, is not how the Hegelianism of the 1940s was discovered to be philosophically inadequate. Rather, it is how the antianthropologism of the Heideggerian perspective changed the function of philosophic discourse for Hyppolite and for other intellectuals who had invested much less than he had in the humanist historicism of the mid–1940s.

Two global perspectives on this development in the French cultural scene are offered by E. P. Thompson and Fredric Jameson. Thompson asserts that the epoch of the thirties and forties was one of great confidence in the power of historical action: the world seemed ripe for change by political means, and people acting in concert could determine their own future. The 1950s, in contrast, brought increased pessimism and complacency as a hardening of the positions of the superpowers left only the unappetizing terrain between them as the field for limited political struggle. Thompson sees the development of the new perspective on history, in which humanity is no longer

---

12. Ibid., 244–245. For some, however, Hyppolite's newly acquired anti-anthropologism did not go far enough, because his understanding of Hegelian contradiction and tragedy might have left open a door through which man could reenter. See Gilles Deleuze, "Analyse de 'Logique et existence,'" *Revue philosophique de la France et de l'étranger* 144 (1934), 457–460, and below, Chapter 9.

the subject, as a reaction to this static structure of contemporary political life. The powerlessness of people confronted by the bureaucratic nightmare of the modern state and the world order maintained by two empires was reflected in a social theory that saw people acting out a role that was not of their own making but that was their necessary function in the largest scheme of things.[13]

Jameson's perspective on the turn in French social theory in the 1950s differs from Thompson's in large part because Jameson is critical of but sympathetic to the theory following the turn, whereas Thompson views it as a massive and dangerous series of mistakes. For Jameson, the reaction against Hegelianism as historicism in France masked the reaction against Stalinism.[14] The Hegelian perspective on historical change, when combined with the Marxist theory of the proletariat, had helped justify the purge trials and in principle could be used to legitimate any form of state terror. The power of states perhaps seemed more fluid to thinkers just after World War II, more open to influence and to being shared. By the 1950s such hopes seemed worse than naive, and many thinkers turned away from a technique for legitimating a power that clearly they and their friends would never possess. It was, during this time, certainly easier to imagine power—and responsibility—coming from elsewhere, that is, anywhere but from ourselves.

Useful as these interpretations are for understanding certain trends within French historiography and psychoanalysis, and the origins of modern structuralism, they do not offer us much help in our attempt to understand Hyppolite's particular turn toward an antianthropological, or at least nonhumanist, position in the 1950s. Thompson and Jameson are concerned with the connection between the development of social theory and ideology, and Hyppolite neither developed nor embraced a coherent theory. Indeed, his new position in many ways helped legitimate his own, nonsystematic approach to the history of philosophy.

The Hegelian legacy that Hyppolite had seemed ready to acquire in the mid-1940s is not an easy inheritance to make one's own. The conception of Hegel as the last philosopher weighed heavily on nine-

13. See E. P. Thompson, *The Poverty of Theory* (London, 1978), 374–379.

14. Fredric Jameson, *The Political Unconscious: Narrative as a Socially Symbolic Act* (Ithaca, N.Y., 1980), 37. Jameson's interpretation would be more persuasive if it were not aimed at making Althusser a closet—or at least a "coded"—anti-Stalinist.

teenth-century and twentieth-century Continental philosophy, especially in light of the Marxist perspective that portrayed the merely philosophical interpretation of the world as an anachronism.[15] French Hegelianism assumed this weight in conceptualizing the validity of philosophy as based on its ability to make sense of significant change over time or to legitimate concrete historical action, even systematic violence, by emplotting it in a larger story of development. This mode of philosophy had its risks, as emerging details made contemporary events ever more difficult to integrate in a larger narrative of history as progress. The best example in this regard is *Humanisme et terreur*, and the risks its author ran become more apparent as the extent of Stalinist brutality emerged in the 1950s.[16] In any case, in a Europe frozen within the Cold War, claims for significant progress and historical reason were all but impossible to make.

By the early 1950s France had almost fully returned to party-dominated republican politics. Gone were the heady days when Liberation meant not only throwing out the Germans but also the possibility of creating a new kind of society. Instead, the Fourth Republic was engaged in a generally defensive politics: its goals had something to do with the attempt to reestablish French dignity and honor, but concretely they had to do with establishing a modern capitalist economy that would allow the French state to maintain substantial political autonomy in a world dominated by superpowers. Most important, France in the 1950s was entering a protracted period of decolonization. Not only would it lose overseas territories, it would be disconnected from them slowly and painfully.

Hyppolite's early work on Hegelianism emerged from the context of the Popular Front and continued during the struggle against fascism. This was a period of great crisis, to be sure, but it was also a period of great hope that resolution of the crisis would mean a fundamentally better world. By the early 1950s dissatisfaction was tied

---

15. Recall Hyppolite's comparison of Marx and Hegel in which the latter figures as the last philosopher: pp. 32–33 above. This idea was an important facet of French Hegelianism generally and plays a crucial role in Kojève's and Weil's work. For a more recent example of the weight that the idea retains for French thought, see the references to Hegel in the closing pages of Michel Foucault's "Le discours sur la langue" (1970), in *The Archaeology of Knowledge*, trans. A. M. Sheridan Smith (New York, 1972).

16. See Sartre's account of Merleau-Ponty's withdrawal from politics: "Merleau-Ponty," in *Situations*, trans. Benita Eisler (New York, 1965), 156–226.

to a new sense of crisis, but it was a crisis without the hope of closure—not a dramatic, agonistic conflict that, through the work of the negative, would bring change and reconciliation, but pervasive, systemic problems that admitted of no definitive solution. Radical political change seemed to have no place in such a world.

When Hyppolite abandoned heroic Hegelianism to be a hopeful Heideggerian, he abandoned a theory of history as progress in favor of a perspective that valued history as a repetition of the Same. For Hegel, as for Freud, repetition is a kind of death, and history made sense only as the effort to advance. Not so, as we have seen, for Heidegger; in his work history is important because in it one can follow the diverse expressions of Being spoken by the greatest thinkers. Those who think and create with words are, Heidegger says, the guardians of language, the house of Being.[17] The greatest thinkers, in their creations of new paths for language, make a clearing in which we can see Being shine forth. The historian of philosophy, in repeating and rethinking their *poēsis* preserves this clearing. Although no longer taxed with showing progress from one thinker to the next, the historian of philosophy still has a crucial task as guardian, repeater, and preserver. If people are the shepherds of Being, the historian of philosophy watches over the best of the flock. Heidegger tells us to learn the poverty of the shepherd, but, among us shepherds, the historian of philosophy has a special wealth to protect and draw upon. By becoming the guardian of the language of Being, Hyppolite could protect the suprahistorical dimension that Hegelian humanism, in his eyes, failed to reach.

Hyppolite's published work after *Logique et existence* makes most sense as an attempt to cultivate this dimension. Hyppolite continued to explore issues in Hegelianism and humanism, but he also turned to contemporary questions in psychoanalysis, Marxism, art, literature, French philosophy, and information theory. Indeed, it is difficult to find rhyme or reason in Hyppolite's choice of topics, to say nothing of his diverse styles of treating them. This difficulty should not surprise us, insofar as Heideggerian hope allows the philosopher to think that almost any text he or she happens upon is an expression of Being, a lost stanza of its poem.[18] Perhaps it is this confidence which dis-

17. Heidegger, "Letter on Humanism," in *Basic Writings*, ed. F. Krell (New York, 1977), 193.
18. This hope, wrapped in semiotic theory and the "interest of scientific responsi-

placed in Hyppolite any effort at consistency.[19] Hyppolite's late work seems to welcome all efforts at philosophy as expressions of the Same; apparent contradictions, or mere unrelatedness, can be dispelled by a philosopher sufficiently open to the light of Being.[20] With this hope, the philosopher can show the interrelatedness of all things in our increasingly specialized world without, however, claiming that these things are the product of human work and struggle over time. Indeed, the idea of bringing together, through philosophy, the increasingly isolated branches of intellectual inquiry is the unifying theme in Hyppolite's work after *Logique et existence*. The will to re-connect, or re-collect, diverse cultural expressions is also dominant in Hegelian historicism, but in Hyppolite's late studies the connections made are not diachronic. Instead, Hyppolite saw philosophy as the field in which the truths of one kind of discourse could be translated into terms that were meaningful for another discourse.[21] In this way, philosophy could, to use the language of Richard Rorty, serve to keep the conversation of culture from breaking down into increasingly isolated language games.[22]

If there was a strategy in Hyppolite's late work, then, it was very different from those we have seen within the Hegelian paradigm. The

---

bility," has been reiterated recently by Hayden White: "We must be prepared to grant that the comic strip cannot be treated as *qualitatively* inferior to a Shakespeare play, or any other classic text." See his "Method and Ideology in Intellectual History: The Case of Henry Adams," in *Modern European Intellectual History: Reappraisals and New Perspectives*, ed. Dominick LaCapra and Steven L. Kaplan (Ithaca, N.Y., 1982), 308.

19. Hyppolite's warm embrace of Althusser's reading of Marx was the most incredible example of his trying to live his dictum from *Logique et existence*, 93: "To know oneself is to contradict oneself." See Hyppolite, "Le 'scientifique' et 'l'idéologique' dans une perspective marxiste," *Diogène* no. 64 (1968), in *Figures*, 370–371, and "Une perspective nouvelle sur Marx et le marxisme," in *La philosophie contemporaine* (Florence, 1971), 339–357.

20. Of course, in Heidegger's own rewriting of the history of philosophy as a Fall some thinkers are more important than others. It would be difficult if not impossible, however, to identify whatever criteria Heidegger used to distinguish those thinkers whose texts deserved to be cared for from those whose works were best left exposed to forgetting.

21. Hyppolite, "La situation de la philosophie dans le monde contemporaine" (1965), in *Figures* 2:1036.

22. The comparison of Bachelard and Althusser in "Le 'scientifique' et 'l'idéologique' " is a good example in this regard.

Hegelian philosophy of history which Hyppolite had embraced—with some ambivalence, to be sure—in the late 1930s and just after World War II was a critical philosophy of legitimation. That is, Hegelianism either legitimated or undermined practices, beliefs, and institutions according to their place in a story of history as progress. Once one knew the structure or logic of this story, one could act in such ways as to foster the right kind of change; that is, one learned the meaning and direction of history so as to participate effectively in it. Of course, Hegelianism could also criticize the status quo effectively for inhibiting the meaning and direction of history, but such criticism did not undermine the notion that ultimately the real was rational and the rational was real; it showed only that the real was becoming rational and that we had a part to play in that becoming.

By the time Hyppolite wrote *Logique et existence*, the stakes had changed. He was no longer concerned with a critical legitimation, nor with the meaning and direction of historical change. Instead, he was interested in how our language is put together—how, to use a word that became fashionable shortly after *Logique et existence* was published, the world is structured. We are no longer the authors of meaningful actions, we are the vehicles of the absolute genesis of Being. The "universal self-consciousness of Being *appears*" in us, we are not the creators of self-consciousness. Indeed, we are its trace.

Obviously, Hyppolite's language here has resonance for us because more recent structuralist and post-structuralist thinkers have adopted similar stances. (In the final chapter of this book, I examine two such stances.) Nonetheless, the abandonment of a humanistic historicism is not the achievement only of structuralism. By the early 1950s Hyppolite was already moving in this direction. In the fifties Heidegger offered a useful language for the retreat from humanism and historicism, which is also a retreat from the idea of people as political actors, as capable of giving meaning to their political participation. Before this retreat Hegelianism provided people who believed in radical change with a philosophy of history which legitimated this belief. After the retreat Heideggerian antihumanism provided a framework of thinking for people who had abandoned the possibility of a politics that we can make meaningful. Even without a meaningful politics, however—that is, in a world, as Heidegger said, where only a god can save us—the philosopher still has something to do. As language is the poem of Being, the philosopher now, as guardian of language, retains an importance that is independent from the pain of negativity, independent of history.

The hope that Hyppolite thinks he discovers in Heidegger is that even in a world in which "there are no new territories to discover," philosophy has a claim to validity.[23] The mission of philosophy is no longer to make sense of, let alone legitimate, change over time but to keep the conversation among diverse disciplines alive or to create the possibility for such conversation if it does not already exist. The only expressions of Being that have to be greeted with real suspicion are those which lend themselves to dogmatic systemization; that is, those which lend themselves to monopolizing discourse, claiming (thus needing legitimation for) an exclusive—historical or logical— suprahistorical validity.[24] It is the fear of such dogmatism which enables Hyppolite to maintain his distance from the *movements* of French cultural life over three decades. Perhaps, though, it is also this fear which prevents him from rigorously articulating his approach to the history of philosophy and the place of Hegelianism in that history and in his approach. It is a fear that eventually leads him to give up history, progress, and heroism to settle for Being, repetition, and hope.

23. Hyppolite, "La situation de la philosophie," 1036.

24. This is especially clear in the summaries of Hyppolite's seminars at the Collège de France, 1964–1968, to be found in *Annuaire du Collège de France* (Paris, 1965–1969).

Part Two

After the End:
Alexandre Kojève

Chapter Four

Absolutes and History

> For Comte, as for Hegel, man can be absolute only in taking
> the place of God: for them, man is absolute, but he is absolute
> only because there is no other absolute than him.
>
> *Alexandre Kojève, 1935*

Alexandre Kojève's work in philosophy was molded, if not forced,
by the exigencies of history. The son of a well-to-do bourgeois family
in Russia, he left Moscow at the age of eighteen in 1920 and, after a
brief stay in a Polish prison, spent most of the decade in Berlin and
Heidelberg. By 1927 he had come to Paris, where he would stay until
his death in the spring of 1968. One could trace the impact of Kojève's
personal experience of the violence of this epoch on his philosophy
of history and politics, but here I explicate how, despite this experience, which might be called intensely historical, he saw himself and
his contemporaries as living in a posthistorical world. In this world
nothing really new occurred; contemporary events were looked upon
as mere "realignments of the provinces" in an increasingly homogeneous and universal global system.[1] The philosopher's task in this
world was to repeat in a pedagogically efficacious way the Science of
Hegel: the final, original philosophy that accounted for itself and the
last act of history of which it was a part.

The major idea of Kojève's philosophy—that history, properly so-
called, is over—confronts the historian who takes it seriously with a

---

1. Kojève, in an interview published in *La quinzaine littéraire* (June 1–15, 1968),
19: "Since this date (1806), what has happened? Nothing at all, the *alignment of the
provinces*. The Chinese revolution is only the introduction of the Napoleonic Code
into China."

paradox. If Kojève is right, then there is no *history* to be written about him. If he is assumed to be wrong from the start, however, then why should one want to write intellectual history about him?[2] As one develops a reading of his work, furthermore, it becomes more difficult to know what it means to take him seriously, as the content of his discourse seems to be at odds with the form and the point of his pedagogy. That is, the ironic component of his writings becomes more important over time, and the philosophic point of his writings less clear. Yet the power of his version of Hegelianism, and the implicit commentary on all historicism which it contains, has a claim on anyone trying to find significance in or give significance to change over time. Or so I shall try to show.

I shall explore the problematics with which Kojève was concerned in all his philosophic work and explicate the shift that occurred in the form of his concern between the 1930s and the 1950s. I focus on his reading of Hegel's *Phenomenology*, which he developed in a series of seminars from 1933 to 1939 at the Ecole Pratique des Hautes Etudes.[3] Later these seminars became quite famous, as they appeared to be a field for cross-fertilization among many of the most important species of French intellectual life. This fame, however well-deserved, does not concern us here; I shall not attempt to measure Kojève's influence on such diverse figures as Merleau-Ponty, Bataille, Lacan, and Fessard. Instead, I try to determine how Kojève develops his particular interpretation of Hegel, and what is at stake in it for him and for us.

What were the concerns with which Kojève came to Hegel in the 1930s? Kojève's early writings show how questions about the connections between philosophy and history—about philosophy's claims to truth given historical change—led him to think through the ways in which action can be meaningful both because of its orientation toward the future and because of the fact of human finitude. It was a configuration of the relation among mysticism, histori-

---

2. There is no contradiction in a historian believing the end of history has been reached, for the task of such a historian would be to recount how this had occurred. The point of doing so would, of course, remain problematic.

3. Notes and texts of Kojève's lectures were assembled by Raymond Queneau (who attended the seminar) and published by Gallimard in 1947 as *Introduction à la lecture de Hegel*. An abridged English version edited by Alan Bloom, is *Introduction to the Reading of Hegel*, trans. J. Nichols (New York, 1969).

cism, and Heidegger's phenomenology which Kojève brought to his reading of Hegel.

Unlike Hyppolite, Kojève adopted extreme philosophic positions and was not content to write a commentary that explored "possible readings" of Hegel's texts. These positions fit into his more general philosophic project. In my treatment of his interpretation of Hegel, in chapter 6, I adopt the categories of Kojève's own central paradigm, the master/slave dialectic. That is, I consider his reading through the prism of the moments of this dialectic—Bloody Battle, Reign of the Master, Triumph of the Slave—which determined his philosophy of history. In chapter 7, I discuss how by the 1950s his concerns had shifted from the question "What does our history mean?" to "How does our discourse work?" Unlike Hyppolite and many other French intellectuals of this period, Kojève did not use a critique of Hegel as a springboard for this shift. Instead, he adopted a rigid Hegelian dogmatism. His introductions to the philosopher's System became the occasion for abandoning the philosophy of history (and politics) in favor of the study of discourse. The "discursive solipsism" of Kojève's late works, however, can be fully understood only through the philosophy of history that led up to them.[4] Thus I show the unity of his philosophic project underlying the shift in his concerns.

The major philosophic interests and intellectual equipment that Kojève brought to his interpretation of the *Phenomenology* can best be determined by studying his early published and unpublished writings.[5] The important texts are his own summary of his dissertation "Die Religionsphilosophie de Wladimir Solowjews" (1930)—originally written under Jaspers at Heidelberg University—published in French in 1934 and a series of reviews published in the short-lived but important *Recherches philosophiques* between 1933 and 1939.

Kojève's two-part article "La métaphysique réligieuse de Vladimir Soloviev" presents what he took to be the philosophical underpinnings of the religious and mystical writings of Soloviev. Most of the article simply summarizes Soloviev's views, but for our purposes,

---

4. I borrow the phrase "discursive solipsism" from Stanley Rosen's review of volume one of *Essai d'une histoire raisonnée de la philosophie païenne*, in *Man and World* 3, no. 1 (1970), 120–125.

5. Something that has not been done by commentators on various facets of Kojève's work or by Patrick Riley and Vincent Descombes in their treatment of his general philosophic project.

Kojève's points of focus are crucial, as they remained at the center of his work over the next two decades. Simply put, his chief interest is in the way a religious thinker takes history into account despite an ultimate concern with the Eternal and in the way that this concern shapes a perspective on human development over time.

Kojève emphasizes the dual perspective that Soloviev adopts toward God, or the Absolute. On the one hand, the Absolute is always already complete and fully self-contained; there is no development essential to this Absolute, because any becoming (the "not yet") implies some imperfection or absence that needs to be worked out or filled. On the other hand, the Absolute is the "work of God," in which the creation, the fall, and the redemption of humanity are necessary facets of the Whole. To reconcile these two visions of God (Kojève calls them pantheist and dualist, respectively), Soloviev turns to the German idealists, specifically to the dialectic of Schelling and the concept of a Man-God.[6]

The concept Man-God allows Soloviev to account for history. History is important, has significance, as the order in which humanity works its way toward the Divine. Only humanity is potentially divine, and in the course of history that potentiality (essence) becomes a reality (existence). Human potential divinity is understood by Soloviev as the immanence of the Absolute in history. The human effort to perfect the world is itself the sign of a "becoming Absolute," which is the temporal facet of the Divine. The *sens* of the becoming of humanity can be determined by its relative nearness to the Absolute which, at least according to one perspective of Soloviev's, is untouched by time, to say nothing of historical change.

This dual perspective on the Absolute or God is not, of course, original to Soloviev, and Kojève points out its debt to German mysticism and romanticism. The force that Kojève sees in Soloviev's version stems from the extreme importance that Soloviev gives to people and their action in the world. Although human freedom depends ultimately on God, it is the freedom, not the dependence, that

---

6. I use the term "Man-God" from Soloviev, although I do not think there is anything necessarily gender-specific about the combination of the human and the divine that Soloviev has in mind.

7. A. Kojevnikoff (Kojève), "La métaphysique religieuse de Vladimir Soloviev," *Revue d'histoire et de philosophie religieuses* 14, no. 6 (1934), 534–544, and 15, nos. 1–2 (1935), 110–152, quotation 115.

Soloviev stresses: "Man is, in a word, almost the equal of God, and nevertheless he is the _same_ being who revolted against God, while appearing in his fall as the finite universe and, in this universe, as historic humanity; . . . he and he alone, in giving himself freely to God, can save this universe; . . . he is, finally, the being who is in each of us, the being in which each of us really and essentially participates— this particular idea of Soloviev is not found with this force and power in Boehme, nor even in Schelling." The importance that Soloviev gives to an anthropological perspective, however, remains contained by the categories of theology. Whereas for thinkers such as Comte and Hegel humanity is absolute because it has replaced God, Kojève points out, for Soloviev human progress is a movement back toward God.[8] The conception of God as the Absolute that knows no becoming is precisely that which allows us to determine whether there is progress.

The significance of Soloviev's dual perspective is clear: by seeing the Absolute as incarnate in Time (Humanity), he places great importance on human history. The structure of history's progress is determined by its End, which is the continual unification of all people in a universal reunification with God.[9] A _dual_ perspective is necessary in Soloviev's metaphysics because without the suprahistorical version of the Absolute, there are no stable criteria by which to judge human actions in the world. The paradoxes that result from having the Absolute exist both in and outside time as facets of a unified and unique God troubled the mystical theologian less than the dilemmas that might have ensued from regarding humanity as having no anchor outside time.

Soloviev's Absolute, both temporal and atemporal, recalls Hyppolite's ambivalence about Hegelian historicism. Hyppolite, too, looked for a way of thinking which would take historical change seriously, but he feared the consequences of making the truthfulness of all values dependent on their realization in history. Both realized the necessity of having a criterion (or goal) for judging whether an action is progressive, and both feared making that goal (nothing more than) the product of (only human) history. Whereas Kojève's Soloviev adopted a mystical solution to this perception of necessity and this

8. Ibid., 124–125.
9. Ibid., 142.

fear, Hyppolite remained agnostic about any solution. Neither option was satisfactory to Kojève, who saw them as abandonments of philosophy.

In Europe after World War I the problem of finding what makes specific change meaningful was not confined to Russian mystics and esoteric commentators on Hegel. On the contrary, for intellectuals facing a world of increasingly rapid and increasingly obscure changes, the search for some criterion of evaluation was an important political, philosophical, and social scientific issue. The absence of such a criterion might condemn one to relativism and political impotence vis-à-vis the status quo. However, given the extraordinary dynamic of modernism and modernization in culture and society, how could one claim to know a criterion of change which was itself immune from change? From the aesthetics of his uncle Kandinsky to the philosophy of social science of his teacher Rickert, Kojève was surrounded by thinkers who were wrestling with this constellation of questions. In a Europe already devastated by a war that had brought many changes but seemed to have no meaning or direction, these questions were neither mystical nor esoteric.

Although in his mystical concerns Soloviev claimed to have something to do with history, it may seem that he remained on such a abstract level as to leave untouched all concrete aspects of human change. Kojève's interest in Soloviev, however, stemmed from the mystical thinker's realization that "concrete change" becomes significant change only when it is understood as part of a meaningful whole. Both Soloviev and Kojève tried to think that which gives meaning to concrete, specific changes, that which makes them properly historical. For the former it was the dual-natured Absolute, and for the latter it would be the End of History.

It is no overstatement to say that all of Kojève's work in philosophy was an attempt to show that an atemporal Absolute—or some historical criterion of judgment—is not necessary for making sense of human actions over time. Kojève tried to demonstrate the position by standing on Hegel's shoulders, that is, by developing an interpretation of the German philosopher in which anthropocentrism and historicism had the highest priority.

In some short reviews written by Kojève in the 1930s we can see what he took to be the most important philosophical problems of the time, and in what direction he thought solutions to these problems were most likely to be found. Kojève discovered in Hegel a language with which to speak to these problems. His reading of the philosopher makes sense—that is, seems not merely idiosyncratic or a simple distortion[10]—only if these problems are first understood.

Kojève wrote short reviews regularly for the annual *Recherches philosophiques*. This journal appeared between 1933 and 1937 and featured some of the most innovative philosophers in France. Publishing the work of Koyré, Sartre, Groethuysen, Aron, Weil, and Kojève, the journal was particularly important as a forum for discussing developments in German existentialism, phenomenology, and *Lebensphilosophie*. Kojève himself was most interested in the conflict between these last two movements.

For Kojève, the conflict between *Lebensphilosophie* and phenomenology—between Dilthey and Heidegger—is a battle over the very existence of philosophy. Kojève sees Dilthey and his followers substituting a "philosophy of philosophy" for philosophy itself. They have given up the quest for metaphysical or ontological truth and are content to study earlier struggles for wisdom. They leave unanswered the questions of why these earlier attempts were worth making in the first place and of how some are better (closer to the truth) than others. The desire to replace philosophy with a metaphilosophical cultural history is, for Kojève, "to want to replace art by criticism, the thing by its idea."[11]

Heidegger, on the other hand, remains a philosopher insofar as he is concerned with Being, with finding universal and objective truths. Indeed, Kojève asserts that Heidegger is the only philosopher since Hegel (with the "possible exception of Marx") to have made any significant progress.[12] He sees Heidegger as the heir to the anthro-

---

10. Patrick Riley shows in some detail how Kojève's "readings" seriously distort important texts: "Introduction to the Reading of Alexandre Kojève," *Political Theory* 9, no. 1 (1981), 5–48. It will become clear in this chapter that Kojève willfully distorted other philosophers—that is, used their texts to make his own points—and I concentrate on the significance of his "distortions" rather than on his ability to remain faithful to precious texts.

11. A. Kojevnikoff, review of Georg Misch, *Lebensphilosophie und Phänomenologie*, *Recherches philosophiques* (1932–1933), 475.

12. The phrase "with the possible exception of Marx" occurs in the longer manuscript of a review of Alfred Delp's *Tragische Existenz: Zur Philosophie Martin Heideggers*, an abridged version of which was published in *Recherches philosophique* (1936–1937), 415–419. The progress that Marx made in philosophy was his conception of work and of ideology, which Kojève would make use of in his reading of the master/

pocentric philosophy of the *Phenomenology.* The advance that Heidegger makes over Hegel is his development—still tentative in *Sein und Zeit*—of a dualistic ontology. Whereas Hegel sketched all the possibilities for monism, Heidegger opens the possibility of forging distinct ontological bases for Nature (*Vorhandensein*) and Humanity (*Dasein*). This dualism accounts for human freedom and action without reducing them to some nonhuman denominator or atemporal Absolute.

What is at stake in this choice between monism and dualism? For Kojève the answer seems to have been the importance of the human in philosophy. A rigorous dualism seems to him to leave open the possibility of an anthropocentric philosophy in which human action will have no basis outside itself and in which history can be *fully* described in its own terms. For moderns, the impulse to monism comes, for the most part, from those who want to integrate the human into the natural, from those who see persons as having no attributes that require an ontology distinct from what other entities in the world need. A humanist or anthropocentric monism does not seem workable to Kojève, for he thinks it entails an anthropomorphic view of nature which cannot properly account for the achievements of modern science.[13]

The importance of the human in philosophy can be translated in Kojève's work as "the importance of history in philosophy." He maintains a critical distance from Heidegger because such a translation is inappropriate to a coherent reading of *Sein und Zeit* and conflicts with important themes in the essays that followed it. In a review written in 1936 Kojève criticized Heideggerian anthropology for unduly emphasizing the contemplative side of the human. Whereas Hegel's "person" is engaged in destructive action that is ultimately creative, Heidegger's "person" is most fully human when he or she

---

slave dialectic. I am deeply indebted to Nina Ivanoff for giving me access to all the unpublished documents used in this section and permission to quote them.

13. See Kojève, "La dialectique du réel et la méthode phénoménologique chez Hegel" (1934–1935), in *Introduction à la lecture,* especially 485–487n. It does not seem that Kojève considered in any detail the alternative provided by pragmatism as an anthropological monism. He certainly had a pragmatist view in regard to politics and ethics ("history is the becoming of truth") but retained "circularity" and correspondence as criteria for scientific truths.

has the opportunity to reflect. The reflective individual can be isolated from history, whereas the Hegelian person has to make history.[14]

An idea common to both philosophers, though, is that humanity is essentially finite. Hegel starts from freedom and historicity, eventually coming to the view that self-consciousness is impossible unless humanity is finite. Heidegger, we are told, starts from the proposition *cogito ergo sum finitus* and, for the most part, by-passes freedom and history. Hegel and Heidegger both reject traditional notions of transcendence in favor of a conception of human autotranscendence, through historical action and reflection respectively. Kojève does not, however, think that this rejection, or for that matter the traditional notions, can be justified by philosophical argument. The choice between atheism (humanity is finite) and theism (humanity is infinite) is, for him, *pre*philosophical. Kojève does identify autotranscendence with freedom, but he emphasizes that one can reject this freedom and seek instead grace through serving God: "The decision for or against freedom is, therefore, to the extent that it is philosophic (that is, fully conscious and thus truly free), a decision for or against an anthropological philosophy (and ontology) which reveals the sense [*sens*] (and essence) of my freedom to my empirical consciousness."[15] In the 1930s Heidegger seemed to Kojève to be heir to the tradition of anthropological philosophy developed by and bequeathed to the modern world by Hegel.

We can see in Kojève's work for *Recherches philosophiques* some of the same themes that were predominant in his article on Soloviev and that would remain crucial in his philosophy. The first of these themes is dualism versus monism. Whereas Soloviev strives to retain a monism in which the temporal (and human) will remain subordinate to and encompassed by the eternal (and divine), Heidegger seeks an independent ontological basis for human activity. Paradoxically, it is Soloviev who attaches the greater importance to history. For him, humanity has to work its way back to God; its action over time is the key element in the salvation of the world. If Heidegger gives up salvation as the product of work, he also abandons any simple notion

---

14. Kojève, manuscript review of Delp, p. 7. Kojève did not attach much importance to Heidegger's category of *Mitsein*.

15. Ibid., 14.

of human action as that which creates significant changes over time. Instead, he sees reflection on that which remains the same through time as the quintessential action.[16]

Kojève never accepted this intellectualization of the human realm. If he used Heidegger as a tool in his reading of Hegel, Hegel also served as an implicit critique for the antihistorical tendencies of Heidegger. The seeds for this critique were already planted in the perspective that Kojève adopted on Soloviev. According to Soloviev, as we saw above, human action is not only creative but directional; that is, action that counts is action in the service of progress, and progress for Soloviev is the unification of all people in a Universal Church. History makes sense as the account of this unification, as the development from the particular to the universal. The problem for Kojève in Heidegger's idea of reflection is that the idea cannot be separated from particularity. It is action that is possible (more likely, even) for the isolated individual.[17] Although Kojève does not accept Soloviev's understanding of an eternal Absolute or God as a final criterion for judging the value of particular human actions, he does retain the notion of a universal achieved over time which will serve as a standard for judging the particular.

Kojève elevates universality to the status of a criterion by which to evaluate particular actions. The True is the Whole, Hegel says in the Preface to the *Phenomenology*, and Kojève adopts this proposition without reservation. The Whole or Absolute is not necessarily a homogeneous End or tension-free resting place. On the contrary, it can encompass a "passionate counterpoint";[18] contradictions are contained but not destroyed within it. Kojève sees our greatest power in the human ability to construct such a whole—whether it be Human-

---

16. See Heidegger's "Letter on Humanism," in his *Basic Writings*, ed. F. Krell (New York, 1977), esp. 193–195, 215, and above, Chapter 1.

17. We shall see in Chapter 6 that Kojève's concern with particularity in Heidegger mirrors his critique of sectarianism in Leo Strauss's understanding of political philosophy.

18. Kojève, "La personnalité de Kandinsky," manuscript (date is illegible). For Kojève the crucial aspect of Kandinsky's paintings—and in this regard he saw them as the expression of his uncle's personality—was their creation of a concrete universality: "The calm and serene equilibrium of a counterpointal and harmonious richness, which remains concrete in its universality." For Kojève on Kandinsky see "Les peintures concretes de Kandinsky," *Revue de métaphysique et de morale* 90, no. 2 (1985), 149–171.

ity in History, the philosopher in a System, or an artist in a work that is fully harmonious. Without this power, he thinks, we would be locked into isolated particularity and unable to make sense of and evaluate change over time.

The task that Kojève set for himself and for philosophy in the 1930s can be described as follows: it is to understand the achievement (realization) of universality without having recourse to any form of theological (transcendent) explanations. We might stress "understanding" and "achievement," because the cognitive process of grasping the *sens* of action is no less important to Kojève than the action itself. Action is not truly human (and hence is mere activity) unless it is understood. This understanding has to follow successful action and cannot be divorced from historical achievement. History without philosophy is blind; philosophy without history is empty.

Thus Kojève brought to his interpretation of Hegel a set of concerns about how one could make meaning out of historical change and how that meaning could guide historical change. Clearly, the "possible exception of Marx" was connected to Kojève's philosophic endeavors. What has come to be called Western Marxism had its birth in an environment very similar to the one from which Kojève emerged in Germany, and parallels can be drawn between his path to Hegel and Lukàcs's Hegelian version of Marxism in *History and Class Consciousness*. Rather than move in the well-traveled direction of Western Marxism, however, our next chapter examines how Kojève articulated his specific concerns in his commentary on Hegel. That commentary and the debates surrounding it provide great insight into how history can be made meaningful and, perhaps, meaningfully.

Chapter Five

Desire, Dialectic, and History

> The disappearance of Man at the end of History, therefore, is not a cosmic catastrophe; the natural World remains what it has been from all eternity.... In point of fact, the end of human Time or History—that is, the definitive annihilation of Man properly so-called, or of the free and historic Individual—means quite simply the cessation of Action in the full sense of the term.
>
> *Alexandre Kojève, 1947*

Insofar as Alexandre Kojève is known outside the circle of scholars of the Hegelian tradition, he is known as the leader of a seminar on the *Phenomenology* which brought together an extraordinary group of writers and philosophers in the late 1930s. Mark Poster sees Kojève as the founder of a "small but very distinguished Hegel cult," and Vincent Descombes places his "humanization of nothingness" at the sources of twentieth-century French philosophy.[1] The one-time Stalinist Jean Desanti, the liberal Raymond Aron, and the new philosopher André Glucksmann all point to Kojève's seminar as the secret of contemporary French thinking about history.[2] In this chapter, I do not trace these various lines of influence but rather concentrate on the interpretation of Hegel that Kojève developed in the seminar, an interpretation published in 1947 as *Introduction à la lecture de*

---

1. Mark Poster, *Existential Marxism in Post-War France: From Sartre to Althusser* (Princeton, N.J., 1975), 8, and Vincent Descombes, *Le même et l'autre: Quarante-cinq ans de philosophie française (1933–1978)* (Paris, 1979), 21–63.

2. Jean Desanti, "Hegel, est-il le père de l'existentialisme?" *La nouvelle critique* no. 56 (1954), 91–109. As Kojève noted on his copy of this article, Desanti's "critique" of Kojève's "subjective" reading of Hegel completely overlooked the connection of freedom and work in Kojève's interpretation. See also Raymond Aron, *Mémoires: 50 ans de réflexion politique* (Paris, 1983), 94–100, and André Glucksmann, interview in *Le nouvel observateur* no. 992 (11 November, 1983), 4.

Hegel. By coming to terms with his idea of the End of History, and the changing functions it has in his teaching, we shall understand better the significance of the connections he made between knowing and history.

Kojève began his seminar on Hegel at the Ecole Pratique des Hautes Etudes, Section des Sciences Religieuses, in 1933. He was asked to give the course as a replacement for his friend Alexandre Koyré, whom Kojève had come to know at Heidelberg in the 1920s. Koyré had become a professor at the Ecole Pratique after leaving Germany, and Kojève registered as a student there in 1926.[3] Although housed within the main building of the Sorbonne, the Ecole Pratique attracted an array of students and professors rather different from that of the central university. It was more hospitable to foreigners than the Sorbonne and in the twenties and thirties was a meeting place for Russian emigrés and German Jews. The courses offered were, to all intents and purposes, open to the public, and although each term began with a registration period, there was no strict requirement that one register in order to attend a class. Nevertheless, the *Annuaire* published by the school and the *Registre des Inscriptions* do provide some idea of who intended to take particular courses and are the best available concrete evidence in regard to students at the Ecole Pratique during the 1920s and 1930s.

Kojève's name first appears in the *Annuaire* for the academic year 1926–27, when he attended Koyré's course on Hegel's religious philosophy. This seminar was part of a series on speculative mysticism in Germany. It concentrated on Hegel's early writings on the unhappy consciousness and on the concept of mediation in the *Phenomenology*.[4] In 1932–33 Koyré again taught on Hegel's religious philosophy, and Kojève was in attendance. This was a comparatively large class, and some of the other participants are notable. Georges Bataille, Henri Corbin, Aron Gurvitsch, Raymond Queneau, Leo Strauss, and Eric Weil all signed up for the course. With the exception of Strauss, who left for England, all attended the continuation of the course under Kojève's guidance when Koyré began a leave to teach at the University of Cairo.

3. Koyré was directeur d'études when he left to teach in Cairo in January 1934. Kojève at that time had the status of elève diplômé.

4. *Ecole Pratique des Hautes Etudes: Sections des Sciences Religieuses, Annuaire (1926–1927)* (Paris, 1926), 51.

What was the immediate context in which Kojève developed his interpretation of Hegel? It was no doubt easier for Kojève to construct his idiosyncratic reading within the open setting of the Ecole Pratique than it would have been at a standard philosophy course at the Sorbonne. Even a partial class list (see Appendix) reveals the diverse character of the seminar. There was a marked presence of surrealism—or at least of thinkers influenced by surrealism—with the participation of Queneau, Lacan, Bataille, and Breton.[5] Father Gaston Fessard, a Jesuit of striking erudition and flaming anticommunism, participated frequently in the discussions, often in opposition to Kojève.[6] Merleau-Ponty attended the seminar in 1937–38, and the Marx-Hegel link that Kojève emphasized was surely no surprise to him or others in the class who were studying the much discussed early texts of both thinkers.[7]

When Kojève assumed responsibility for Koyré's seminar, he made use of some of the key themes in the latter's interpretation of Hegel.[8] Yet the way in which Kojève presented them was wholly different. Kojève pushed these ideas to their limit and attempted to show their plausibility as a correct reading of a classic philosopher. If Koyré's reading of Hegel is original, Kojève's is violent; if the former sheds light on difficult texts, the latter explodes them. In this regard it is a complete mistake to try to understand or evaluate Kojève's work on the basis of whether it gets Hegel right—whether the commentary translates the original. On the contrary, Kojève finds in Hegel a language he can appropriate in order to speak to the philosophical issues that most concern him. This appropriation is itself Hegelian insofar as it results from a confrontation with Hegel's texts which aims to realize their deepest meaning but also to point out difficulties in them

5. Breton's name does not appear in either the *Annuaire* or the registration list, but Kojève spoke of his attending the seminar in his 1968 interview in *La quinzaine littéraire* 53 (1–15 July 1968), 19. Although technically students, these participants in the seminar had already started publishing and making names for themselves in French cultural life.

6. Private correspondence between Fessard and Kojève, especially Kojève to Fessard, 21 June 1936.

7. See above, Introduction, 13–15.

8. See, for example, Alexandre Kojève, *Introduction à la lecture de Hegel* (Paris, 1947), 434n–435n, hereafter *ILH*. I use the translation of James H. Nichols, Jr., *Introduction to the Reading of Hegel*, ed. A. Bloom (New York, 1969), 158n–159n, hereafter *IRH*.

that Hegel himself left unsolved. Kojève himself is quite direct about this. In a letter to a critic from *Les temps modernes* he describes his interpretation as an *"oeuvre de propagande destinée à frapper les esprits."* Unlike Koyré, Kojève is not concerned whether his issues were the same ones that Hegel thought crucial when he wrote the *Phenomenology.*[9]

As we saw in the Introduction, Koyré develops a historical anthropological reading of Hegel based upon a consideration of the Hegelian notion of time. This notion is a paradigm for historical thinking insofar as it organizes future, present, and past as temporal dimensions *for us.* Hegel's great originality, according to Koyré, is to give primacy to the future. The significance of any "now" is to be found in its future and in the connection of that future to the past of the now. The future is that which is hoped for, worked for, or, most generally, willed by people; the past is what people choose from time-gone-by to make a present more meaningful. Hegelian time is history as apprehended by persons; Hegelian knowing is the discursive form of this apprehension.

Koyré shows that Hegelian time is history for humanity, but he does not try to specify in any detail what is properly human. Kojève begins with the question "What is the Hegelian person?" and answers it by explicating the structure of human desire, in contradistinction to the needs or demands of the animal. Human desire is the desire for recognition (*reconnaissance*), which, according to Kojève's Hegel, alone can lead to self-consciousness. Human desire, properly so-called, has as its object another desire and not another thing.[10] Thus it is an animal desire that draws one to the *body* of another but a human desire that is expressed as the wish to be desired, loved, or—most generally for Kojève—recognized by another.[11]

This distinction is not merely an attempt to call "properly human"

9. Kojève to Tran-Duc-Thao, Paris, 7 October 1948. Kojève's most significant overt departure from Hegel was his rejection of Hegel's monism in favor of a nature/history dualism. Thus Kojève, in contrast to Hegel, tried to show the independence of the historical from the natural. Important in this regard also is Kojève's use of Marx and Heidegger to understand Hegel.

10. Hegel's analysis of Desire, *Phenomenology*, trans. J. B. Baillie (New York, 1931), 225–227, did not have the dualist form that Kojève stressed. This form was crucial for Kojève because it was one of the bases for his fundamental distinction of the natural from the historical.

11. *ILH*, 13.

those desires which are directed at nonmaterial or "higher" things. Kojève also discusses the human desire for objects, but in this case he speaks of a desire that is mediated by another's desire: "Desire directed toward a natural object is human only to the extent that it is 'mediated' by the Desire of another directed toward the same object: it is human to desire what others desire, because they desire it. Thus, an object perfectly useless from the biological point of view (such as a medal, or the enemy's flag) can be desired because it is the object of other desires. Such a Desire can only be a human desire, and human reality is created only by action that satisfies such Desires: human history is the history of desired Desires."[12] Natural objects, then, are "humanized"—become part of history—as they acquire some function in the interplay of deflected desires.

How, then, is desire characterized as an object? What does it mean for human desire to be satisfied? Kojève's description of desire as "the presence of an absence" seems to make matters more difficult rather than to offer any firm ground upon which we can build. The essential distinction of human desire is that it does not consume its object. The satisfaction of a human desire is therefore creative, because its object is empty (an absence). To make the same point somewhat differently: the satisfaction of human desire requires some form of mutuality (the loved one "returns" the love) or social recognition of an object's value (the value of a medal is appreciated by another; the enemy fights to keep its flag). When satisfaction occurs, something new is introduced into the world (a useful object becomes beautiful; two individuals become a couple). For satisfaction to endure, the desire *qua* object has to be preserved, albeit in an altered state. The simultaneity of preservation and change (negation) marks the dialectic of human desire. The effort at satisfaction *and* conservation demands that this dialectic be linked with the development of self-consciousness.

Of course, a person—even a Hegelian person—does not have only properly human desires. The *désir de reconnaissance* coexists with purely animal needs. For Kojève's Hegel, there is a crucial conflict between *les désirs humains* and *les désirs animaux*. The latter are always in the service of preserving the life of the individual, whereas the former are not necessarily attached to objects that contribute to

---

12. Ibid. Translation, slightly modified, from *IRH*, 6.

his or her continued existence. The "proof" of the predominance of the human over the animal can be found in one's willingness to risk one's life for the sake of some form of recognition, to decide self-consciously that it is preferable to die than to live without the satisfaction that comes from this recognition. The will to risk one's life knowingly is *the* sign of a person's "humanness" for Kojève. Clearly, animals other than humans are often in situations where their lives are at stake. Risk itself is not sufficient proof of humanness; the risk has to be in the service of a desire for another desire. Kojève concludes as follows:

> Therefore, to desire the Desire of another is in the final analysis to desire that the value that I am or that I "represent" be the value desired by the other. I want him to "recognize" my value as his value; to "recognize" me as an autonomous value. In other words, all human, anthropogenetic Desire—the Desire that generates Self-Consciousness, the human reality—is, finally, a function of the desire for "recognition." And the risk of life by which the human reality "comes to light" is a risk for the sake of such a Desire. Therefore, to speak of the "origin" of Self-Consciousness is necessarily to speak of a fight to the death for "recognition."
>
> Without this fight to the death for pure prestige, there would never have been human beings on the earth.[13]

Humans properly so-called, then, emerge from this bloody struggle whose goal is not a final destruction of the other but acceptance by the other.

This account of Kojève's response to the question of what defines the human has been abstract insofar as it has spoken generally of the human versus the animal in terms of their respective desires. Kojève uses Hegel's story of the master/slave dialectic to structure his own treatment of these terms and to make them more concrete. We saw in Chapter 1 how Hyppolite used the section of the *Phenomenology* on the unhappy consciousness as a figure for the book as a whole. Similarly, for Kojève the master/slave dialectic is the key to understanding the *Phenomenology* and Hegel's work generally. The section concerned has an allegorical function for Kojève insofar as he uses it to speak to almost all of the philosophical problems that arise out of Hegelian thinking.

13. Ibid. 14. Translation, slightly modified, from *IRH*, 7.

The story of the master/slave dialectic is fairly straightforward;[14] indeed, I have already touched on some of its crucial aspects in my description of Hegelian desire. Hegel describes the confrontation of two persons, two "consciousnesses," who have forged their identities in isolation from other people. Upon meeting, each sees the other as a threat to his or her individual existence, and, more important, each seeks to dominate the other so as to be more certain of this existence. (Hegel speaks here of "self-certainty.") The two struggle for domination, for the recognition of the strength of their respective individualities. The loser of the struggle is the one who decides that life is more important than the recognition originally sought. This person abandons the fight and is made a slave who recognizes the sovereignty of the master. In other words, the loser allows the animal desire for self-preservation to take precedence over the human desire for recognition.

The slave is forced to work on behalf of the master, and the latter enjoys the fruits of the former's work. The master's desires are acted upon by the slave, and the master experiences satisfactions without mediation. The slave, on the other hand, has to labor for the satisfaction of his or her desires *and* those of the master. Here, then, is the domination of the slave: being forced to work, to produce, for the master while living with the fear that he or she will be put to death if the efforts do not meet with approval.

The victory of the master, however, is only apparent. True, the slave works to produce what is desired, but this is not what the master risked his or her life for. The work of the slave satisfies only the animal desires of the master. The recognition that the latter was willing to die for now comes from *merely* a slave, and hence it is not the recognition that can provide self-certainty. The slave's "self" is not made of the same stuff as the master's, and hence, from the master's perspective, the slave cannot really appreciate him or her. Thus the hierarchy established by the struggle for recognition prohibits the satisfaction of properly human desire. Kojève describes the inability of the master to be satisfied as follows: "But the Master fights as a man (for recognition) and consumes as an animal (without having worked). Such is his inhumanity. Through this he remains a

---

14. See Hegel, "Lordship and Bondage," in *Phenomenology*, 229–240; Kojève's commentary, "En guise d'introduction," *ILH*, 12–34.

man-of-appetite [*homme de la Begierde*] (which he succeeds to satisfy). He cannot transcend this level because he is idle. He can *die* as a man, but he can only *live* as an animal."[15]

For Kojève, the position of the master is an *impasse existentiale*, whereas the slave's actions constitute the germ of historical development. The slave has been shaken out of a naive *sentiment de soi* by the threat of death with which he or she is forced to live and under which he or she has to work. The complementary poles of fear and labor are the crucial formative elements of the slave's consciousness. The fear of the master is, Hegel says, the beginning of wisdom,[16] and it is through the transformation of the natural (given) world on behalf of the master that the slave *qua* worker can find a form of satisfaction which will be not an impasse but progressive. The master's satisfaction, on the other hand, can be repeated but not deepened.

Meanwhile, as Hegel shows, the slave works: "By serving he cancels in every particular aspect his dependence on and attachment to natural existence, and by his work removes this existence away.... Labour...is desire restrained and checked, evanescence delayed and postponed.... The consciousness that toils and serves accordingly attains by this means the direct apprehension of that independent being as its self."[17] Kojève's comment on this passage is worth quoting at length:

Only the slave can transcend the given World (which is subjugated by the Master) and not perish. Only the Slave can transform the World that forms him and fixes him in slavery and create a world that he has formed in which he will be free. And the slave achieves this only through forced and terrified work carried out in the Master's service. To be sure, this work by itself does not free him. But in transforming the World by this work, the Slave transforms himself, too, and thus creates the new objective conditions that permit him to take up once again the liberating Struggle for recognition that he refused in the beginning for fear of death.[18]

Through work, through the changes seen in the natural world as the results of these efforts, the slave can begin to attain a degree of sat-

15. *ILH*, 55.
16. Hegel, *Phenomenology*, 237.
17. Ibid., 238.
18. *ILH*, 34. Translation, slightly modified, from *IRH*, 29.

isfaction: the slave can see himself or herself in his or her creations. This form of satisfaction is progressive or historical insofar as the work that has been accomplished can be built upon.

For Kojève, the dynamic of mastery and slavery is the motor of history: domination sets history in motion and equality will end it. As history arises out of this dialectic, so does self-consciousness and finally truth. The field upon which the two battle for recognition, Hegel says, "is that native land of truth ... that kingdom where truth is at home."[19]

The master/slave story functions for Kojève as a fundamental code that allows the philosopher to organize the field of human relations historically: first there is the Bloody Battle; then comes the Reign of the Master and the formation of the slave; and finally, the Triumph of the Slave. The difference between the master/slave dialectic and the dialectic of the unhappy consciousness points to the crucial difference between the perspectives of Kojève and Hyppolite. The story of the unhappy consciousness emphasizes the psychological pain of individual development, in the search for community by the wounded self. The story of the master and the slave—at least in Kojève's hands—asserts that there is no human self prior to social interaction. The human is always a product of struggle or of work. Rather than stress the personal suffering of growth through alienation, the master/slave dialectic underlines physical battle, fear, recognition, and, most important, work and death. In Kojève's reading, the social and political perspective always has priority. Alienation may be a fundamental psychological phenomenon, but only a person living in society has a psyche.[20]

In Kojève's strong emphasis on the master/slave dialectic we can discern his view that Marx and Heidegger are the two philosophers of note after Hegel.[21] Kojève's understanding of this dialectic as the

19. Hegel, *Phenomenology*, 219.

20. I do not address here the question of whether Hyppolite or Kojève had more textual support for their respective emphases on sections of the *Phenomenology*. In any case, to answer this question fully one would have to develop a complete interpretation of the *Phenomenology* (to determine what counts as textual support). The question would then arise whether *this* interpretation had as much textual support as either Hyppolite's or Kojève's. I have already noted that Kojève himself was not interested in developing a "correct" reading of Hegel.

21. See above, Chapter 4, 89 and note 12. Kojève noted that Heidegger took up the Hegelian theme of death but failed to account for History (struggle and work). Likewise, Marx accounted for History, but neglected death: *ILH*, 575n.

motor of history allows him to assimilate the struggle for recognition with class conflict. Furthermore, as we shall see, his discussions of work and slave ideologies are a reading of Hegel's articulation of the history of philosophy and of religion through the Marxist concepts of labor and false consciousness.[22] Likewise, Kojève's emphasis on the existential results of the experience of mortality in the struggle for recognition borrows heavily from Heidegger's early work. Kojève's conception of Hegelian time adds to Koyré's ideas the theme of a person's essential finitude, a theme that is so important in *Sein und Zeit*.[23]

In what follows I explicate Kojève's reading of Hegel through the three moments of the master/slave dialectic: Bloody Battle, Reign of the Master, Triumph of the Slave. The published account of Kojève's seminar follows the *Phenomenology* section by section, but the schema used here is not foreign to his interpretation. Indeed, by organizing the material in this way I underline the connection Kojève made between philosophy and history, which he thought was the decisive contribution of Hegel to the history of philosophy.

Bloody Battle

Kojève's—even Hegel's—claim that the origin of the human is to be found in bloody confrontation is hardly original. The most important predecessor is Hobbes, whose idea of the state of nature as a war of all against all is surely a point of reference for Hegel's master/slave dialectic.[24] For Kojève's Hegel, however, the struggle for recognition is not only at the origin of human community but at the very foundation of the self—of humans, that is, in contradistinction

---

22. See below, 113–116. In two review articles published just after World War II, Kojève made clear the importance that the Hegel/Marx connection held for him. See "Christianisme et communisme," and "Hegel, Marx et le christianisme," *Critique* 3–4 (1946), 308–312 and 339–366.

23. See *ILH*, 53, 338n, 379–380, 388n, 487, and especially, "L'idée de la mort dans la philosophie de Hegel," 529–575.

24. In Leo Strauss's *The Political Philosophy of Hobbes* (London, 1936), the author notes that he and Kojève "intend to undertake a detailed investigation of the connection between Hegel and Hobbes" (58n). Although the study never materialized, the two authors did correspond at length on this subject.

to animals. The origin of community is coextensive with the origin of the human, properly so-called. Persons do not exist outside communities unless they are separated from them, and, Kojève adds, that means they do not exist outside history. The struggle for recognition is the basic dynamic of society—as well as of self-consciousness—and as long as this struggle continues, social relations are not static. They *become* static only as the *result* of the struggle; only after the struggle is complete is it possible to separate the social from the historical.

The only properly human element that precedes the Bloody Battle is the desire for recognition. As we saw above, for Kojève the essential facet of this human desire is that it has as its object another desire. More generally, desire is always mediated, and the mediating term is always another desire. This formulation is helpful because it leads to the question "What makes an object desirable?" Kojève's answer to this question reveals the values according to which he thinks history is made and judged.

Kojève's response to the question is simple: an object is desirable because "recognized" others desire it. The flag of the enemy is worth fighting for, but only if the enemy cares about it enough to fight (and if the enemy is sufficiently respected). Once the opponent is willing simply to give it up, the flag becomes a mere piece of material. Why does anybody fight over flags? Kojève replies, "to attain recognition." Is recognition, then, desirable in a more absolute way than everything else? Does it play the role of some ahistorical Good that is desirable in itself, not because anybody desires it?

Recognition cannot be made a transcendental concept, if only because it has no content outside the field of social relations. Instead, it is bound up with Kojève's conception of a person as always already mediated by others. That is, because recognition is coextensive with the human, one can not talk about persons *qua* human without situating them in a sociohistorical context. Even the individual ego, according to Kojève, can be discussed in its particularity only in terms of its *separation* from the social. Without the mediation of others, the *human* ego does not exist: "Real and true man is the result of his interaction with others; his I and the idea he has of himself are 'mediated' by recognition obtained as a result of his action. And his true autonomy is the autonomy that he *maintains* in the social reality by the effort of that action."[25] There is no autonomous identity that one fights to protect in the primordial struggle; instead, this identity is constructed piecemeal from this Bloody Battle and the struggles and work that follow it.

Clearly, the desire for recognition which becomes manifest in the Bloody Battle is at the origin of both self-consciousness and history. The two always go together, and there is no history (only the chaos of events) without self-consciousness, as there is no self-consciousness (only dreams and madness, or the chaos of consciousness) without history. Here we can see the distance between Kojève and Hyppolite. The problem that Hyppolite saw as absolutely crucial for modern philosophy—the connection between historicity and history—does not even arise for Kojève. For the latter, the problem, in the sense of a confusion, is to think one can talk separately about either history or historicity.

Thus a wide range of issues that we have already seen as part of the Hegelian revival in the 1930s does not appear in Kojève's work. The first manifestation of *human* desire is for him the beginning of history, and so the surrealist attempt to use Hegel to bring the instinctual depths up to the level of history should not be confused with Kojève's analysis of desire. Likewise, the attempt by certain Marxists to see "the dialectical method" as Hegel's great contribution to the history of philosophy finds no support in Kojève.[26] Nor does Kojève view the dialectic, like some existentialists, as first and foremost a reflection of personal experience. Instead, he sees it as the framework for all historical change.

Kojève emphasizes that the struggle for recognition is "bloody," and because the figure of the initial battle serves as the model for all historical development, it is important to ask why the desire necessarily manifests itself in *violent* confrontation rather than in some less extreme form. One cannot answer simply that the Bloody Battle serves as the basic myth in the *Phenomenology* and then point out the connection of violence and the sacred in myths of founding. Although the master/slave dialectic does indeed function to some extent as a foundational myth, Kojève emphasizes that the violence of the

25. *ILH*, 21. Translation from *IRH*, 15.
26. See, for example, *ILH* 460, 527.

struggle is by necessity repeated throughout history. It does not have only a symbolic or an allegorical function.

The importance of violence for Kojève is that it evinces the willingness to take radical risks. That is, violence in itself is glorified not because of its cathartic or purifying function but because in some situations the resort to violence shows the will to die rather than to submit to a particular way of life. Self-conscious risk shows that a person has triumphed over his or her natural (animal) tendency toward self-preservation.

The importance of this valorization of risk becomes clear in its implications for the understanding of historical development generally. History is, in large part, "the story of bloody struggles for recognition (wars, revolutions)," and it is always written by the (ultimate) winners of these struggles. At the start of a war or a revolution, however—when there are at least two sides willing to fight—no one side can be said to be in the right.[27] The right is decided by the historians, or, more simply, by the writers employed by the winners. Kojève, like Hegel, accepts Schiller's dictum *Die Weltgeschichte ist das Weltgericht*, there is nothing independent of historical development—or prior to the struggle for recognition—which can serve as a criterion to evaluate particular actions.

Kojève's valorization of risk is a double-edged sword. On the one hand, he tends to respect political violence that accepts death as a necessary result of failure, but, on the other, he dismisses the merely verbal violence so typical of the French intellectual scene as so much empty noise. Indeed, "intellectual" for Kojève is a term of derision, for insofar as everyone knows that the individual designated by this word *only* speaks, his or her words have no force. The intellectual is a "spiritual animal" because he or she neither triumphs as master nor works as slave.[28] The intellectual's attempt to be disinterested or objective carries no weight for Kojève, who underlines the role of desire in all work and struggle. The intellectual's embrace of the Good, the True, and the Beautiful as eternal values is ridiculed by Kojève as a dishonest attempt to hide from history.

27. See Kojève, *Esquisse d'une phénoménologie du droit* (manuscript date Marseilles, 1943, published Paris, 1981), 377–383. For a brief outline of this book in relation to Kojève's work see Michael S. Roth, "A Note on Kojève's Phenomenology of Right," *Political Theory* 11, no. 3 (1983), 447–450.

28. See *ILH*, 93.

Kojève's emphasis on risk and on the test of violence fell on receptive ears in France in the late 1930s. The generational conflict was clear when Julien Benda's *Trahison des clercs* was answered by Paul Nizan's *Les chiens de gardes*. Whereas the former defended a traditional view of the intellectual as the defender of universal values, the latter put forward an angry call for committed thinkers and writers. Although verbal calls for commitment should not be confused with actual political commitment, it did seem increasingly difficult to remain detached from political affairs during the heady days of the Popular Front and the struggle with fascism. Of course, by the end of 1940 detachment was a thing of the past: one had to choose sides or be placed. In this context, the philosophy of engagement became common currency, and when Kojève's commentary appeared in 1947, his readers were prepared for his denunciations of the *merely* intellectual.

The pretension of disinterest has no merit at all for Kojève's Hegel because it is only through interest—passion—that people will risk their lives to change the conditions of their existence. The ideal of calm detachment is for him the image of death or at least the image of a *merely* biological (natural, animal) existence. The struggle for recognition, which is the origin of the human, remains as a criterion for separating those willing to participate in historical life from those content with the repetition of the natural. Kojève describes Hegel's view as follows: "Man will risk his biological *life* to satisfy his *nonbiological* Desire. And Hegel says the being that is incapable of putting its life in danger in order to attain ends that are not immediately vital—i.e. the being that cannot risk its life in a Struggle for *Recognition*, in a fight for pure *prestige*—is *not* a truly *human* being."[29] It is through risk that one steps from the animal to the human, from the natural to the historical.

The acceptance of violence and the valorization of risk seem to lead us only to a muscle-bound philosophy of struggle meant to celebrate warriors who battle without fear. The fascistic resonances of this philosophy are not unimportant, despite Kojève's insistence that he was presenting a Marxist reading of Hegel.[30] Yet one must remem-

29. Ibid., 169. Modified translation from *IRH*, 41.
30. In this regard I note the influence of Carl Schmitt on Kojève's understanding of politics. Schmitt is cited in Kojève's book on Right, and Kojève delivered a lecture on colonialism and capitalism at Schmitt's invitation. I am currently collecting their

ber that the Bloody Battle is but a moment of the master/slave dialectic, and that the persons who will make history are those whose fear of death leads them to give up the struggle and become slaves. Kojève insists that it is the confrontation with death which enables the slave to make history self-consciously.

The fear of death which leads a person to give up the struggle reveals the slave's own ties to the natural, but it reveals them to him or her as well as to us. Slaves imagine themselves as being-no-longer and thus experience the contingency of particular existence. Victorious masters are never forced to expand their consciousnesses this way and so are more tightly bound to the given world (the here and now) than are the slaves. The slave's initial brush with death provokes a deep intuition of human finitude. Kojève goes so far as to say that this situation gives the slave the capacity to act historically.[31] Initial weakness will be an ultimate strength as the slave is forced to live with the realization of his or her own mortality.

It is in this moment of the master/slave dialectic that Heidegger's influence on Kojève is most apparent. Kojève himself tells us that it is possible to understand the *Phenomenology* only after Heidegger writes *Sein und Zeit;* more specifically, after the analysis of human finitude that *Sein und Zeit* contains.[32] Heidegger underlines the crucial role that the consciousness of death plays in authentic being-in-the-world, and Kojève makes use of this perspective in his reading of the master/slave story. Here also is a theme from Kojève's early writings on Soloviev. For the Russian mystic, there are two facets of the Absolute, the eternal and the temporal. The former guarantees the sense of the latter; the eternal is a firm criterion that allows one to judge history *from the outside.* In his early writings Kojève exposes the problems that this dual perspective on God and history entails. In his version of the master/slave story the slave learns to give up any guarantees, any judgments from the outside, through the reali-

---

postwar correspondence. Poster describes the possibility that Kojève "ontologizes violence" in *Existential Marxism,* 11; Descombes describes Kojève as having a "terrorist conception of history," *Le même et l'autre,* 27.

31. See *ILH,* 175–176.

32. Ibid., 527n. Kojève claimed not that Heidegger's analysis of mortality was original but that his emphasis on the role of human finitude helped us to understand Hegel's powerful but brief discussion of the role of death in the master/slave dialectic. See Hegel, *Phenomenology,* 237.

zation of essential human finitude. The slave's surrender in the Bloody Battle saves the possibility of (self-conscious) historical development.

The slave's rude confrontation with finitude, of course, does not itself enable him or her to assume freely the burdens of history. There are other burdens to shoulder. First and foremost, slaves learn how to serve. They give up struggle and begin to work. Meanwhile the masters rule.

The Reign of the Master

To understand the dynamics of the Bloody Battle for recognition, it was necessary to come to terms with the desire that led the combatants to risk their lives. Similarly, the first thing we must explicate in order to comprehend the rule of the master is the satisfaction the winner finds in having been victorious and in being served. Although the loser of the battle is obviously not satisfied *qua* loser, it is also important to note the possibilities for satisfaction that he or she creates *qua* worker. The development of the consciousness of the slave/worker is a central facet of Kojève's approach to Hegel—and is what can be correctly characterized as Marxian in this approach— and the connection between work and ideology is an important part of the master/slave story.

Masters are left in an "existential impasse" by victories in the struggles for recognition. Acknowledgment received from slaves, because it comes from *mere* slaves, cannot satisfy. The work done for the masters satisfies only the natural desires of the masters, that is, it satisfies them *qua* animals. Because they do not work, they cannot raise themselves above this level of satisfaction. They can only repeat the Bloody Battle with others and never progress. As Kojève characterizes the master, "He can *die* as man, but he can live only as animal."[33]

Kojève explores the contradictions of the master's situation in more detail in his *Esquisse d'une phénoménologie du droit*.[34] His point is that the code of the master is based on a notion of strict equality (among those who count as human, that is, slaveholders) which limits

---

33. *ILH*, 55.
34. In para. 40, 274–281. See Roth, "A Note on Kojève."

interaction to a minimum. For a master there are other people only *qua* masters; to be a master, however, is to be idle, to have others work for you and satisfy your needs immediately. As a rule, exchanges among masters do not take place, because their order is based on equality not equivalence. Only with the division of labor inherent in what Kojève calls the bourgeois rule of equivalence would one want to exchange and be capable of exchanging with another. Insofar as there are interactions or exchanges, they reduce the master to playing the role of a mediator among slaves. (My slaves have cut wood, yours have grown oranges; we can exchange wood for oranges.) The ideal of the master is self-sufficiency and, as a result, isolation.[35] The master's desires should be immediately satisfied by the slave. Insofar as this ideal is realized, the master has no reason to change; more accurately, he or she has no reason to initiate change.

The idle, uncreative master is for Kojève the emblem of satisfaction. He sees the independence of autarky as a kind of death, because for him human life is essentially characterized by the will-to-change. The master does not live in what Koyré described as Hegelian time, in which the future has priority; Hegelian time is the temporality of desire, the master's time is the rhythm of satisfaction. Satisfaction for the master requires the preservation of his or her "now," which in the end amounts to the conversion of the human condition begun by the Bloody Battle into a natural condition.

The single element in the master's way of life which is not assimilated to the natural is the willingness to risk his or her life for recognition. Thus the master is human only *qua* warrior, and this quest for more recognition is simply the quest for more slaves and perhaps more land. The master lives between risk and idleness; the boundary of each of these activities is death—death in bloody battle or death in immediate satisfaction.

The loser of the Bloody Battle, as we have seen, is marked by the confrontation with death. The realization of finitude is not abstract knowledge recalled for philosophical conversation among fellow-slaves. It is instead the yoke under which slaves live, the omnipresent fear that keeps them working for the master. The satisfactions that

35. Kojève thus completely anticipated the critique of his Hegel interpretation by Dennis J. Goldford, "Kojève's Reading of Hegel," *International Philosophic Quarterly* 22, no. 4 (1982), 275–294. It seems that Goldford had not read the recently published *Phénoménologie du droit* before writing his article.

the master experiences immediately are always delayed gratifications for the slave. First, there is service to the master; to work, the slave must learn to suspend desire.

Slaves are first and foremost workers.[36] They act in the world to satisfy not their own instinct but those of an other.[37] To do so, the slave has to expand particular, immediate consciousness so as to comprehend the needs of those being served as well as to manipulate the natural world successfully. Kojève concludes that the faculty of understanding—the cognitive base of technology—arises out of forced labor: "What is a natural desire in the master (desire to eat, for example) is only an 'abstract idea' in the slave, who acts to satisfy a desire without feeling it himself. He works, therefore, as a result of something unreal, of an idea which is a project to be accomplished. And this is why his work essentially transforms the natural world. Consequently, wherever there is work, properly so-called, there is also necessarily Understanding [Verstand], that is, faculty of abstract notions."[38] Slaves are thereby educated (gebildet) by work and achieve a mastery over nature as they acquire the technical ability to make what masters are perceived to want. Slaves qua workers are the emblem for historical progress in the Kojèvian-Hegelian schema of history.

With the introduction of the idea of "progress," however, the master/slave story becomes more complex. We can see without difficulty the difference between the master and the slave. Why is the work of the latter progressive? What does it progress toward?

Slaves certainly live in Hegelian time: their lives are a series of projects, and the dimension of the future always has priority for them. Unlike masters, slaves live for (and by) change, and they create change through work. But why does Kojève call this change "progress?" How can he justify seeing the humanized world created by the slave/workers as better than the natural world they negated? Recall that for Kojève there is no nonhistorical Absolute that—like Soloviev's perfect God—can serve as a criterion for evaluating historical change.

We can begin to answer these questions—which are the essential

36. Kojève placed the following introduction from Marx before the introduction to *ILH*: "Hegel grasps *work* as the *essence*, as the proven essence of man." The quotation is from the *Economic and Philosophic Manuscripts of 1844.*

37. See *ILH*, 171.

38. Kojève, "Hegel, Marx et le christianisme," 354–355.

ones confronting the Hegelian (modern) conception of historical change—by returning to Kojève's conception of human desire. The changes that slaves initiate in the natural world and in their own consciousnesses by their work are sublimations of the desire for recognition; the failure to satisfy this desire in the Bloody Battle forces the desire into other avenues. Thus slaves/workers become masters of nature rather than masters of other people; they recognize themselves in the fruits of their labor. Yet they remain slaves in the eyes of the masters, and the fear of death remains omnipresent. Finally, the workers have to gain the recognition of or kill the masters, not so that they will in turn be slaveholders but to realize the satisfaction of mutual recognition. This mutuality is the goal, then, of the historical change initiated by work; satisfaction on a universal level of the *désir humain*, which Kojève will call freedom.

I underline here that the Hegelian conception of historical change is inseparable from a theory of the subject. I do not say "grounded in a theory of the subject," because it would be equally true to say that the conception of the subject is grounded in a theory of history. Thus the history of psychoanalysis in France, for example, must be understood in light of the resurgence of Hegelianism: Lacan's understanding of personal development owes much to Kojève's vision of historical change.[39] The link between psychology and history is most evident in Kojève's emphasis on the master/slave dialectic as the origin of self-consciousness as well as of historical development and on the End of history as the satisfaction of desire.

Of course, recent critics of the Hegelian theory of historical change have not neglected its ties to a theory of the subject. Instead, they have emphasized that the wholeness which is the telos of both personal and historical development should be rejected. In the last chapter of this book we shall see some of the problems that arise for thinkers who want to abandon a telos of development but do not want to renounce political judgment that can be made meaningful. Here, we need recall only the function of this telos in Kojève's reading of the master/slave dialectic. Kojève's emplotment of the story is based

---

39. See especially the dialectical account of development in the "Rome Discourse," translated in Anthony Wilden's *The Language of the Self* (Baltimore, Md., 1968), and Wilden's discussion of Kojève's influence on Lacan, 192–196, 218–219, 306, 308.

on a retrospective judgment of the value of various kinds of action and, ultimately, on a conceptualization of the freedom that is achieved in history. Without a concept of the ultimate product of history, there are no criteria for judging human action unless one is willing to put one's faith in an suprahistorical Absolute. Having rejected this faith, Kojève looks to the satisfaction that is the product of history in order to understand how that satisfaction has been constructed.

This concept of universal satisfaction, this goal of historical development, is *for us*, not something that consciously animates the work of the slave. Kojève does not, though, neglect the question of why *slaves* think they are working or of how the ideational realm is connected to the realm of labor. Generally speaking, the histories of Art and Religion are considered in the *Phenomenology* as parts of an ideal universe that slaves construct because of the absence of the full satisfaction of mutual recognition. More important, this ideal universe expresses the goals of slaves/workers—the direction of historical progress—in disguised form.

Kojève presents in detail Hegel's account of "slave ideologies," from Greek stoicism to bourgeois liberalism.[40] Perhaps the most important of these is Christianity. All of these ideologies are attempts to reconcile in thought the contradictions present in the life of the slaves. A real reconciliation requires the reinitiation of the struggle for recognition. The slaves are not prepared for this risk (they are afraid), so they create a fiction that makes sense of, justifies, the fact that they desire recognition and freedom but continue to live in servitude.

The fiction of Christianity confronts this contradiction by emplotting it in a larger narrative that shows that living in contradiction is necessary for everyone: all existence implies contradiction because the world of existence is in tension with the Other World, the Beyond.[41] Workers live in servitude despite their desire for freedom, but they should not necessarily act to free themselves. All who live in this world live in servitude; even the masters serve, when seen in their *real* role, that is, in relation to the Beyond. There is no need to struggle to change *this* world, because "in the Beyond, in the only

40. "Slave ideology" is quoted from Kojève, who defined ideology as "something which can *become* true by Struggle and Work, which will make the World conform to the ideal. The test of Struggle and Work makes an ideology true or false." *ILH*, 117.
41. *ILH*, 182–184.

world which really counts, one *is* already free and *equal* to the master (in the Servitude of God)."[42]

For Kojève's Hegel, Christianity is a crucial stage in the evolution of the consciousness of the slave because it affirms the values of freedom and equality. It is *only* a stage, because it displaces these values from this world into the next. In the heavenly realm, these values are already realized:

> Without Struggle, without effort, therefore, the Christian realizes the Slave's ideal: he obtains—in and through (and for) God—*equality* with the Master: inequality is but a mirage, like everything in this World of the senses in which Slavery and Mastery hold sway.
> Certainly an ingenious solution, Hegel will say.[43]

The solution to the contradiction of the slave's existence is too easy. For Kojève, the promised liberation is "metaphysically impossible," because it does not come through bloody struggle.

Christianity itself reveals this impossibility insofar as the liberation it describes is not a freedom from servitude. It promises equality, but equality before God the Absolute Master. The ideology of Christianity does not negate the condition of slavery; indeed, it facilitates the internalization of the master and thus the universalization of servitude. The equality of brotherhood offered by Christianity, Kojève emphasizes, presupposes subservience to the Father.[44]

The new and absolute master is recognized for the same reason as the human master: fear of death. Absolute servitude is the price paid for eternal life—the contingency and finitude of existence can be dismissed as not real, whereas the Beyond (that is, the beyond time, beyond death) preserves all. Human masters are defeated by transferring the recognition they received to God, who promises an escape from finite existence. Only when the possibility of the human as a synthesis of master and slave is realized, and salvation is seen as the product of human work and not of God's grace, can the ideals of Christianity be true for (and in) this world. As Kojève says, the heav-

---

42. Ibid., 182.

43. Ibid. Modified translation from *IRH*, 55.

44. Kojève, perhaps following Weber, saw the internalization of the master as an essential facet of capitalist development. The bourgeois, he said, is his own slave. *ILH*, 194.

enly realm can be realized only through history.[45] Until such time, Christianity provides an effective rationalization and consolation for the slave; the contradictions, however, remain.

From this perspective, Soloviev's conception of a dual Absolute appears in a new light. For Soloviev, a suprahistorical criterion (pure perfection) is necessary to judge the relative progress of human action. From the Kojèvian perspective on Christianity, however, this necessity appears to be a vestige of the fear of death. The Absolute as suprahistorical criterion (as judge) is a substitute for the master. Only when the fear is conquered, and the master deposed (or dissolved), will people be free and know that they are their own judges.[46]

The Triumph of the Slave

The Triumph of the Slave is first and foremost the triumph of equality over hierarchy, the idea of equality having been introduced into history through the projections of slave ideologies. With Christianity, the concept of the individual is linked to equality: the individual is a synthesis of the universal (divine) and the particular (profane). The idea of the incarnation is the most powerful figure of this synthesis, for then the Universal takes the corporal form of a particular man: God is an individual. The supreme proof of his being *qua* individual is his death on the cross.

The "truth" of Christianity for Kojève's Hegel is contained in its ideas of equality in a Universal Church and of the Incarnation. The image of the God who becomes a man is converted by Hegel into the image of heaven descending to earth. Christian love will be realized through historical action:

> For Hegel, Love is mutual recognition, in opposition to the Struggle for prestige (the duel). In Love, conflicts are not essential; differences, while being marked, do not become radical oppositions. Where there is no Love, conflicts grow, the situation is untenable, everything must be destroyed. But we cannot *begin* with Love; the Master/Slave conflict is essential

45. In a letter to Strauss written after Kojève received Strauss's book on Hobbes (published in 1936).

46. The step, according to Kojève's Hegel, taken by the French Revolution and the judgment of the Terror.

and primitive. Love can only exist between equals. This situation of absolute equality can occur only in the perfect (universal and homogeneous) State to which history leads.[47]

The State replaces the Church in this secular translation of Christian categories. The *dure parole* of Christianity that God is dead itself points to this secularization, to the Hegelian conclusion that judgment comes not from some Beyond but from the History that is the result of human struggle and work and the acceptance of death. For Kojève, the truth of Christianity is that it was "the becoming of atheism."[48]

The becoming-of-atheism is the process of liberation from the Absolute Master. It is the acknowledgment of the universal equality of individuals; freedom is found in this equality. For Kojève, Marxism provides the schema for understanding history as a movement from class conflict (the master/slave conflict at the level of collectivities) to a society without classes. The freedom of a rigorous equality is the freedom of citizens equal before a law they have made themselves. In his *Esquisse d'une phénoménologie du droit*, Kojève goes so far as to describe the citizens of the ideal, fully developed socialist state as having no relevant specificity. In the universal State or Empire—the Endstate—there will be no further need for warriors, no distinction between ruler and ruled. All humans will be citizens, with no relevant political and social distinction among them.[49] This rigorous equality/equivalence enables Kojève to describe the final State as homogeneous.[50]

What is the content of the freedom of equality that Kojève describes? Our initial freedom, our historical freedom, is our ability to negate, to initiate change through struggle and work. At bottom, this ability is a product of our desire for recognition; the desire is sublimated into culture (ideology) and dominion over nature because the

---

47. *ILH*, 260.

48. Ibid., 256.

49. Kojève, *Esquisse d'une phénoménologie du droit*, 578, 580. Hence the major distinctions between the Greek state and the socialist state: 1) there were no slaves or masters in the latter as there were in the former; 2) there were no barbarians outside the socialist state, in opposition to whom the citizen was defined.

50. In a letter to Strauss (19 September 1950), Kojève did distinguish between the "sick"—those who need to be locked up—and the "healthy" members of the final state.

fear of death prohibits direct attempts at satisfaction. In the socialist state described by Kojève, this desire *is* satisfied, because equality there means the universal satisfaction of the desire for recognition. The reservoir of desire that had fed the sublimations is dried up; there is no longer any reason for humans to negate. Our historical freedom, then, after the achievement of equality is completely empty.

With the achievement of equality comes the long-delayed satisfaction of the slave, and satisfaction is, for Kojève, a kind of death. If people are satisfied in the Endstate, they will no longer negate, because they will have no properly human desires to act on. The master/slave dialectic is complete, and as this dialectic is the framework for all historical change, History, too, is complete. This does not mean that nothing happens in the world. Instead, it means that when persons cease to act as humans—to risk their lives or to work for recognition—there is no reason for significant new creations. Kojève speaks of the End of history not for some metaphysical reason but because in principle humanity is fully satisfied: "Certainly, the end of history is not a limit imposed on man from the outside: history is, if one wants, unlimited. Because man can negate as much as he wants, and he ceases to negate and change only if he no longer wants to do so. He only completes his development, then, if he is perfectly *satisfied* . . . by what he *is*; or, more exactly, by what he *has done*— since he has *created* himself (by negating what did not satisfy him, externally and internally)."[51] The point is not that all people are now happy or that complete freedom exists throughout the world. It is rather that the idea of universal equality in a homogeneous state is introduced during the epoch of the French Revolution, and all subsequent battles of import are fought for this same goal. The principle of universal recognition can no longer be coherently rejected; what remains to be done is "merely" the implementation of this idea—a technical but not a historical problem.

Kojève's idea of the End of history draws on both Heidegger and Marx, "the only significant figures in post-Hegelian philosophy." He projects Heidegger's conception of the essential finitude of persons onto the historical plane, arguing that history, because it is the project of human action, is also finite. If this is not the case—and here Kojève accepts Heidegger's critique of a standard version of Hegelianism—

51. Kojève, "Hegel, Marx et le christianisme," 347.

people can flee from the consciousness of their mortality by identifying themselves as part of the story of the infinite progress of History. The satisfaction that will come in the End is assimilated explicitly to Marx's *Reich der Freiheit*, "where men (recognizing each other mutually and without reserve) no longer struggle, and work as little as possible (Nature being definitively tamed, that is to say, harmonized with Man)."[52]

When Kojève first wrote of the realization of the realm of freedom, he was not pointing out that the final liberation had already taken place. Rather, this realm had been fully described (by Hegel), and the process of its realization mapped out (by Napoleon). We could now know the End of history, but—as Kojève wrote in 1946—the actualization of this End, the ultimate proof of our knowledge, still depended on our action: "In our day, as in the time of Marx, Hegelian philosophy is not a truth in the proper sense of the term: it is less the discursive revelation equivalent to a reality than an idea or an ideal, i.e., a "project" to be realized and therefore proved by action."[53] The interpretation of the Hegelian ideal thus had the status of political propaganda. And as this ideal pretended to account for all historical possibilities, the stakes in the conflict among interpretations could not be higher. As Kojève emphasized: "We can say that, for the moment, every interpretation of Hegel, if it is not more than small talk, is only a program of struggle and work (one of these 'programs' is called *Marxism*). And that means a work of Hegel interpretation has the significance of a work of political propaganda. . . . It is possible that the future of the world, and therefore the meaning and direction of the present and the significance of the past, depends in the final analysis on the way in which we interpret Hegelian texts today."[54] From Kojève's perspective just after the war, then, the Triumph of

---

52. *ILH*, 380, 435n. Riley shows how Kojève injected his own ideas of recognition into Marx's conception of the "realm of freedom," in "Introduction to the Reading of Alexandre Kojève," *Political Theory* 9, no. 1(1981), 16–17. Following Marx's claim that the shortening of the workday was the crucial step toward the realm of freedom, Kojève would later see Henry Ford as one of the great "prophets" of Marxism: "Marx est Dieu, Ford est son prophèt," *Commentaire* 9 (1980).

53. Kojève, "Hegel, Marx et le christianisme," 365.

54. Ibid., 366. Kojève distinguished between a commentary and an interpretation. The former starts from the text only to rediscover the thought of the author, whereas the latter starts from the thought in order to discover the text: compte rendu of G. R. G. Mure's *A Study of Hegel's Logic*, in *Critique* 54 (1951), 1004.

the Slave was not yet definitive. Struggle and work would continue, but the End—mutual recognition among rigorously equal citizens— was in sight.

The Kojèvian version of heroic Hegelianism is based on the belief that Hegel gives us a complete account of the meaning of history. Kojève's answer to the question "What is the human?" can now be developed more fully. A human is that being who is what he or she is not yet. He or she is history and lives *qua* human by giving priority to the future. But how can we know a being who "is not yet"? This is the problem that Kojève addressed in his dissertation on Soloviev. For the religious thinker, the problem is transformed by the existence of a God outside history. According to Kojève, Hegel rejects this alternative in favor of a philosophy that grasps the realization of the "not yet." We can know the human only through history, and, given the priority of the future in historical time, we can *know* history only if it is essentially complete. This is the dilemma that Koyré had pointed out in 1934: "Thus, the dialectical character of time alone makes possible a philosophy of history; but at the same time the temporal character of the dialectic makes it impossible. Because the philosophy of history, like it or not, is an immobilization. . . . The philosophy of history . . . would be possible only if history was over; only if there was no longer a future; only if time could be stopped."[55] Kojève accepted the force of this argument and—at least through the mid-forties—was willing to assert that historical time was in the process of stopping.

Perhaps one's first reaction is that the idea of the end of history is not serious, that it is a transparent attempt to stop the realization of certain historical possibilities and to reify the status quo into an Absolute. This has been, of course, the classic criticism of Hegel's political philosophy and its supposed glorification of the Prussian state. The Kojèvian response to such criticism is that Hegel may have been wrong about Napoleon and Prussia, but he has been right about the End of history becoming evident in a universal and homogeneous state. In other words, we can accept Marx without disturbing the fundamentals of Hegelianism.[56]

---

55. Koyré, "Hegel à Iéna" (1934), in *Etudes d'histoire de la pensée philosophique* (Paris, 1971), 189.

56. Kojève's interpretation was not accepted by orthodox Marxists. Jean Desanti, who in party publications often protected the pure from threatening ideologies (see

Kojève's insistence on the End of history is tied to his view that Hegelianism is "understanding history as the becoming of truth."[57] A key term in the Hegelian view of history is "the cunning of Reason." This term points to the way in which the *sens* of history can remain hidden beneath events, to the fact that a series of events can seem to mean one thing but from a retrospective appreciation of the *longue durée* have another signification. We can know the *sens* of history only retrospectively, even anachronistically. If such a retrospective view is in principle never definitive, if history has no End, then we are left with the skeptical position that history, despite what we may wish, makes no sense, that one can never KNOW what is progressive.

Kojève rejects this skepticism, but he refuses to make use of transcendent categories to provide criteria for judging historical change "from the outside." He regards the use of such categories as "theological" insofar as one has to believe in their value independently of occurrences in the world and as their own development cannot be accounted for. He thinks that the rejection of both skepticism and theology leaves a single alternative, a historicism that accepts the finitude of historical development, understanding history as the becoming and the realization of truth.

What, then, does truth mean in Kojève's version of Hegelianism? Clearly, it is something that results from history, but as one can say the same thing about error, this tautological route does not take one very far. Truth is differentiated from error by its success. Action, in the strongest sense of the word, aims at changing the world. The actions that succeed in changing it definitively form the basis of our understanding and of our judgments. Action that is destructive is judged as bad, but if this destructive action (negation) creates something new upon which to build, it is judged as good—or at least as a success. To judge action knowingly, Kojève concludes, one must do so from the standpoint of *la réalité definitive*: "Something which

---

note 2 above), bitterly attacked Kojève's reading for giving too much importance to man and not enough to his material context. He suggested Lenin's reading of Hegel's *Logic* as an antidote to Kojève's insidious influence: "Hegel, est-il le père de l'existentialisme?" 91–109. The East German response was, as one might expect, more straightforward: "The great return to Hegel is only a desperate attack against Marx...a revisionism of fascistic character;" in *Deutsche Zeitschrift für Philosophie* 3, no. 1955, 357. I borrow this quotation from Iring Fetcher's introduction to the German translation of *ILH* (Stuttgart, 1958).

57. *ILH*, 249.

exists is good insofar as it exists. All action, being a negation of existing reality, is therefore bad: a sin. But a sin can be pardoned. How? By its success. Success absolves crime because success is a new reality which *exists*. But how to judge success? For that it is necessary that History be finished. Then one sees that which endures in existence: definitive reality."[58] One can see what endures in reality only from the perspective of the End of history. If reality is never definitive, then our knowledge of it will be always contingent, and we cannot know the degree of contingency because there is no standard by which to measure it.

The problem of establishing a criterion by which to judge historical change has been fundamental in twentieth-century social thought. Among Marxists, this dilemma has been much obscured by the amount of attention given to the related issue of historical determinism. From the middle of the nineteenth century onward, Marxists and those concerned with Marxism have argued extensively about the connections between various levels of historical change. The most conventional form of this argument has to do with the extent to which the base causes changes in the superstructure. Much ink, and more than a little blood, has been spilled by partisans of a more or less deterministic historical materialism.

With the development of Western Marxism the nature of this debate changed. Lukács's *History and Class Consciousness* was the decisive text. Published in 1923, the book argues that history must be considered as a totality, and only then can the "antinomies of bourgeois thought" be understood as expressions of a particular historical culture; only then can one see revolution by a class that embodies universal history as the answer to the questions of relativism plaguing social science.

The development of Lukács's thought and its relation to the tradition of Western Marxism has been examined in detail elsewhere.[59]

58. Ibid., 95.
59. The literature on Lukács is enormous. For connections with our subject see Jean Hyppolite, "Aliénation et objectivation: A propos du livre de Lukács sur *La jeunesse de Hegel*," in *Figures de la pensée philosophique* (Paris, 1971), 1:122–145; Merleau-Ponty, "Marxisme et philosophie," in *Sens et nonsens* (Paris, 1947), 253–277, and *Aventures de la dialectique* (Paris, 1955); and Lucien Goldmann, *Les sciences humaines et la philosophie* (Paris, 1952), *Recherches dialectiques* (Paris, 1959), and *Lukács et Heidegger* (Paris 1973). More generally, see Perry Anderson, *Considerations on Western Marxism* (London, 1976), and *In the Tracks of Historical Materialism* (London,

Here I note only that Kojève's End of history can be understood in light of the Western Marxist concentration on historical universality, or totalization. Kojève's concern with totality is also a concern with time. For him, the final state that people produce in history is the universal; as a product of history, the universal dialectically contains the past, and, being final, it does not lack a future. Such a state—which in the late thirties Kojève thought was being realized—is the standard for judging and inspiring historical action.

The problem of a definitive reality from which to judge historical action recalls the discussion of a logic of history in Merleau-Ponty's *Humanisme et terreur*. Merleau-Ponty wanted both logic and contingency; that is, he invoked contingency in describing as "revolutionary" certain historical periods in which the political sphere was contested while also invoking a logic of history to describe the long-term progress toward humanization.[60] From a Kojévian perspective, this was merely an attempt to have the best of both worlds without attending to the difficulty of the connection between logic and contingency. Revolutionaries acted *as if* they knew the End of history, and logicians of history wrote *as if* they knew that contingency did not run too deep. In both cases, the "as if" evidenced more a wishful than a serious thinking.

One need not turn to existential Marxism to find this kind of wishful thinking. The assumption of historical progress is an essential facet of modern political theory, both in liberalism and in the various Marxist denominations. How was one to find the progressive route in the late 1930s? Even if one was clear that fascism and Nazism were the enemies of progress, one did not know immediately with whom one should join in struggle. Were the fascists the last gasp of capitalism who would reveal contradictions and create revolutionary conditions before disappearing, or were they important historical figures in their own right who had to be defeated immediately with any and all possible alliances? If one was a communist, did one join with conservative capitalists in a popular front against fascism? If one was

1983); Andrew Arato and Paul Breines, *The Young Lukács and the Origins of Western Marxism* (New York, 1979); Martin Jay, *Marxism and Totality: The Adventures of a Concept from Lukács to Habermas* (Berkeley, 1984); Andrew Feenberg, *Lukács, Marx, and the Sources of Critical Theory* (Totowa, N.J., 1981); and James Miller, *History and Human Existence: From Marx to Merleau-Ponty* (Berkeley, Calif., 1979).

60. See above, Chapter 1.

a liberal, did one join with authoritarian communists in order to smash an even greater threat? How could one know which threat was the greater? There are countless formulations of these questions, and all of them require some form of judgment about the direction of history. All judgments about the progressive and the reactionary require either some notion of the End toward which history is (really) going or a conception of the natural purpose or final cause of the human. For Kojève, the latter is discredited as a vestige of theological thinking, whereas the former's implicit assumption of the End must be converted into an explicit determination.

According to Kojève, Hegel negates the style of "as if" philosophy characterized by Kant and replaces it with a complete reading of history.[61] In its effort to accomplish this completion, Hegelianism is a competitor to Christianity. The latter purports to offer knowledge in the form of a revelation by an absolute Other, whereas Hegelianism purports to present a *connaissance-de-soi* that is circular or reflexive insofar as it accounts for its own origins. Both are absolute philosophies in the sense that they give a total account of the world, and Kojève insists that there is no mid-point between knowledge through an atemporal Absolute (Other) and knowledge through a re-collection of history (Self). The choice between the two is radical: "The decision is absolutely unique; and as simple as possible: it is a matter of deciding for self (i.e., against God) or for God (i.e., against oneself). And there is no 'reason' for this decision other than the decision itself."[62] The attempt to retain a suprahistorical Absolute alongside a historicism (the problem of Soloviev thus appears again) is merely the symptom of an inability to decide.

Why, though, does the decision for historicism imply a conception of the End of history? Without such a definitive reality, Kojève asserts, historicism is simply a genre of relativism, and philosophy (including the philosophy of historicism) loses its raison d'être.[63] Philosophy,

---

61. See Kojève's *Kant* (Paris, 1973); also Riley, "Introduction to the Reading of Kojève," 31; Hans Vaihinger explicitly developes the "as-if-ness" of Kantianism: *The Philosophy of "As If"* (London, 1935).

62. *ILH*, 293.

63. Kojève, *Essai d'une histoire*, 1:51. Note the similarity of the argument here to Strauss's critique of historicism in *Natural Right and History* (Chicago, 1950), 25ff. In a long letter to Strauss (7 July 1957), Kojève explained how circularity (completeness) transformed the relativism of historicism into certain knowledge.

that is, has to give up its claim to provide discursive truths and be content—like the Diltheyans whom Kojève attacked in his early reviews—to explicate the various proposals made or questions posed by people who called themselves philosophers.

Thus for Kojève the End of history makes meaningful both historical action and philosophic reflection. Historical action is significant (that is, really historical, really human) insofar as it contributes to the actualization of the End of history. Likewise, philosophic reflection is meaningful insofar as it can still make claims to discursive truth based on its comprehension of historical action in light of the End of history.

Kojève's seminar on the *Phenomenology* ended, fittingly, in 1939. Not until 1947 did Queneau publish notes and texts from the course, by which time the philosopher's influence had been felt and had provoked important criticism. (I examine the most important critic, Leo Strauss, in the next chapter.) Not long after the publication of his commentary, moreover, Kojève began to view the proximity of the End of history not as an occasion for celebration but as the ironic condition of his own discourse.

Chapter Six

No Guarantees: Irony and the End of History

> To believe in progress is not to believe that progress has already taken place. That would be no belief.
>
> —*Walter Benjamin quoting Franz Kafka, 1934*

Most critics of Kojève have taken one of two approaches to the interpretation of Hegel which culminates in the End of history. The first argues Hegel never said *that* and then criticizes Kojève for willfully distorting the ideas of a more reasonable philosopher.[1] The second claims the End of history is not necessary to save historicism from relativism, or if we do need this concept to make judgments about historical change, we certainly have not experienced the ending of history.[2] I examine neither in any detail, because neither engages Kojève on his own terms.[3] I emphasized, however, that Kojève was well aware of the personal or even violent nature of his reading of

1. This is Riley's approach in "Introduction to the Reading of Alexandre Kojève," *Political Theory* 9, no. 1 (1981), 5–48. Tran-Duc-Thao's Marxist critique was the most important contemporary example in this regard: "La phénoménologie de l'esprit et son contenu réel," *Les temps modernes* 36 (1948), 493–519.

2. See, for example, Michel Darbon, "Hégélianisme, marxisme, existentialisme," *Les études philosophiques* 4, nos. 3–4 (1949), 346–370. Mikel Dufrenne thought that God saved us from relativist historicism, whereas Jean Desanti settled for Marx (as revealed by the Party): Dufrenne, "Actualité de Hegel," *Esprit* 17, no. 9 (1948), and Desanti, "Hegel, est-il le père de l'existentialisme?" *La nouvelle critique* no. 56 (1954), 91–109.

3. A new step in Kojève interpretation is taken by Barry Cooper, *The End of History: An Essay on Modern Hegelianism* (Toronto, 1984). Cooper accepts Kojève's notion of the Endstate and uses it in a very interesting way to "make sense of our modernity." On the connection of this usage to Kojève's work as a whole, see my review of Cooper in *Political Theory* 13, no. 1 (1985), 148–152.

Hegel.[4] The Kojèvian response to those who claim that we cannot have *knowledge* of historical change but that we can still speak reasonably about it echoes Hegel's response to Christianity: without doubt an ingenious solution....

One response to Kojève should be examined in detail, however, because through its intelligent and complete opposition to the Kojèvian perspective it clarifies the stakes involved in the interpretation of Hegel. This is the response of Leo Strauss. Strauss and Kojève knew each other in Berlin in the 1930s, and after leaving Germany they maintained a correspondence over forty years.[5] In 1950 Kojève—in response to Strauss's request—reviewed the latter's commentary on Xenophon, *On Tyranny*. This review was published together with Strauss's response in subsequent editions of the book. These texts and the surviving correspondence enable us to see the force of and the dilemmas in Kojève's perspective on history and the possibility of its closure.

Strauss's objections to Kojève's reading of Hegel fall into two categories. The first is based on the view that without a teleological philosophy of nature, history can be given no order, nor can we know if it is "one and unique," a single process. The second criticizes the fundamental value Kojève attaches to the universal satisfaction of the desire for recognition, asserting that it is the quality, and not the universality of recognition which counts. Strauss does not attack the idea of the End of history as such; rather, he tries to show that this concept does not do the job Kojève assigns to it. It will not allow the philosopher to determine reasonably the value of specific historical actions.[6]

Strauss points out the philosophy of nature implicit in Kojève's reading of Hegel. The primary distinction between the human and the natural clearly presupposes a conception of nature, but, more

4. In addition to the letter to Tran-Duc-Thao (Paris, 7 October 1948), cited in Chapter 5, I note Kojève's marginalia to an article by Aimé Patri, "Dialectique du maître et de l'esclave," *Le contrat social* 5, no. 4 (1961), 231–235. Patri wrote: "Under the pseudonym of Hegel, the author [Kojève] exposed a personal way of thinking"—Kojève added "bien vu!" In the preface to his (unpublished) history of philosophy and Hegelian wisdom, Kojève wrote: "Finally, the question of knowing if Hegel "truly said" what I have him say would seem to be puerile" (8).

5. With Victor Gourevitch, I am currently assembling the complete correspondence between Strauss and Kojève for publication. I have translated the quotations from Strauss' letter of 22 August 1948 from the original German.

6. Strauss to Kojève, New York, 22 August 1948.

important, this conception allows Kojève's Hegel to organize the field of historical events. In other words, the theory of a desire that begins history and a satisfaction that closes it is a form of *Naturphilosophie*, even though Kojève conceives of this theory in contradistinction to all species of philosophy of nature. If not for the naturalist base, Strauss argues, there is no reason to assume that history does not repeat itself indefinitely or that there are not many different histories with no underlying unity: "How can one possibly show the necessary uniqueness of the historical process? Moreover, why should it not lead to a temporally final, earthly cataclysm . . . resulting in a repeat of the historical process, in whole or in part? Only a teleological concept of nature can be of help here. As long as nature does not order or guide history, one arrives at a radical contingency, as in Kant." If a hidden concept of nature gives direction to the master/slave dialectic, then "the underexposure of *Naturphilosophie* is exposed."[7]

In Strauss's criticism is a theme crucial to his philosophy as a whole: historicism that divorces itself from a philosophy of nature results in either incoherence or relativism. Kojève hopes to meet Strauss's objection without relinquishing his theory of history, by using the End of history as a standard of judgment. Both agreed on the necessity of such a standard. As Strauss wrote in *Natural Right and History*, "To the extent to which the historical process is accidental, it cannot supply man with a standard, and . . . if that process has a hidden purpose, its purposefulness cannot be recognized except if there are transhistorical standards. The historical process cannot be recognized as progressive without previous knowledge of the end or purpose of the process."[8] Although both Strauss and Kojève agree on the need for some stable criterion of judgment, they are radically opposed in regard to what that criterion will be. The knowledge of the end or purpose of the historical process can be known, Kojève tells us, because the process is essentially complete. This knowledge is itself a product of the historical process, not something transhistorical by virtue of its participation in eternity. Kojève has to (and does) accept the complaint that he is advocating the worship of success (although he wants to substitute "honor" for "worship"), because he endorses Schiller's dictum that *die Weltgeschichte ist das Weltgericht.*

7. Ibid.
8. Strauss, *Natural Right and History* (Chicago, 1950), 274.

Strauss does not confine himself to criticizing Kojève's criterion of judgment because it is the product of historical development. He also questions the value of the End of history as Kojève conceives of it. The essential feature of this final state is that in it, the fundamental human desire is satisfied because there is universal recognition. Strauss points out an ambiguity: is Kojève claiming that humanity is satisfied in this Endstate, or that it should be satisfied therein? Kojève has to affirm the former, because he has no criterion other than the satisfaction itself for establishing the "should." In the Endstate, that is, "is" and "ought" must coincide, and it is one of the principal tasks of the philosopher to describe how they do so.

According to Strauss, the final coincidence of "is" and "ought" in an Endstate of universal recognition omits the essential facet of the human. "In the Endstate great deeds are impossible," he points out, and the best among persons will never accept definitive mediocrity, even if the Endstate created conditions in which all are equal. Strauss summarizes his disagreement with Kojève as follows: "In any case, if not all men become wise, the final condition for all men will be identical with the loss of their humanity/humaneness [Menschheit-Menschlichkeit], and this cannot reasonably satisfy them. The fundamental difficulty is shown here: on the one hand, the Endstate is characterized as the state of warrior-workers . . . on the other hand, it is said that at this stage there are no wars and as little work as possible (in the strict sense, indeed, there will be no work at all since Nature is definitively subjugated)."[9] According to Strauss, only if the fundamental (or the highest) human desire is for wisdom will an Endstate—ruled by the wise—satisfy what is best in humanity. Even if history is going in the direction Kojève claims, therefore, the satisfaction it brings to people might not coincide with making them wise—unless we are willing to equate wisdom with idleness. By failing to make wisdom a component of the end of history, Kojève does not provide an idea of universal satisfaction, because philosophers will be satisfied by nothing less than wisdom.[10] The mastery of nature is the triumph of technology, but this victory does not show that people have discovered the highest goal in the service of which to

9. Strauss to Kojève, 22 August 1948.

10. I note that for Strauss the philosopher's dissatisfaction would be particularly grave, as the philosopher was among the best of men.

employ their technē. Indeed, the "progress" that Hegelianism applaudes may threaten the possibility of this discovery by destroying the conditions in which philosophy can exist.

The debate between Strauss and Kojève about the role of history in philosophy is also a debate about the role of philosophy in history; that is, about the value of philosophy for historical change and political action. This is the theme of their *Auseinandersetzung* in the early 1950s in regard to Strauss's commentary on Xenophon's *Hiero*. Their dialogue raises the essential questions about the desire and responsibility of the philosopher vis-à-vis the political-historical realm and introduces Kojève's final claim that this realm has already been completed in the definitive triumph of us slaves.

Hegel identifies the history of philosophy with the philosophy of history because he believes that persons necessarily become (self-) conscious of the changes created in them by their actions in the world. Self-consciousness, although stimulated by philosophy, tends naturally to grow. Kojève here separates his own position from Hegel's; Kojève thought that philosophy, far from being an extension of human nature, has always to struggle against a natural human tendency to remain the same. If self-consciousness grows in history—and, in turn, promotes historical development—it does so because of the "incessant efforts" of philosophers.[11] Thus Kojève admits the possibility that people will be satisfied with the "security of their well-being" in an efficient State without worrying at all about the realization of universal recognition; he also admits the possibility that some will prefer the perfection of an "absolute silence" to the wisdom of a complete and coherent discourse.[12] These two historical possibilities can be described as antiphilosophical, and if either is realized, the End of history will look quite different from the conception of Kojève's Hegel.

Kojève sees the philosopher's task in politico-pedagogic terms. Philosophy depends on politics and can also serve to guide it. Dependency derives from the fact that philosophers have to begin the process of

11. Kojève, *Introduction à la lecture de Hegel* (Paris, 1947), 398, hereafter *ILH*.

12. Ibid., 278. In this text he refers to the stasis described by Nietzsche and the wisdom of silence described by Buddhism. Kojève remained interested in the "wisdom of silence," and this is the subject of his correspondence with Georges Bataille reprinted in *Textures* 6 (1970), 61–71. See also Kojève, "Préface à l'oeuvre de Georges Bataille," *L'arc* 44 (1971), 36.

reflection from a given historical reality created, in large part, by politics. If philosophers are not to live in isolation, furthermore, they must coexist peacefully with the polity, at least to the extent that it will permit them to philosophize. Philosophers can serve as guides for politics on the basis of what Kojève sees as their three advantages over other members of the polity: expertise in dialectic or discussion; liberation from prejudices, which permits a greater appreciation of historical reality; and ability to see the whole rather than to simplify through abstraction.[13]

Will philosophers *want* to be political persons? It is in their response to this question that the point of disagreement between Strauss and Kojève becomes clear. For Kojève, philosophers, like all persons, desire recognition. They attain it, however, not through bloody battle but through dialectic or discussion. It is through discussion that wisdom (or progress toward it) becomes manifest and is admired by those who can understand what is being said. It is as pedagogues that philosophers can most easily come into conflict with the state, which itself is pedagogic to the extent that its authority is not exclusively based on violence. Kojève concluded:

> Consequently, to want to influence the government to accept or establish a philosophic pedagogy, is to want to influence the government in general; it is to want to determine or co-determine its policy as such. But philosophy cannot renounce pedagogy. Indeed, the "success" of the philosophic pedagogy is the only "objective" criterion of the truth of the "doctrine" of the Philosopher (at least of its anthropological part)....
>
> If one does not want to be content only with the subjective criteria of "evidence" or "revelation" (which do not do away with the problem of madness), it is then impossible to be a Philosopher without wanting to be at the same time a philosophic pedagogue.[14]

Philosophers must assume responsibility for their pedagogy, and that responsibility is, in large part, political. The retreat from this responsibility is for Kojève the mark of intellectuals, who do not accept the *risk* that comes with philosophizing and whose political responsibility has to be forced on them by others.[15] Thus philosophers, in contrast

---

13. Kojève, "L'action politique des philosophes," *Critique* 41 and 42 (1950), 139.
14. Ibid., 145. I have closed the parenthesis after "madness." There was no closure in the text printed in *Critique*.
15. Ibid., 183: see also 48, 141.

to intellectuals, want to be political persons to the extent that they want to be philosophers.

Strauss's view of the philosopher vis-à-vis politics is diametrically opposed to Kojève's. If Kojève belongs to the Hegelian tradition in which the highest form of philosophy is the state philosophy, Strauss belongs to the tradition that underlines the need to *force* the philosopher to return to the cave in order to rule. Not that Strauss thinks philosophers are without the advantages that Kojève attributes to them—both agree on the *capacity* of philosophers to guide the polity. For Strauss, however, philosophers who want to rule, who desire recognition, cease for that reason to be philosophers.[16] It is not that philosophic inquiry needs to be conducted in solitude but that the demands of the political are always in conflict with the requirements of the philosophical. If philosophers are more adept at discussion, political persons have to know when to stop talking and get back to work; if the former are liberated from prejudices and thereby have a view of the whole, the latter share in the prejudices (opinion) of the community and know their own place. Perhaps *the* lesson of political philosophy, for Strauss, is that the conflict between politics and philosophy is irremediable; to forget this conflict is to invite disaster in both domains.

Strauss offers his own teaching not as a prophylactic against the possibility of an apocalyptic marriage of philosophy and politics but as a protest against the acceptance of their union as eternal. For him, modern thought is founded upon this marriage, and its implications form the fundamental assumptions of contemporary life. The "idea of progress," the idea that by combining theory and practice we are solving the most important problems, is born of this unholy union. Modern thought is concerned with the triumph over Necessity (Nature or *Fortuna*) as the crucial step toward the solution of these dilemmas. Strauss points out, though, that the modern tradition has almost nothing to say about the world people will live in after this step is taken. The realm of freedom provides satisfaction and protection, but it offers no clues for happiness or excellence. In a passage

16. See Strauss, "Restatement on Xenophon's *Hiero*," in *On Tyranny*, rev. and enl. ed. (Glencoe, Ill., 1963), 218. My entire discussion of the Kojève-Strauss dialogue in this section owes much to Victor Gourevitch, "Philosophy and Politics," *Review of Metaphysics* 22, nos. 1 and 2 (1968), 58–84, 281–328.

in Strauss's *Thoughts on Machiavelli*—underlined in Kojève's own copy—the author summarizes his view of modern philosophy:

> The new philosophy lives from the outset in the hope which approaches or equals certainty, of future conquest or conquest of the future—in the anticipation of an epoch in which the truth will reign, if not in the minds of all men, at any rate in the institutions which mold them. Propaganda can guarantee the coincidence of philosophy and political power. Philosophy is to fulfill the function of both philosophy and religion. . . . The domination of necessity remains the indispensible condition of every great achievement and in particular his [Machiavelli's] own: the transition from the realm of necessity into the realm of freedom will be the inglorious death of the very possibility of human excellence.[17]

If philosophers participate in the struggle against nature at the expense of contemplation of the natural, they forget the basis of philosophy. When the goal of all human effort is the triumph over nature, victory removes the very ground of the human.

Strauss thus rejects Kojève's political criterion for a successful philosophy. Although he agrees that a standard of judgment is necessary, he denies that history or modern self-consciousness can satisfy this necessity. Instead, he affirms, an independent transhistorical standard must be based on the supposition that there is an "eternal and unchangeable order in which History occurs, and which is in no way affected by History."[18]

Kojève's review of *On Tyranny* asks how this supposition can be legitimated. How can the philosopher's "subjective certainty" of a natural order be differentiated from the paranoid's certainty that everyone is out to get him or her? Given Strauss's insistence on the self-sufficiency of the life of the philosopher[19]—the philosopher's indifference to the admiration, even the welfare, of other people—and on the natural limits on the number of persons capable of being philosophers, the possibilities of intersubjective certainty are practically

---

17. Strauss, *Thoughts on Machiavelli* (Chicago, 1958), 298. Kojève underlined the last sentence of this passage and noted in the margin: "cf: Kojève."

18. Strauss, "Mise au point," *De la tyrannie* (Paris, 1954), 343. I translate from the French edition because its final paragraph (approximately two pages) is not contained in the English edition.

19. Strauss, "Restatement on Xenophon's *Hiero*," 214, 219. See Gourevitch's discussion, "Philosophy and Politics," 80–84.

nonexistent. The shared beliefs within a sect (or school) of philosophers—to say nothing of political scientists—are clearly not an adequate form of legitimation, even if friendship and loyalty among the sect's members alleviate some of the existential dilemmas resulting from this inadequacy.[20]

For Kojève, the appeal to an eternal and unchangeable order provides a stable standard only as long as people agree about the significance of the order. The order does not effectively command agreement, and insofar as people do not agree, the appeal does not provide a solution to Strauss's problem of relativism; it seems only to substitute obscurantism for nihilism. To use a metaphor that Strauss had borrowed from Schopenhauer via Weber: *Naturphilosophie* is not a cab that one can stop at one's convenience. How can moral certainty or self-satisfaction avoid the problem of criteria of judgment? Strauss's apparent inability to respond to this question gives further weight to Kojève's view that a discursive appeal to a natural order is ineffective, because even if such an order exists Kojève does not see how we can speak reasonably about it. One can choose silence—one can even call this choice an openness to Being—but otherwise one either chatters in a modern way, or one is a Hegelian.[21]

Strauss's critique of the modern tradition, though based on an approach to philosophy and history very different from Kojève's, raises problems that the latter confronted in his first articles on Soloviev. Translated into the language of Soloviev, Strauss is asking if the End of history has really come to coincide with the suprahistorical Absolute that is the ultimate criterion of judgment. With this question, indeed, Strauss is expressing his profound doubts about whether humanity can ever create its own salvation through history.

Kojève rejects the possibility of using a suprahistorical criterion for judging historical development. He chooses what he calls philosophic knowing through a re-collection of history and rejects what he calls theological knowing through a suprahistorical Absolute.[22] Strauss em-

---

20. Strauss, "Restatement on Xenophon's *Hiero*," 218.

21. Kojève to Strauss, September 19, 1950.

22. The distinction between theological and historical knowing runs through all of Kojève's work, and he regarded the "choice" between the two modes as fundamental and prephilosophical. See, for example, his review of Alfred Delp's *Tragische Existenz*, in *Recherches philosophiques* 5 (1936–1937), 415–419; *ILH*, 293; "Hegel, Marx et le christianisme," 347, 363–364; *De la tyrannie*, 242 (*On Tyranny*, 161). See also Strauss,

phasizes that this choice obliges Kojève to recognize the End of history as salvation, even if this result fails to reach humanity's highest aspirations. Kojève accepts the obligation because he holds fast to the view that salvation can come to us only from ourselves. Even as Kojève's view of the quality of the supposed salvation approaches Strauss's, as we shall see, he does not try to escape from its source.

The dialogue between Strauss and Kojève does not end in reconciliation, which is to be expected, for both are philosophers willing to accept the apparently unhappy implications of their respective positions. In response to Kojève's claim that through Hegelianism we see the completion of history, Strauss asks whether it has been worth the effort. Kojève's only reply is that the End is the *result* of the effort, so we have to recognize it as worth the effort or withdraw (preferably in silence) from historical reality. In constructing his version of Hegelianism, he makes such a withdrawal philosophically impossible, for to go beyond history for Kojève means learning to live with the results of history. As Hegel writes in the preface to the *Philosophy of Right* "there is less chill in the peace which knowledge brings." By the end of the 1940s, when the end of history seems less a goal one wants to achieve than a world one must learn to live within, Kojève shifts from a concern with historical recognition through struggle and work to a concern with reconciliation—via philosophy—with the "posthistorical world" of former slaves.

It is not at all clear that Strauss's critique of Kojève's End of history was instrumental in changing the function of that concept in the latter's philosophy as a whole. It is clear, though, that the function did change by the mid–1950s, as Kojève reappraised the positive potential of his historic present. During the seminar on Hegel and in the *Esquisse d'une phénoménologie du droit*, Kojève discusses the End of history as both necessary and good. As Kojève does not think that the Endstate has been fully realized, he is self-consciously making propaganda to persuade others to work for the Endstate. Although never losing his conviction that the world is becoming "universalized

"Jerusalem and Athens: Some Introductory Reflections," *Commentary* 43 (1967), 45–57, and "On the Mutual Influence of Theology and Philosophy," *Independent Journal of Philosophy* 3 (1979), 111–118. In Kojève's copy of the typescript of Strauss's lecture "What Is Political Philosophy," Kojève wrote "Strauss = Theology," alongside Strauss's discussion of political theology.

and homogenized," he describes it in his late works in critically ironic rather than in Utopian or prophetic terms. The realm of freedom turns out to be the final example of the cunning of Reason.

The transition to this new approach to the End of history can be seen in two book reviews published in 1952 and 1956. The first is a compte rendu of three novels by his friend and editor at Gallimard, Raymond Queneau. Kojève wants to show that the heroes of these books are posthistorical wisemen, *Sages,* insofar as they are fully satisfied with their lives and self-conscious of this satisfaction. A disinterested proletarian, a poet who does not publish, and a pacifist soldier, these are the *Sages* displayed by Queneau. Each lives in what Kojève, following Hegel, calls the *Shabbat de l'homme,* humanity's definitive repose following the completion of all struggle and work. Queneau's heroes live in the self-conscious satisfaction that there is no longer anything for which to fight or work.[23] Indeed, in the posthistorical world there is nothing left to do except perhaps to know that there is nothing left to do.

Playful resignation in the review of Queneau becomes more bitter in a 1956 critique of two novels by Françoise Sagan.[24] The subject is again our posthistorical condition, but instead of talking about the end of desire in satisfaction and resignation, Kojève points to the replacement of desire by impotence and boredom. The posthistorical world is empty of challenge, let alone risk and struggle.

Kojève's critical or playful resignation vis-à-vis the contemporary world appears to be nothing more than the nihilism of the bourgeois intellectual which he so strongly criticized in the commentary on Hegel.[25] However, his position cannot be described simply in these terms, nor can it be fully assimilated to the more general phenomenon in the mid-fifties of the retreat from heroic politics. Indeed, Kojève's vision of the posthistorical world must be understood in the context of his own activity in this world. Shortly after the end of World War II he became a civil servant, and for about twenty years worked for

23. Kojève, "Les romans de la sagesse," *Critique* 60 (1952), 396.

24. Kojève, "Le dernier monde nouveau: Françoise Sagan," *Critique* 111–112 (1956), 702–708. It should be noted that Kojève's ironic treatment did not assume that Sagan intended her characters to be posthistorical.

25. See above, 106, and *ILH,* 93 and esp. 132. The distinction between the intellectual and the philosopher is also underlined in the debate with Strauss: see "L'action politique," 48.

the Ministère des Finances et des Affaires Economiques. He began working for the government not only because—as he wrote to Strauss—"Suez and Hungary are more interesting than the Sorbonne" but because through his work he was able to contribute to the actualization of his Hegelian theory of history.

Even if the march of World Spirit was essentially complete, all nations did not yet participate equally in the Endstate. Kojève concentrated his efforts on this technical—in contradistinction to historical—problem, by working to develop a policy that replaced the vestiges of European colonialism with a more equitable system of trade between industrialized and developing nations. This system, or at least Kojève's contribution to it, took the form of proposals for preferential tariff arrangements combined with a rigorous foreign aid program.[26] The conflict between North and South was more problematic in his view than class conflict within industrialized countries, for the latter was disappearing as an increasing percentage of surplus value was being directed to the working majority (if only to create conditions in which they could buy more products and hence promote economic growth).[27]

Thus Kojève attached himself to the tradition that put philosophy at the service of the state. He sought no academic appointment, for to him the idea of the Academy was a vestige of the Platonic view that the highest form of knowledge depends on a separation of the philosopher from history.[28] His work during the day for the government was of a piece with his philosophic labors at night and on the weekends. Kojève saw philosophy as a form of life, but this life, though more comprehensive (universal) than others, should not be radically distinct from them.

---

26. A summary of Kojève's governmental work was prepared in 1977 by the Ministre du Commerce Extérieur, and I have consulted this document. See also Kojève, "Kolonialismus in europäischer Sicht" (1957), a lecture delivered in Germany at the invitation of Carl Schmitt, part of which was published in French in *Commentaire* 9 (1980), 135–137. An English translation appeared in the *Collegian* of St. John's College (Annapolis, Md.) in 1964. Kojève himself published a concise summary of his views in this regard in "Nécessité d'une révision systématique des principes fondamentaux du commerce actuel," *dévelopement et civilisations* 19 (1964), 44.

27. Kojève was fond of saying that the only real capitalist nations were in the East, because there more than anywhere else surplus value was extracted from workers for the purpose of investment.

28. Kojève, *Essai d'une histoire raisonnée de la philosophie païenne* (Paris, 1972), 2:143.

Kojève's work in philosophy (in a narrower sense) took the form of studies in the history of philosophy aimed at beginning an "encyclopedia of Hegelian wisdom." The history of philosophy he reads through Hegelian glasses: the thinkers who count are the ones who make significant progress toward the completion of philosophy in Hegel's work. There are five: Parmenides, Heraclitus, Plato, Aristotle, and Kant. After Hegel, we can organize their contributions into a systemic, or reasoned, history of philosophy: "The System of Knowledge is nothing less than an *'a priori construction'* ... of the history of Philosophy. . . . But the "com-prehension" (*Be-griefen*) of a process is possible only *at its end*, as it were, the process becomes 'comprehensible' (and can therefore be *definitively* 'comprehended') only at the moment that it is *complete*."[29] Kojève's history of philosophy, then, will be a *re-connaissance* of the steps of philosophical progress from the standpoint of the last stage.

Kojève's *Essai d'une histoire raisonnée de la philosophie païenne* is an attempt to provide access to Hegelian wisdom by re-collecting a history leading up to it. The history with which he is concerned is no longer that of bloody battles and work but that of discourse which speaks of others and itself speaking about others.[30] He is concerned with philosophy as a reflexive discourse that aims at universality. His perspective is always a Hegelian one, accounting for the history of the discourse in light of World History while also accounting for itself in this light. Kojève wants to show how the circle of philosophic discourse can be (and has been) closed, how the love of wisdom is finally requited and is not a senseless longing.[31] He does so by defining philosophy as a discourse and then by showing that its discursive "possibilities" have been either actualized or shown to be impossible.

This history of philosophy organizes the field of total and reflexive discourse according to the connection it can (and does) establish between eternity and time: The "Thesis" of Parmenides is that "the Concept is Eternity," and the "Antithesis" of "Heraclitus" that "the Concept is non-Eternity." The subsequent history of philosophy is the attempt to reconcile these positions, which Hegel ultimately accomplishes in his "Synthesis" that "the Concept is Time."[32] The

29. Ibid., 1:17. Kojève plays here with the French verb "comprendre."
30. Ibid., 84.
31. Kojève, *Kant* (Paris, 1973), 37.
32. Kojève's schema went as follows: The "Socratics," which included all philos-

Synthesis is definitive insofar as it enables us to situate all previous philosophic responses as stages in the development of the Concept, and in so far as it accounts for all chronologically posterior responses as repetitions. Given the range of philosophic discourse that Kojève defines, nothing new can be said by a philosopher *qua* philosopher.

This effort to close the circle of philosophy has explicit parallels with the arguments about the End of history. Indeed, Kojève tells us that the latter is a necessary condition for the former. Yet even if history and philosophy have an End, how can we be sure that we know what it is or that the story we tell about it retrospectively is the only (or even the best) one that can be told? Kojève responds that if our story is universal—if it accounts for everything essential and itself—then to ask if there is a better story to be told makes no sense. The complaint that there can be more than one story ("that's only *your* interpretation") is not effective against Kojève insofar as his (Hegel's) is a story that takes multiplicity into account. This Big Story—Hegel's philosophy/wisdom—unifies the diversity of philosophic discourse just as the Endstate unifies the diversity of human action into a coherent Whole.

The point common to the Big Story and the Endstate is universality. We saw in Strauss's critique and in Kojève's two book reviews that the universality which closes history is the death of excellence and of action in the strong sense of the word. Similarly, the universal System that closes philosophy (or transforms it into wisdom) marks the death of human discourse. In the realm of freedom, or the post-historical world, one sees the "re-animalization of man." As Kojève writes in a note to the second edition (1962) of the commentary on Hegel:

> If Man becomes an animal again, his arts, his loves, and his play must also become purely "natural" again.... But one cannot then say that all this "makes Man *happy*." One would have to say that post-historical animals of the species *Homo sapiens* (which will live amidst abundance

---

ophers after "Heraclitus" and until and including Kant, tried to put the Eternal in relation with our world: Plato, the Eternal in relation with Eternity outside of Time; Aristotle, the Eternal in relation with Eternity in Time; Kant, the Eternal in relation with Time. Hegel completed the history of philosophy by saying the following: The Concept is Time. The diagrams on pp. 139 and 141 of vol. 1 of the *Essai d'une histoire* are helpful. Kojève put the name of Heraclitus in quotation marks to indicate that one need not think the name designates an individual.

and complete security) will be *satisfied* [*content*] as a result of their artistic, erotic and playful behavior, inasmuch as, by definition, they will be satisfied [*contenteront*] with it. But there is "more." "*The definitive annihilation* of Man *properly so-called*" also means the definitive disappearance of human Discourse (*Logos*) in the strict sense.[33]

Thus in the definitively posthistorical era the Big Story and the Hegelian wisdom it contains will eventually disappear; and, as Kojève adds to this same footnote, this era is the one we live in. The *fin de l'histoire* has already arrived, but it appears as mere form without content, rituals without faith, and the absence of action properly so-called. The final stage of world history and the end of philosophy which coincides with it make possible universal satisfaction, as they signal the death of all properly human desire.

Thus Kojève transforms his portrayal of the Endstate as the triumphant ascension of humanity into a portrayal of the End of history as a final decadence in which humans are distinguished from other animals only by their pretentiousness. Kojève joins his early Marxist-Hegelian vision to what we can call a Weberian perspective of the rationalization of life: the closure of the End of history is an iron cage in which functionaries without spirit and spiritualists without function can coexist peacefully. Kojève would add that the noises they make—even if called "social science"—should not be confused with coherent discourse.

A crucial question arises for us in this shift in Kojève's work from a militant Hegelianism intent on *promoting* a theory of historical change and political action to this final, bleak vision of the impossibility of genuine change and the end of action: Why does Kojève continue to do philosophical work *after* the end? A psychological answer to this question, interesting though it might be, does not concern us here. Instead, our problem is how his philosophy of history accounts for its own continuation after (by its own account) the pos-

33. Kojève, *ILH*, 436n. Modified translation from *Introduction to the Reading of Hegel*, trans. J. Nichols (New York, 1969), 159n–160n. The quotations within this passage refer to a statement Kojève made in the first edition, part of which I quote on the first page of this chapter. Kojève's discussion of the "definitive annihilation of man" might be usefully compared with Foucault's declaration of the imminent "disappearance of man" in *Les mots et les choses* (Paris, 1964). In this regard see Vincent Descombes, *Le même et l'autre* (Paris, 1979), 131–139.

sibilities for the extension of self-consciousness have already been exhausted.

Kojève does not, like Hyppolite, mediate his Hegelianism with another philosophic system or vision that undercuts the connection between knowing and history. On the contrary, if his Hegelianism as such changes at all, it is to become even more dogmatic. Kojève does not waver in his commitment to understand history as the becoming of truth, even if the truth that finally has become is painful and frightening.

There are, however, important changes in the form and content of Kojève's philosophizing which result from his transition from a militant to a resigned perspective on historical change. His late work is concerned with the limits and possibilities of philosophy as a discourse, as opposed to his earlier emphasis on the meaning of historical change. This shift in subject matter coincides with a change in the form in which he expresses these concerns.

Kojève's vision of historical development, like that of Hegelianism and Marxism generally, follows a "Comic" archetype or Romance paradigm. Historical change is emplotted in this paradigm as aiming ultimately at the reconciliation of contradictions and the resolution of contradiction. Hayden White's description of the Comic conception of history in Hegel and Marx fits Kojève's early work perfectly:

> Hegel's Comic conception of history was based ultimately on his belief in the right of life over death; "life" guaranteed to Hegel the possibility of an ever more adequate form of social life throughout the historical future. Marx carried this Comic conception even further; he envisioned nothing less than the dissolution of that "society" in which the contradiction between consciousness and being had to be entertained as a fatality for all men in all times.... This conception did not envision humanity's redemption as a deliverance from time itself. Rather, this redemption took the form of a reconciliation of man with a nature denuded of its fantastic and terrifying powers, submitted to the rule of technics, and turned to the creation of a genuine community.[34]

---

34. Hayden White, *Metahistory: The Historical Imagination in Nineteenth-Century Europe* (Baltimore, Md., 1973), 281–282, quoted by Fredric Jameson, *The Political Unconscious* (Ithaca, N.Y., 1981), 103n.

In Kojève's early writings on Hegel the Endstate provides criteria for determining how the forms of social life became "even more adequate." The final form of social life is one of rigorous equality or, as Kojève puts it, where the citizens' being is equal to their function.[35] Like the great utopian theorists before him Kojève wanted to portray— or, as he said, make propaganda for—a human condition in which there was an absolute convergence of the particular and the general; their convergence would be the triumph of Reason. Like Hegel and Marx, however, Kojève thought of himself as a realist apprehending in thought a process being actualized in history. All three made sense of change over time through the Comic mode.

This Comic mode remains intact despite Kojève's change in perspective during the late 1940s. Although the "genuine community" is for Kojève translated into either the triumph of snobbism or the omnipresence of the American way of life,[36] he retains the structure of emplotment characteristic of the Comic paradigm. It is the Comic with a difference, however, and that difference is Irony.

It is not surprising that Kojève adopts an Ironic mode, because the trope of irony is the dialectical form par excellence.[37] It is, moreover, a mode of particular use to philosophers who write for (or to) a select group of readers or who, as he put it, want to "play" with discourse.[38] It is also a pedagogically useful mode insofar as it can be used to awake an audience from its dogmatic slumbers. In a letter to Strauss, Kojève described how difficult this task had become; even when he tried to be as "paradoxical and provocative as possible," the posthistorical auditors at his lecture remained passive and docile.[39]

35. Kojève, *Esquisse d'une phénoménologie du droit* (Paris, 1981), 585.
36. *ILH*, 436.
37. See Kenneth Burke, "Four Master Tropes," *A Grammar of Motives* (New York, 1945) Appendix D. On the ironic resignation in Hegel's understanding of history and absolute knowing, see Michael Allen Gillespie, *Hegel, Heidegger and the Ground of History* (Chicago, 1984), 114–115.
38. See Kojève, "L'empereur Julien et son art d'écrire," manuscript (1958), 1; a translation of this essay was published in a collection in honor of Leo Strauss, *Ancients and Moderns: Essays on the Tradition of Political Philosophy in Honor of Leo Strauss,* ed. J. Cropsey (New York, 1964). This essay deals in large part with the use of irony in philosophy, a problem about which Kojève often wrote to Strauss in the 1950s.
39. Kojève made much of "play" in his 1968 interview, "Entretien avec Gilles Lapouge," in *La quinzaine litteraire* 53 (1–15 July 1968), 18–19, but he had already concluded that after the end of history, play, too, would disappear (*ILH*, 436n).

But what is the point of being paradoxical and provocative after the End? After it is all over, what good is pedagogy? Why prepare four volumes on the history of philosophy, and hundreds of pages on "discourse, time and the concept," after the animalization of man?

Kojève tells us all contemporary philosophy that attempts to recover a wisdom or truths prior to Hegelianism is, consciously or unconsciously, "tainted" by the last great philosopher. And those wanting to go beyond Hegel have, until now, "succeeded only to isolate certain aspects or fragments of Hegelianism, and in letting them pass, wrongly, for a new 'whole.' "[40] In other words, these attempts have brought about no progress: "But these diverse, so-called "philosophical" attempts at advance and retreat have had practically no influence on the ('profane') mass of those who are content to be where they are. But where they are (me and you included in this situation) is in the midst of 'Hegelianism.' It certainly matters very little whether this situation is called 'Marxist,' 'Leninist,' 'Stalinian (?),' etc., or the legacies of Hegel. What matters is that each of us today needs to know what Hegel said in order to achieve self-consciousness in his own situation such as it is."[41] Kojève wrote, then, to facilitate our understanding of Hegel and hence to promote self-consciousness.

Kojève's pedagogic efforts to establish a Hegelian self-consciousness for our time must be read *against* his nihilistic description of the animalization of man. The former project makes no sense if the latter is definitive. On the contrary, "self-consciousness" has a specific function in the Kojèvian schema of historical change. To have progressed from one stage of history to the next, it is necessary to have self-consciousness of the earlier epoch or, as Kojève put it, "it was necessary that at each dialectical turn there was a *Philosopher* ready to take consciousness of the newly constituted reality."[42] Without the stimulus to self-consciousness provided by philosophy, humans

---

40. Kojève to Strauss, 29 March 1962.

41. Kojève, "Le concept, le temps et le discourse: Essai d'une mise à jour du *Système du savoir* hégélien," manuscript (dated "1952–19   "), 3. This manuscript, and that of the second introduction to the system of knowledge, were recovered and put into clearly legible form by Bernard Hesbois. See his thesis on Kojève's System, "Le Livre et la Mort: Essai sur Kojève" (Thèse, Université Catholique de Louvain, 1985).

42. "Le concept, le temps et le discours," 3–4.

tend naturally toward stasis, to withdraw into what they are already sure of, and to reject even the possibility of the new. The self-consciousness provided through philosophy has been a necessary condition of historical progress, just as historical progress has nourished self-consciousness.

Yet the self-consciousness that Kojève was promoting in his final philosophical labors was the knowledge that further historical progress after Hegel has necessarily not been possible. The "proof" of this knowledge was twofold: the *fact* that no real or significant historical progress has occurred since Hegel's time, and the necessary limitation of self-consciousness and discourse to possibilities already systematically detailed by Hegelianism. After 1948 Kojève did not address himself to the former proof but concentrated his work on the latter. Here again is the shift in questions, from "What does our history mean?" to "How is our discourse put together?" Kojève's late work concentrated on showing how the system of philosophic knowledge—the totality of the True—was completed with Hegel. In other words, he detailed the way the System is put together. The difficulties inherent in this enterprise were formidable, if only because it is not clear why we need Kojève to show us, one hundred twenty-five years after the fact, how the limits of philosophic knowledge had been reached. Kojève was acutely aware of this dilemma and went to great lengths to submerge the point of view of "his own time," but his response—to the effect that Hegel's vocabulary is difficult for twentieth-century readers—was not adequate.

Kojève does not explicitly address *why* it should matter if we, after the End, know that Hegel succeeded in closing the circles of history and philosophy. We can see that it matters to the philosophy of Kojève, however, because his philosophy has a profound commitment to self-consciousness and its extension. This commitment makes sense, *according to the Kojèvian reading of Hegel*, only if self-consciousness is tied to progress. The step taken by his friend Strauss—the commitment to philosophy as a form of knowing divorced from historical change and political commitment—Kojève rejects as a vestige of theological/Platonic reasoning. Thus Kojève's effort to open the path of self-consciousness to an understanding of our contemporary (Hegelian) situation itself counts against his claim that this situation can lead nowhere. The effort to close the circle of Hegelian wisdom and to communicate that closure to others allows for an opening as wide, or as narrow, as the self-consciousness to which this effort is addressed.

Here is the irony found in the form of Kojève's late works: the "discursive solipsism" of his introduction to Hegelian wisdom is willfully disconnected from any discussion of historical development, but it makes sense (according to a Kojèvian analysis) only in light of its connection to self-consciousness, and self-consciousness (again according to Kojève) is inseparable from historical development.[43] Without the dialectical tension provided by history, self-consciousness tends toward dissolution. Thus the commitment to the possibilities of self-consciousness reveals a commitment to the possibilities of history. It is not the task of philosophy to enumerate these possibilities, but the effort of the owl of Minerva to take flight again points to their existence in a night that will know another dawn.

This view of Kojève's philosophy keeps alive the dialectical tension in its development, showing how his work can be appropriated by either a militant modernism or a playful postmodernism. The former appropriation concentrates on Kojève's early work, where we find the philosopher of *engagement*, the thinker who connects human desire to the totalizing project of politics. There may be a nothingness at the core of our being, but this is an absence we can fill by work and struggle. The story of that effort is a Comic resolution of heroic proportions. Bloody Battle dominates the action, but the success of mutual respect and equality redeems the violence of what some now euphemistically call "the process." The philosopher is a militant because he or she brings others into the direction of the movement, the movement of history itself.

The postmodern appropriation of Kojève concentrates on his late work. Barry Cooper seriously uses Kojève's late, bleak vision as a vehicle for coming to terms with the impossibility of politics—of meaningful action and discourse—in the contemporary world. More playful postmoderns can find in Kojève's late work an ironic detachment from questions about the significance of change over time which makes *depassé* all efforts to find the meaning in history and thus *give* history a meaning. Kojève's view that history is dead fits in well with

---

43. I borrow "discursive solipsism" from Stanley Rosen's review of vol. 1 of *Essai d'une histoire raisonné*, in *Man and World* 3 (1970), 120–125.

the contemporary trope of the death of philosophy, the death of literature, and, of course, the death and disappearance of Man.

If the militant appropriation of Kojève fails the test of sophistication in our ironic age, the postmodern appropriation fails the test of Hegelian reflexivity which was so important for Kojève. The postmodern perspective fails to account for itself speaking or writing, that is, and —as we shall see in the final chapter of this book—it fails to account for its own (lack of) critical capacities. The irony in Kojève's late work points to possibilities it cannot articulate more directly. Philosophy for Kojève can be only its time reflected in thought. As the times in which Kojève writes seem to change, the function of the End of history in his philosophy also changes. The point of the reflection of philosophy, however, is to provide a self-consciousness that can initiate action which will further change the times. Kojève does not, like many other thinkers, adopt a stance of tragic resignation in the face of a world that to him resembles a more and more comfortable prison. Nor does he insist that a prison in which all are equal is no longer a place of unfreedom. These are merely different versions of the End of history added to the long list of suprahistorical Absolutes that Kojève unmasked as slave ideologies.

This discussion of the possibilities of history may seem merely an attempt to avoid the *dure parole* of Kojève's Hegel that history is dead, or to appropriate the philosopher for a "progressivist" vision that Kojève himself finally rejects. The latter would be fully in keeping with the spirit of Kojève's own style of commentary, but it is not exactly my purpose here. Instead, I emphasize that without this reading of the ironic turn in his late works, the death of history in his Hegelianism has the same function as the death of God in the slave ideology of Christianity. In both cases, death brings the greatest power, and that power is yet another form of the rule of the Master. The death of God as a man on the cross creates the conditions for universal equality in an ultimate servitude to the Absolute Master. The End of history in the closed circle of Hegelianism substitutes History, one and complete, for God as the Absolute.

The commitment to self-consciousness evinced by Kojève's late philosophy works against such a substitution. Its ironic form distinguishes it from other slave ideologies and recalls to the reader the connections among philosophy, self-consciousness, and historical change. Kojève cannot provide an alternative program for historical development, nor can he escape the burden of history altogether by tuning the ears of an elect to the call of an atemporal Being. Neither option is possible for philosophy insofar as its discourse can no longer be separated from Time and insofar as its knowledge is dependent on, and posterior to, historical development. The theme that runs through all of Kojève's work is that without this development philosophy will disappear, without the self-consciousness provided by philosophy the dialectical turns of history will be stalled. Thus Kojève remains a philosopher long after he is a militant, and thus he is not satisfied with being a technician of the Endstate. The *dure parole* of Kojève remains a *parole*—participation in the conversation of philosophy. His work to continue that conversation is the sign of his struggle against the last Master, History.

Part Three

Progress and the
Elimination of Sens:
Eric Weil

Chapter Seven

From Certainty to Participation

> The path of those who want to forget is not open to the man who does not want to be an animal.
>
> *Eric Weil, 1950*

The weight of Eric Weil's "cross of the present" was the product of the pull of the past and the force of the future; his philosophy labored under, but was also nourished by, the burden of history. Like Hegel, Weil thought that philosophy's task was to find the rose in this cross. For the earlier philosopher, however, the rose was the consciousness of the completion of history in the triumph of Reason, whereas for Weil it was the possibility of preserving the openness of history to meaning and direction, to *sens*. Weil's task was a particularly modern one insofar as it was the result of the triumph of progress, a victory that paradoxically left us exposed in new ways to the terrible power of sophisticated violence.

In 1933, when Weil was twenty-nine years old, he left Germany to settle in Paris. His philosophic formation had been guided by the neo-Kantian perspective that dominated the German academic scene in the twenties, and he wrote his dissertation under Ernst Cassirer on Pietro Pompanazzi, an Aristotelian philosopher of the Italian Renaissance.[1] Weil later wrote of the crisis in German intellectual life between the wars as one of the major roots of French philosophy in the 1940s. He described this crisis as a facet of the loss of faith in

---

1. Eric Weil, "Des Pietro Pomponazzi Lehre von dem Menschen und der Welt" (diss. Hamburg 1932). See also his "Die Philosophie des Pietro Pomponazzi," *Archiv für Geschichte der Philosophie*, 41, nos. 1–2 (1932), 127–176.

science, as part of the general perception that Reason had led to violence or at least had proved incapable of preventing economic crisis and social destruction.[2] Throughout his life Weil was concerned with the connections between Reason and Violence, between progress and the destruction of *sens*. In much of his work through the mid-fifties he spoke to these connections through the concepts of French (especially Kojève's) Hegelianism but in his late work returned to a neo-Kantian moral philosophy that tried to provide the individual with a reasonable basis to hope that these connections would be transcended.

Like many philosophers who were deeply influenced by Hegel in the 1930s, Weil attached great importance to history as the domain in which truths are found. Not only was he concerned with the goal of philosophy of history—drawing universal knowledge from the diversity of change over time—but he also focused on the historian's effort to piece together particular stories while maintaining a fidelity to the Real. Although he never abandoned his interest in history, he substantially changed the perspective from which he confronted the historical in the late 1950s. We can characterize this shift as the transformation of a political into a moral concern with history, although the full significance of these terms will become clear only in the course of this chapter.

Weil's major work, the *Logique de la philosophie* (1950), and two smaller books, *Philosophie politique* (1956) and *Philosophie morale* (1961), are focal points of this chapter, but I also consider his voluminous collection of articles and the analyses of Hegel (1950) and Kant (1963) where appropriate. Starting from the Kojèvian idea of the End of history, Weil struggled to make sense out of what was still happening in the world—despite the fact that history was, so to speak, over. This struggle to preserve the question of meaning eventually led him to seek refuge in a Kantian moral philosophy that remained connected to history but sought to preserve a sanctuary against the ravages of time.

When Weil arrived in Paris, the Hegelian revival was already well under way. Within a year he was publishing reviews in *Recherches*

2. Eric Weil, "The Strength and Weakness of Existentialism," *The Listener* 8 (1952), 743. See, on this same theme, Weil, "Wider den Okkultismus," *Literarische Welt* 7 (1931), reprinted in *Zeitgemasses aus der Literarische Welt von 1925–1932* (Stuttgart, 1963), 348–352, and more generally, "Questions allemandes," *Critique* 1, no. 6 (1946), 526–539; 2, no. 12 (1947), 456–466; 3, no. 13–14 (1947), 65–80.

philosophiques, and he soon established lasting—if stormy— friendships with Koyré and Kojève. Enrolled as a student at the Ecole Pratique des Hautes Etudes, he attended Kojève's seminar on Hegel from 1934 to 1938.[3] During this time Weil published his first full-length article in French, "De l'intérêt que l'on prend à l'histoire."

The question with which Weil was concerned in this article remained at the center of his philosophic project for the following forty years: What leads a person to be concerned with his or her past? He tried to determine in what measure a person is a historian; that is, whether our humanity requires us to turn to the past to fulfill ourselves as persons.

It is the present that leads Weil's individual to turn to the past; as individuals we do so to find ourselves and our "situation." We come to see ourselves as connected to a past and begin to explore this connection in order to orient our actions in the present. Of course, it is not necessary for us to orient our actions in the present; it is quite possible simply to go about our affairs. Once the question "Why *these* affairs?" arises, though, people need a way to give meaning and direction to their decisions and actions. Once they begin the attempt to give meaning and direction, they feel the presentness of the past to be a powerful source of and threat to the very identity of the person making the attempt. As Weil says:

> What am I? First of all, I am not me. The world where I live, the customs that I am, the language in which I speak—I have not chosen them. They are the products of human activity, but it is not I who produced them; at my birth I am in these conditions, but I have not chosen this birth. However, I cannot speak of these conditions without knowing others, I cannot grasp my life without knowing that there are other forms of life, I do not know that I speak a specific language before having learned that there are many of them. Only by questioning the form and *sens* of other lives can I look for a *sens*, a form, a unity in my own life.[4]

Thus it is our desire to give a *sens* to our existence after realizing the contingency of our particular form of life which leads us to explore

---

3. *Annuaire* and *Registre des Inscriptions, Ecole Pratique des Hautes Etudes—Section des Sciences Religieuses*, 1933–1939.

4. Weil, "De l'intérêt que l'on prend à l'histoire," *Recherches philosophiques* 4 (1935), reprinted in *Essais et conférences*, vol. 1 (Paris, 1970), 220, hereafter *E.C.*

our connection with the past. The past can help us as individuals both to situate our particularity and to weave decisions that alter its dimensions into a fabric of diverse but integrated meaning.

Although Weil has now answered his initial question, he goes on to pose another that sets him apart from many Hegelians: How can one justify—be satisfied with—the *sens* that one thinks one has found in the past? If it is the desire to escape from isolated particularity which leads us to the past, how can our point of view on the past escape this same problem of particularlity? How, in other words, do we get a history out of all the histories that individuals find when they turn to the past?[5]

In one sense this is a problem that concerned both Hyppolite and Kojève. The former saw Hegel's great contribution as his story about how the isolated ego developed into the universal subject, the latter was predominantly concerned with how the triumph over particularity was realized in historical reality. Weil shared their suspicion of particularity and saw the "interest" in history as a major facet of the effort to overcome it.[6] But he went further in asking how one can come to terms with the fact that there is more than one way to escape from individual isolation. The response that there is a story—Hegel's *Phenomenology*—which integrates all these routes did not satisfy Weil, because we still need to know why Hegel's is THE story. How did the philosopher knowingly choose between "competing universals"?[7]

Weil's answer in "L'intérêt" is preliminary, as he is more concerned to point out the problem of competing histories than to propose solutions. How do we confront our particularity? Weil answers that it is "reason," embodied in language, which saves us from isolation. Indeed, for Weil it is a serious error to view the individual as separate from others in particularity. Insofar as we can speak with those around

5. *E.C.*, 222–228.

6. Ibid., 229–230.

7. In this early article Weil spoke of the problem of competing points of view, not of "competing universals," and in this regard he cited Max Weber, not Hegel. However, Weil's discussion of reason and history as a response to this problem was surely meant to evoke Hegel. Weil's later comments on the philosophy of history deal with the problem of competing universals (e.g., *Philosophie politique* [Paris, 1956], 226), and this is the theme of his "Le particulier et l'universel en politique," *Christianisme social* 71, nos. 1–2 (1963), 13–28, reprinted in *Philosophie et réalité: Derniers essais et conférences* (Paris, 1982), 225–240.

us and come to grasp our own specificity, we are not truly isolated.[8] Thus, for Weil, reason permits the isolated individual to expand— rise above, perhaps—the particularity of a point of view through discussion with others. Is "reason," however, more than discussion itself? And is discussion more than a cleaned-up version of history, which, as we saw in our analyses of Hyppolite and Kojève, in a Hegelian schema can simply be identified with reason?

This Hegelian schema is not appropriate for Weil because he is asking why we are interested in history rather than what is history, or even what is reason. The interest in history is an aspect of the search for meaning and direction, a crucial facet of our desire to know our identity and the possibilities for change. Weil's later work is preoccupied with this quest for *sens*, for an orientation in or justification of a form of life. History draws our interest because it can help provide this orientation and lead to a reconciliation with the present. The problem for philosophy is to make a coherent whole out of the multiplicity of orientations and reconciliations; to do so would be to reveal the reason in the quests for *sens*.

This quest for *sens* is not an abstract or metaphysical project of interest only to philosophers. Weil's concern here intersects with an important current in modern historiography and sociology (to refer to just two disciplines), namely, the study of mentalities and values. Simply put, the quest for *sens* is the effort people make to give reasons for doing what they do, to give meaning—for themselves and others— to their activity. Weil's interest in this process is self-consciously construed as part of the process itself—the attempt to grasp the quest for *sens* is the *sens* of philosophy.

Thus the quest for *sens* is a form of the search for legitimation. Weil does not limit himself to an inquiry into the logic for validating behavior but rather is concerned with the ways in which people see their desires and identities in relation to the past. They can do so in the form of causal statements or of attributions of responsibility: "I am depressed because nobody can love me," or "It's the fault of my oppressive conditions that I am so aggressive." But Weil tends to concentrate on the use of narratives to convey legitimacy—legitimacy

---

8. "De l'intérêt," *E.C.*, 229–230. Weil's emphasis on "discussion" may recall the notion of the "ideal speech situation" that is so important for Jürgen Habermas. Habermas's ambiguous connections to Hegel and Kant are reminiscent of Weil's own relations to these philosophers.

not as a validation but as meaningfulness: "Why did I become a writer? It all started when my mother gave me this book.... " The kind of legitimacy conveyed by a narrative does not persuade another person that he or she would have acted in the same way given the same conditions, but it does allow other people to understand why you act as you do given the diachronic context for your actions. For Weil, we turn to history to provide stories in which our actions have meaning. Insofar as these stories can be shared, we are not confined to particularity. Insofar as the stories are not unique, however (that's only *your* story), we do not escape conflict.

Weil never fully embraced, as Kojève did, a Hegelian perspective on change over time, nor was he content, as was Hyppolite, to explore the rich possibilities within Hegel's oeuvre. In his question about the legitimacy of an account of the meaning and direction of history, we can see both the traces of his formation in the neo-Kantian atmosphere of German philosophy in the 1920s and the roots of his later, explicitly neo-Kantian turn. Weil's interest for us here is in the way in which he poses this question (and others like it) to—even within—the Hegelian philosophy of history as developed in France. His contribution to that development, as well as his late turn away from it, helps us understand more clearly the trajectory and legacies of Hegelianism in France.

Earlier investigations of the human quest for meaning and direction had an impact on Weil's development of the theme, and they are not difficult to locate. Certainly traces of *Doktorvater* Cassirer's analysis of our use of symbolic formations, and of Max Weber's discussion of the social role of tradition and religion, can be found in Weil's philosophy.[9] Here, however, I discuss not the various influences on his thinking but how his own "interest in history" develops in relation to his concern with how we give meaning and direction to our lives.

9. Cassirer's view that we give meaning and direction to our existence through our spiritual activity can be seen in the structure of Weil's *Logique* as the possibility of our giving *sens* to our lives through the diverse categories of philosophical expression. Weil compared his own understanding of the human point of view vis-à-vis history with Weber's idea of our "decision" to turn to history for specific reasons ("De l'intérêt,"' *E.C.*, 213, 218), and he considered the philosophical bases of Weber's general perspective in *Logique de la philosophie* (1950; Paris, 1974), 263–281—page references in text are to this work. The implication of the fact/value distinction is a theme of much of Weil's work, and its connection to the choice between reason and violence is the subject of his "Science in Modern Culture, or the Meaning of Meaninglessness," *Daedalus* 94, no. 1 (1965), 171–189.

Weil's major work, *Logique de la philosophie,* charts the development of the *sens* of philosophy. The map of the categories of philosophical reflection it provides is organized "logically"; that is, according to a necessary sequence based on hypothetical conditions (e.g., *if* one progresses from Category A, then the progression must be to Category B). Implicit in this organization is a Hegelian perspective on historical change which is now familiar: following Kojève, Weil accepts the idea that history has *in principle* been completed because it has become comprehensible.[10] For him, this notion means that the meaning and direction of history have been apprehended by Hegel. There is still much work to be done to realize fully the idea of history as the ascent to freedom and universality, but—unless history is absurd—the End of the work is now in sight.[11]

Weil takes more seriously than either Hyppolite or Kojève the fact that this last sentence is hypothetical. He takes more seriously the possibility that history has no meaning and direction, and he tries to integrate this possibility as a problem for philosophical reflection. He is concerned, in other words, with the willful rejection of the search for wisdom, with the self-conscious rejection of the End of history in absolute knowledge, freedom, and satisfaction: "I know that what I am doing is wrong, I am not trying to set an example or create anything, I am only trying to get what I can." The rejection of reason has to be confronted by a philosophy that is not willing to reduce history to the progress of scientific knowledge. The choice between reason and the irrational is itself never "reasonable."[12]

The most extreme and important form of the choice against reason is the choice for violence. All of Weil's postwar philosophical work is marked by the shadow of violence, the Other of philosophy. Hegel and his heirs are also concerned with violence, of course, but as a tool in the service of history as reason.[13] Although Weil attends to

10. *Logique,* 54–55. We shall see that Weil went on to say that this principle—and with it a meaningful history—can be rejected through violence (*Logique,* 83–85).

11. Weil, *Hegel et l'état* (Paris, 1950), 36, 77–79, and *Logique,* 54–55.

12. *Logique,* 56. Nor did the choice of reason, for Weil, fulfill a natural purpose, as Kant thought it did in "Idea for a Universal History from a Cosmopolitan Point of View."

13. Kant also configured violence as being in the service of progress, not as reason's self-unfolding but as a realization of man's natural ends. See, for example, the fourth Thesis of the "Idea for a Universal History" and Yirmiahn Yovel's discussions of violence and the "cunning of nature" (a phrase he borrows from Weil's late work) in *Kant and the Philosophy of History* (Princeton, N.J., 1980), esp. 140–153.

this facet of historical development, he underlines the possibility of violence as an alternative to reason.

This alternative is the willful maintenance of isolated particularity. Hegelianism in all its forms tells a story of the development of the isolated ego to some form of integrated universality. This development is the path of reason, and it provides criteria for judging the "underdeveloped" or the "incomplete." Weil does not reject this story, but he recognizes that it can be, and is, rejected. To call this rejection "unreasonable" or "irrational" is to use terms that have significance only within the story of reason's development or within the context of a reasonable discussion that is itself being rejected.

Weil thus modifies the Kojèvian-Hegelian conclusion that history, properly so-called, is over. He agrees with this conclusion insofar as it says that *in principle* it is now possible to know the direction, the End, of historical progress. For Weil, however, this possibility means only that history *can* be terminated.[14] He emphasizes that one can know in what direction the train of history is traveling and still choose not to climb on board; one can try to slow the train, moreover, with acts of violence, not even attempting to provide an alternative destination. Weil is committed to finding the *sens* even in this rejection of *sens* (77).

Our own century gives us no shortage of examples of what Weil means by this rejection of *sens*. Although at least the structure of the *Logique* was already conceived before Weil left to fight with the French armies in World War II, the experience of this conflict and especially of the Holocaust surely added a painful urgency to the philosopher's concern with the rejection of meaning and direction in favor of violence. In our own day we know forms of terrorism—terror not in the name of virtue or even as a dirty means to a glorious end, but terror that feeds on itself and does not even attempt to point to a world where terror will no longer be necessary. This is the kind of violence that Weil had in mind.

The *Logique de la philosophie* begins from a consideration of the decision against violence in favor of discourse. It acknowledges this decision as free or absurd, but as discourse, it figures itself in this

---

14. In *Hegel et l'état*, Weil emphasizes that for Hegel the condition among states is not yet rational and thus not yet definitive (77–79). Still, the goal of history—the rational condition—is in sight (102).

option against violence. Weil takes the basic desire of the philosopher *qua* philosopher to be the desire to eliminate violence (20), because violence as the rejection of discourse eliminates the possibility of philosophizing. The relation of philosophy and violence, however, is not symmetrical: violence is a problem for philosophy, but philosophy is not a problem for those who choose violence.

The link between violence and philosophy is history. Only by coming to terms with the varieties of historical experience can philosophy understand violence as a human expression and situate it in a coherent whole. History and philosophy, for Weil, are thus inextricable:

> It is only in his history that man is revealed to himself; it is only in his discourse that he becomes conscious of this revelation.
>
> We must, then ... affirm not only the identity between philosophy and the history of philosophy, but even that of history itself and philosophy. Being understood beginning from violence and aiming toward coherence, the man who has chosen discourse understands himself only in his accomplishments [*réalisations*], in what he has *made* in the world, and in what he has *made* of himself (69).

The person who has chosen discourse has begun the search for meaning and direction, the self-conscious form of which is philosophy striving to replace violence with coherence.

Weil's concern with violence relates to his earlier study of the human "interest" in history. We turn to the past, he told us, to situate ourselves in the present and find our way to the future. In the *Logique* he underlines that to engage in this process is to renounce violence, that the search for *sens* implies an openness to the other—to that which questions the legitimacy of our own way of life—which the threat of violence would negate. The choice for discourse in the face of violent aggression, however, would simply be a choice for self-sacrifice. The asymmetrical relation between violence and discourse forces the philosopher to leave open the recourse to violence in order to protect the possibility of later discussion. In the face of violent action, discussion cannot be pursued.[15] Ultimately, therefore, Weil

15. Weil noted that in the face of war, a liberal democracy can not exist as such: "Le sens du mot 'Liberté,' " *Critique* 4 (1948), E.C., 109. In a similar vein he notes that France's big mistake was to confuse the two Germanies—Culture and Power—thereby speaking to the former when it should have been struggling against the latter: "Le problème des deux Allemagnes," *Critique* 4, no. 27 (1948), 718–722.

figures a collective choice against violence as a necessary condition for philosophy, that is, for the search for meaning and direction.

The choice for discourse in the *Logique* is a choice for coherence and ultimately for universality. Universality is Weil's criterion of truth: the power of a discourse is the extent to which it can coherently integrate a range of phenomena and be persuasive to a community that has rejected violence. History presents the great challenge to universality as it continually produces new phenomena to be integrated and is the field in which the process of persuasion takes place. The quest for *sens* is the construction of a coherent story of the past in the present, a construction undertaken with consciousness of the possibility of a renewal of apparently senseless violence.

The *Logique* explicates the basic categories of philosophy, of the self-conscious or reflexive search for meaning and direction. Each category is developed out of an "attitude," a nonreflexive form through which a person unconsciously makes sense of his or her actions. Thus the book means to account for all of the possibilities through which people have given (and can give) a *sens* to their lives. For this reason it has been variously called a *Phenomenology of Spirit* for our times and a "Prolegomenon to Any Future Chuzpa."[16]

What is the theory of history implicit in the book? Weil offers a logic not a history of philosophy, but the development of the former depends on the latter. The interest in history is tied to the desire for meaning and direction. In the account presented in the *Logique*, history is initially experienced as the loss of meaning and direction, as the loss of the certainty that one's way of life has a *sens*. Certainty is the origin and end of historical development. The antehistorical attitude of certainty discussed by Weil is the naive, unreflective belief in the mores of a community. This form of belief can be preserved only through isolation, through the refusal to recognize otherness. History—either as the consciousness of different cultures or epochs, or as the rude confrontation with another society—undermines certainty by forcing the question "Why do we live *this* way?" Why is our form of life better than theirs?

16. François Chatelet compares Weil's *Logique* with Hegel's *Phenomenology*, and Leo Strauss describes the book in the terms quoted in a letter to Kojève (4 June 1956). A more sober analysis of the book, and a useful introduction to Weil's philosophy as a whole, is provided by Gilbert Kirscher, "Eric Weil: La philosophie comme logique de la philosophie," *Cahiers philosophiques* 8 (1981), 25–69.

For Weil, the appearance of these questions marks the beginning of history and philosophy. It marks, that is, the beginning of the quest for *sens*. This conception of beginning is crucial for understanding all Weil's work. Philosophy starts from certainty as a "lost object"; this means that philosophy starts not in some species of Cartesian radical doubt but from the feeling in a community (probably, of an individual in a community) that its form of life can no longer *go without saying*. The effort to legitimate a form of life through discursive reasoning thus becomes the highest task of philosophy. Philosophy should respond to the desire of people to live in certainty, to find the path back to the lost object. Weil puts it this way:

> Certainty must become the inheritance of all men. It is necessary to make men *content*; not only to show them the truth; not only to show them how a system of apprehending falsity is false in itself. Their opinions must be understood not only insofar as they contain something false, but insofar as they contain something true. The discourse of the sage [*sage*] must not remain the pure negation of every position, it must be filled with substance. . . . Man must be convinced in his life, he must know what he can hold [*s'en tenir*] on to on every occasion. There is the false, but there is also the true. Only he who can have the certainty of being in the true is really at home in life, and he can lose this home, if he is left to the uncertainty of opinion. It is in life and not only in discourse that the true and the false must be separated.[17]

The inheritance of certainty—a heritage to be acquired, one that must come to be—will coincide with contentment. It will not be the product of an isolated philosopher's work but must be developed out of the unreflective opinions of the community. Philosophy is not only critical or negative, it must provide access to truths. "Truths" here means ways of life that can be discursively legitimated. Philosophy provides access to ways of life by giving accounts of how the way we live (want to live) has meaning and direction. The wisdom of philosophy, in other words, must be both communicable and capable of integrating nonphilosophy, the beliefs and practices of the community. The process of integration is discussion within the community of its own *sens*.

17. *Logique*, 108. On the beginning of philosophy out of the loss of certainty, see the discussion of Koyré above, 6–7.

The suspension of certainty, like the renunciation of violence, is a necessary condition of discourse as the search for *sens*. In both cases, Weil underlines, it is an openness to difference which permits the possibility of finding, sharing, and legitimating meaning and direction for one's existence. If the goal of this search is the rediscovery of a life of certainty, violence remains an omnipresent threat that can cut off the pursuit of reason through discussion in a senseless, mute destruction. Whereas discourse is an expression of the need for legitimation, violence is the affirmation that no legitimation is possible in a world where particular force rules.

The *Logique* shows how the various categories of philosophic reflection approach the lost object of certainty, and how they fail to reexperience it or recreate it. The most important example in this regard is the discussion of the category "the Absolute," which is dominant in Hegelian philosophy. According to Weil, the limitation of this category is its conception of reconciliation as a complete and total discourse rather than as a development in the life of the community— rather than as practical changes in the ways people live. When Weil talks of the category of the Absolute, he has in mind a story of human development which takes into account all possibilities and reveals history as the becoming of truth. The category of the Absolute does not end the development of philosophy, because even a total and complete philosophy will be (and has been) rejected. In what Weil calls the "scandal of reason," the Absolute, in its truly mighty coherence, is rejected because people remain unhappy; reconciled in thought, they remain estranged in their being in the world. Even peace and freedom when fully articulated will be rejected, to say nothing of equality and fraternity. The truth of a universal discourse makes sense of the world for philosophy, but it does not change this world for humanity. Home in community is not found, and even after the universal values have been made clear, we remain violent, alone, and empty: "On the one hand the accord is total with the absolutely coherent discourse...which is recognized as Reason. On the other hand, there is an emptiness, a feeling of abandonment and of unhappiness as absolute as is the absolute satisfaction of Reason in Reason. This feeling is precisely the result of this satisfaction; a mute despair arising from the knowledge that as soon as man begins to speak, he speaks necessarily in terms which imply satisfaction; that to speak reasonably is to be satisfied."[18] If the truth does not set us free and fulfill us, how can it—and why should it—be spoken? The promised land of Reason-at-home-with-itself provides the order of coherence, but for humanity it remains alien soil, the ground of our alienation.

Weil does not consider revolts against the claims of the Absolute as abandonments of philosophy but as further developments in its logic, developments that—when they have any positive content—are aimed at the reconnection of reasonable discourse and the life of the community. The final category of philosophy proper, Action, re-establishes this connection. The category of Action conceives the actualization of reason in the world, and so it points to the Marxist appropriation of Hegel. It ends philosophy in the effort to unify "life and discourse," theory and practice. If the category of the Absolute thinks the totality of the world coherently, Action will make this world coherent; the former conceives of what the satisfied individual must be, the latter thinks of the action necessary to create the conditions of satisfaction. To paraphrase the sentence from Marx's *Theses on Feuerbach* that Weil certainly had in mind here: freedom has been interpreted, now freedom has to be realized. But whereas Marx saw that realization as a post-philosophical task, Weil's category of Action makes changing the world the completion of philosophy.

This self-conscious attempt to realize discursive knowledge by changing the conditions of the community's life is the final stage of the philosophy of history implicit in the *Logique*. Through the category of Action, philosophy aims to grasp history in order to recreate the conditions of certainty and contentment which were initially lost. If there is an extra-historical category of philosophy, it is *Sens*, the category through which the idea of history itself is thought and each stage given meaning and direction. I emphasize that for Weil, history is development from naive certainty in community life to self-conscious action that creates the conditions for knowing participation in this life. More accurately still, history is a key facet of our being-not-at-home but is also the way to a genuine homecoming. Philosophy, as the "science of *sens*," should help us find our way.

The theory of history implicit in Weil's *Logique*, though certainly

18. Ibid., 351. The word "reasonably" was added to the final sentence in the revised edition.

not completely foreign to the Hegelian schemas in the works of Hyppolite and Kojève, has important differences from them. The theme that runs through the work of all three is that history is the ascent to universality and self-consciousness, although Weil's work emphasizes fully articulated particularities (in contradistinction to "homogenization") within a final universality. For Hyppolite, this process is chiefly the result of alienation—human self-estrangement pushes us toward some form of community. For Kojève, the struggle for recognition is the motor that drives us from the isolation of particularity to a state both homogeneous and universal. Although "alienation" and the "master/slave dialectic" play important roles in Weil's conception of history, neither idea is primary. History is not only determined by its end in universality; for Weil, it is irremediably marked by its origin in loss.

The word "origin" has received so much adverse commentary recently that it is worthwhile to pause and examine just how the lost object of certainty conditions history and historical consciousness. Weil's discussion of the naive certainty in the beliefs and practices of a community does not allude to some golden age preceding the corruption that we know too well. Instead, it points to a form of life that is continually at work alongside historical consciousness. There are always particular beliefs and practices that can "go without saying," that are not subject to discursive legitimation or historical confirmation. These practices and beliefs—we call them "traditions"—give meaning and direction to the members of a community. Historical consciousness, the most developed form of which is philosophy, strives to provide this same meaning and direction through discursive reasoning or narrative. "Certainty" is logically anterior to "discussion" in Weil's book, because discursive reasoning always exists in the context of unquestioned beliefs or traditions that are a condition of communication. The point of historical development or philosophical progress is not to undermine these traditions but to achieve self-consciousness of one's participation in them. The task of philosophy is to recreate through discourse the possibility of full belonging-ness.

Thus in Weil's work the description of history as the ascent to universality has the added significance that the ascent is the attempt to *re*-discover a life informed by meaning and direction. This attempt is not only a response to the loss of the immediacy of *sens* but also an expression of the choice against violence, which Weil takes to be the refusal of the possibility of *sens*. The story of historical development is not, though, a progress from violence to *sens*; the effort to be at home in the world and the revolt against this reconciliation are *always* present in change over time. Indeed, Weil emphasizes that as human power to make the world our own increases, so too does our capacity for destruction: "Thought must be quite advanced for someone to be able to declare that he draws his revolver the moment he hears the word 'culture' " (60).

Violence and certainty, then, are two shadows of philosophy throughout history. Philosophy preserves the questions of *sens* as an alternative to violence and in search of a shared or communicable certainty. It does not create the search for *sens*, for this search is the product of the loss of a shared community, and it is taken up by people who want—even need—to give meaning and direction to their lives. There is no postulate of an ontological necessity for a constant search for meaning and direction. The feeling of the loss of community—which may be, to paraphrase Freud, a refeeling—is always a possibility when there is significant change. Weil emphasizes the loss as well as the condition of relative certainty which is necessary for measuring any feeling as a loss. Whenever we speak, we imply a community of understanding, but we also imply the need to rearticulate that community, because it does not *go without saying*.

Let us note the difference between this conception of philosophy and history and Kojève's. The search for *sens* in Kojève's philosophy is over, and it is declared a success. For Weil, the existence of violence in what should be the posthistorical world expresses the need for history, the need for meaningful action to make us at home in the world.[19] The violent rejection of the modern world, which philosophy declares unreasonable, is the refusal of the closure of history in the coherence of a totalizing story, what Weil calls an Absolute. For Weil, the "violent rejection of the modern world" is not a hypothetical or abstract possibility but instead a human reaction to the rationalization or systematization of the world. We have already confronted the extreme forms of this rejection, which reveal more profoundly than

---

19. Kojève was, of course, well aware of the existence of "posthistorical violence." This was not for him an expression of the need for history but could simply be considered a sickness: "In the endstate, the healthy 'Automaton' is satisfied...and the 'sick' will be locked up" (Kojève to Strauss, 19 September 1950).

in earlier periods in history the importance of the choice of reason against violence.[20] Indeed, Weil writes that a logic of philosophy "was possible only beginning from the moment where violence had been seen in its purity," that is, only when the importance of the will to meaningful coherence, and its opposition, have become fully clear (83).

Weil's conception of the choice between reason and violence should not be understood as a rejection of the Hegelian attempt to incorporate violent action into the story of history as the realization of Reason.[21] Like anybody who takes politics seriously, Weil recognized that violence can be defeated only on its own terms (408). Indeed, as we have just seen, the last category of philosophy for him is Action, which aims to reunite discourse and life—to realize the Absolute for us— employing violence when necessary in the service of a reasonable happiness. In contrast, the concept of violence in his idea of a primordial choice is not a variation on the Hegelian cunning of reason but rather a rejection of reason itself, a rejection of the possibility of giving to our lives a meaning and direction that can be shared in discourse. Weil's political philosophy is preeminently concerned with this rejection in its effort to think the reconciliation of philosophy and action in the uncertainty of a historically viable community. Weil's turn to political philosophy continues his reflection on the problem of the completion of philosophy by finding the path of action that can create a life of reasonable happiness out of the perfect coherence already promised in discourse by Hegelian philosophy.

20. The category of "Work" is that through which philosophy understands the rejection of coherence. Weil here clearly has in mind Nazism as a form of the violent rejection of modernity (*Logique*, 355–357).

21. *Hegel et l'état*, 31.

Chapter Eight

From Uncertainty to Nostalgia

Outside of certainty, desire is fear.

—*Eric Weil, 1950*

In the previous chapter we saw how Weil's *Logique* contains within it a philosophy of history which sees the search for meaning and direction emerging from a community that has begun to question its own legitimacy. Philosophy is sustained by the desire for *sens* while its fundamental condition is the feeling of uncertainty, of the absence of meaning and direction. This absence, coupled with the choice against violence, makes philosophy possible.

In this chapter we see how the conditions out of which philosophy emerges are also fundamental to politics as Weil conceives it. Politics belongs to the realm of uncertainty, which is for Weil also the realm of history. In his *Philosophie politique*—considered in the first part of this chapter—he explores this realm and examines the possibilities for posing the question of *sens* therein. In the second part of this chapter we see how his *Philosophie morale* attempts to find a guarantee for the possibilities of politics and history. This attempt escapes the condition of uncertainty which Weil himself had seen as fundamental to all philosophical reflection. The "nostalgia for certainty" that animates Weil's moral philosophy expresses a weariness with history and with the possibilities of finding meaning and direction within it.

Politics and the Possibility of Sens

Weil's conception of the political begins not with the individual but with the community, the whole in which reflection finds people always already embedded. The "priority" of politics is based on this fundamental tie between the individual and the community. From the political perspective, we exist *qua* individuals only when we are separated—or separate ourselves—from the life of the community.[1]

The community is the vehicle for certainty, for the traditions that give meaning and direction to the daily lives of its members. The form of this certainty is revealed to the philosopher only after its content has begun to slip away. That is, certainty becomes a problem for philosophical reflection only after people feel troubled by doubt. The *Philosophie politique* considers the loss of certainty in the context of historical progress. More specifically, the loss is figured as one of the results of society's fundamental achievements: mastery over nature.[2]

One of the chief characteristics of modern society is its effort to protect its members from violence while it creates the conditions through which "legitimate" desires can be satisfied. Society is organized to confront the dangers and enjoy the benefits of nature (that which is outside of the social). The staggering sophistication of this organization and its technological successes have rightly produced a confidence in the power of society to solve the problems it considers important. Here, though, arises the central political issue for Weil: How does one decide which problems are really important? The individual, as a member of society, though benefiting greatly from the increasingly efficient techniques of social organizatin, has no criterion other than efficiency for judging their relative value. Weil thinks that the result is one of the basic dilemmas of our life in common today: "The result for the individual is that nature, meaningful in itself for traditional thought, is transformed into matter and material. A society is born which knows no sacred in the traditional sense. . . . The modernity of our society, objectively the progressive stuggle with external

---

1. Weil, *Philosophie politique* (Paris, 1971), 21. See also "De l'intérêt que l'on prend à l'histoire," *Essais et conferences* (Paris, 1970), 1:215 (hereafter *E.C.*); "Le cas Heidegger," *Les temps modernes* 22 (1947), 137.

2. Weil used "society" in a technical sense, the sense that political philosophy traditionally gives to "civil society."

nature, is expressed on the plane of subjectivity as the painful division of the individual between what he is for himself and what he does and possesses; between what he considers as his value, and what he must exhibit as value to others, to society."[3] The effort to organize society undermines continuity in a community's beliefs and practices. The meaning and direction provided by these traditions cannot be found in the ideology of technological progress even if this ideology becomes a tradition.[4] Humanity in modernity exists within the domain of uncertainty.

Weil does not, however, join the antiscientific chorus and claim that the mistake has been to attempt to master nature in the first place (*Politique*, 101). The problem for him is that power over nature is necessary but not sufficient: technological mastery provides the member of society with *"free* time," but it does not educate the citizen to be free.[5] Indeed, the more free time made available to the social individual, the greater alienation becomes, because society values the achievements of work. Private life, Weil notes, becomes increasingly divorced from social role in the modern world because individuals abandon the attempt to give meaning and direction to their lives through public, political action. They strive instead to preserve some private haven in which the possibility of *sens* is not automatically denied in favor of the reality of efficiency or success (*Politique*, 100–101).

Thus, despite the achievements of society in protecting its members from violence and in providing a sophisticated technology of satisfaction, people feel forced to look for meaning and direction outside the social sphere. Weil is thinking not of the happy marginality of those who would abandon the advantages of society for a more "natural" or "meaningful" lifestyle but of those who are divided between their appreciation of society's techniques and their need to justify or make sense of them.

3. *Politique*, 97. See also "Masses et individus historiques," in *Encyclopédie française* vol. 11 (1957), pp. II. 10–10 through II. 12–15; *E.C.* 2:266.
4. The role of a tradition of progress or of modernism has recently been discussed in great detail. I have discussed some of the related issues in "Opening a Dialogue between Cultural Conservatism and Modernism," *democracy* 3, no. 4 (1983), 55–59, and in a review essay in *Telos* 62 (1984–1985), 218–222. Weil addressed this same theme in "Tradition and Traditionalism," *Confluence* 2, no. 4 (1953), 106–116.
5. The theme of Weil's "Education as a Problem for Our Time," *Confluence* 6, no. 1 (1957), 40–50.

In the *Politique*, Weil tries to show how this need for meaning and direction can be reincorporated into the public realm; that is, how the need for *sens* becomes a political factor in the state. In this regard he is tilling the same soil as Hegel in the *Philosophy of Right*. Hegel also describes the tremendous power of civil society, "which draws men into itself and claims that they work for it, owe everything to it, and do everything by its means."[6] The appearance of the state for Hegel is the appearance of the Idea in history; the realization of THE *sens* that the members of society found wanting in their pursuit of merely private ends.

If there is a parallel in the structure of Weil's and Hegel's political philosophies, there is also a crucial difference in the content of their concerns. Whereas for Hegel the problem is the development of a reasonable/organic community out of a technically rational society, for Weil the issue is the dissolution of community in the face of a society that is dominant. This difference stems from their respective historical positions, Hegel writing during (and for) the consolidation of the modern Prussian state, Weil writing during the dissolution of states and the growth of empires or of a global system. But more fundamentally, the difference stems from their respective conceptions of the role of philosophy vis-à-vis history.

Philosophy's task, Hegel tells us in the Preface to the *Philosophy of Right* is to "find the rose in the cross of the present, and thereby to enjoy the present."[7] Weil expresses this as philosophy opening a path to meaning and direction through reconciliation with a historical community. Whereas Hegel's political philosophy would achieve this reconciliation by finding the thread of Reason that ties history together, however, Weil's work underlines the problem that such a reconciliation presents to the modern citizen and philosopher. Hegel's philosophy closes the history that leads up to it in the effort to show the completion of Reason (certainty in the concept) in the present, whereas Weil's work shows how the question of *sens* opens up history, preserving philosophy and politics, albeit in the precarious domain of uncertainty.

We can situate Weil's emphasis on the question of *sens* in relation to the Kojève/Strauss dialogue discussed in Chapter 6. Like Strauss,

---

6. Hegel, *Philosophy of Right*, trans. T. M. Knox (Oxford, 1952), 276.
7. Ibid., 12.

Weil thinks that a reasonable person need not—perhaps should not—be satisfied in the Endstate. However, Weil's agreement with Strauss does not extend as far as the latter's position in the debate between Ancients and Moderns. Weil, that is to say, wants to integrate his philosophy into modern thought and practice, not revolt against them.[8] Weil accepts the principle of modern political equality and the use of science the better to control nature. The achievements of modern politics and science make possible his question of *sens* as a demand not only of an elite of philosophers but of the members of a community.[9]

Thus Weil participates in the Hegelian tradition to the extent that he accepts the premise that what is actual is rational, and that philosophy must take its bearings from historical progress (which means that the philosopher must organize change over time as progress). Like Kojève, he sees philosophy as part of the process of universal enlightenment, but he adds that philosophy has to continue to search for the *sens* in this process. Kojève sees no need for such a search, because for him all *sens* is contained in the definition of Universal. For Weil, however, even the achievement of an integrated global politics will not destroy the desire for meaning and direction and thus not remove the basis for posing the question of *sens*.

We can also situate Weil's approach in the context of a more general concern in the twentieth century with totalization and various forms of totalitarianism as realizations of the ideology of historical progress. Whether in the form of Frankfurt School anxiety about identity theory and one-dimensionality or neo-Tocquevillean fears of social homogenization, modern social theory has been at least as concerned about the fast pace of "progress" as it has about the lack of it. Weil's question of *sens* is another attempt to refuse closure in a system of rationality or in a completion of history. In the *Politique* he looks at the possibilities for finding a place for this question in modern political life.

Weil is not, however, offering a critique of historical progress. He

---

8. Toward further comparisons with Strauss see Weil's analysis of the link between the appearance of the idea of natural right and the history of the idea of history in "Du droit naturel," *Nouveaux cahiers* 15 (1968), 37–46; *E.C.*, 1:175–198.

9. *Politique*, 127–128. See also "Christianisme et politique," *Critique* 9 (1953), 748–776, and "Science in Modern Culture," in which Weil emphasized that modern politics and science provide the conditions for posing the question of *sens* but cannot provide an answer to it.

associates neither with the neoromantics in German sociology who point toward the virtues of community against the vices of society nor with more recent thinkers who want to show how what we call Progress is really a more systematic form of domination. Weil accepts progress as a Hegelian (and, eventually, everyone else) must accept significant historical change. He also shows that this acceptance does not fulfill a desire for meaning and direction which is itself an important ingredient in historical development. The presence of that desire points to the absence of complete totalization, as it indicates to the philosopher an important project for politics.

The *Politique* poses the question of *sens* at the level of the state, the level at which a community makes self-conscious decisions. The state is the integration of the technically organized ("rational") society with the living traditions of the ("reasonable") community. The principal task of the state—whether it knows it or not—is the education of its citizens, because it is through a political education that the integration of society and community develops. The government of a state does not have to decide to play this pedagogic role; it is, Weil says, educative by necessity: "Government will therefore necessarily be educator, whether it wants or knows it. It cannot help but influence the rationality of citizens, their morals, and the *sens* they give to their existence. Government makes impossible or inevitable certain moral decisions if only because of its influence on their way of working. Government must search for the reconciliation among the universal of reason . . . the universal (rational and technical) of understanding, and the concrete and historic universal of the morals of the community."[10] Of course, Weil is well aware that the state's officials do not think of themselves in these terms, but he maintains that their specific action has the function of reconciling these three demands. The "universal of reason" is the demand that justice be done; the "universal of understanding" is the demand for efficiency or progress; and the "universal of a community's moral" is the de-

10. *Politique*, 194. The pedagogic role of the state concerned Weil from the start: In "Questions allemandes," he described the German tragedy in terms of the failure of the state to politically educate the citizens and of its effort to keep politics in the domain of experts and away from citizens (*Critique* 13–14 [1947], 71; see also "L'anthropologie d'Aristote," *Revue de métaphysique et de morale* 56 [1951], 283–315; E.C., 1, especially 24–26; and "Guillaume II et la détermination de l'histoire," *Critique* 5, no. 36 [1949], 551).

mand of custom or of the evolving mores of a people. The actions of a government must strive to satisfy the exigencies of all three while preserving the polity.[11]

By what criterion, however, is a government to weigh the demands of the three universals? Weil considers a baldly pragmatic criterion but sees it as offering only the opportunity for eliminating certain possibilities; within the range of potentially successful decisions, hard choices still must be made.[12] How can such decisions be justified? How can we know that they lead to an education, in contradistinction to a corruption, of the citizenry? How can the meaning and direction of political action be ascertained when there is basic conflict among the demands of reason, rationality, and the traditions of a people?

Weil turns to history in order to speak to these classical questions of political philosophy. He reminds us of the decisions and attempts at justification that have been made, the criteria that have been invoked. The principles of political action cannot be discovered in a frozen frame of political life. They have to be grasped as they appear when citizens or rulers discuss what is to be done. Those who participate in discussion share a language; they share a form of life. They search for truths they can live with, and as citizens renounce violence among themselves (*Politique*, 203). Access to political discussion is, according to the principle of the modern state, the possibility of making rational decisions in common.

Discussion, for Weil, is at the base of political life. It is the model for the nonviolent reconciliation of community and society, reason and rationality, in a *vie sensée*. The effort to solve common problems through discussion is crucial in his political philosophy because it implies both the recognition of difference and the refusal of violence. Discussion requires the suspension of isolated certainty in the interest of preserving the possibility of community; it requires the acceptance of uncertainty and otherness in exchange for the security from violence that the polity provides.

---

11. The problem of doing so was the subject of "Machiavel aujourd'hui," *Critique* 7, no. 46 (1951), 233–253; *E.C.*, 2:189–217; and "Politique et morale," *Cahiers de l'I.S.E.A.* ser. M, no. 14 (1962), 3–15; *Philosophie et réalité: Derniers essais et conferences* (Paris, 1982), 241–254 (hereafter *P.R.*).

12. The issue of success/failure vs. good intentions as criteria for judging action concerned Weil greatly: See *Politique*, 177, 196; *Philosophie morale* (Paris, 1961), 124, 183–85; and *Hegel et l'état* (Paris, 1950), 53.

The renunciation of violence, then, is contemporaneous with the renunciation of certainty: politics and philosophy begin only after both are given up or at least displaced.[13] What some observers might now call language in an intersubjective situation, Weil's "discussion," has the same bases as politics generally. The choice against certainty and violence underlies all discussion and politics. This is not a naïve view of politics as pristine and separate from violence on the part of the philosopher. On the contrary, the nonviolence of citizens is viewed as neither natural nor necessary. It is, rather, their attempt—always only partially successful—to make a clearing for discussion within the context of an uncertain and violent world.[14] The self-education of citizens and government through participation as discussion is their progressive politicization, their path from natural, individual violence to life in common—community.

Here we return to one of our initial considerations in the *Politique*. The principle of discussion is an acceptance of uncertainty in exchange for nonviolence, but as we saw above, nonviolence is not enough for the political person. At the level of society the individual is protected from violence by the efficiency of technical organization, but this protection has no positive content. The alienated individual can look for meaning and direction only in private life. The state in Weil's philosophy is supposed to be the political level proper for this search, but we see now that discussion—the fundamental principle of the modern state—is also drawn from the merely negative condition of protection against violence (the violence not of nature but of the aggressive certainty of other people). Weil reiterates, however, that protection is not enough:

> Neither violence nor nonviolence furnishes this *sens* according to which men live, find their way, and are satisfied. This *sens* is present only in the historic morals, these morals that violence wants to unify for the benefit of one among them, and that nonviolence negates all together as obstacles to rational and peaceful collaboration.
>
> Henceforth the task is to create a world in which morality can live

13. One might speak of the displacement of violence from domestic to foreign policy. Weil, however, does not do so, and his comments on the world organization, or interstate relations, are the weakest discussions in the *Philosophie politique*.

14. On the political use of violence see "Machiavel aujourd'hui," and "Philosophie politique, théorie politique," *Revue française de science politique* 11 (1961).

with nonviolence, a world in which nonviolence is not simply an absence of meaning and direction (*Politique*, 233, 234).

How, though, can positive *sens* be found in the *morales historiques* when it is the commitment to positive *sens* that is given up in exchange for nonviolence? Is not the ground of *sens* removed when discussion takes the place of both an automatic belief in tradition and a firm criterion for decision making?

The ground of *sens* is removed if we consider ground as "foundation." If, on the other hand, we consider ground as "condition of possibility," then the ground remains, and it is history. The initial choice of discourse instead of violence is made sensible in the contemporary world by historic conditions that make possible a coherent universalization of the principle of discussion. The Hegelian conception of history as the simultaneous ascent to the universal and growth of alienation points to the possibility that the search for *sens* will be a shared quest—shared, Weil thinks, not only as a mutual victimization through bloody struggle but also as the response to a common need for meaning and direction in conditions that can be understood through discussion. It is the need and desire for *sens* that, according to Weil, keeps history alive and hence prevents philosophy from being closed in an Absolute system or a superior technique. The death of history, properly so-called, would for him not have been an occasion for Kojèvian irony or postmodern playfulness, because its death rattle would have been the resurrection of the agony of absolute violence. Like Kojève, Weil might have thought he saw in the 1940s the possibility of the end of history, but instead he rethought the possibilities for its remaining open to the question of *sens*.

We have now come to the limit of Weil's political philosophy: politics, through the principle of discussion in the state, can preserve the question of *sens* within the context of nonviolence and uncertainty. The classic questions of political philosophy are not answered by Weil's philosophy. There is no guarantee that discussion will result in the Good, only that as long as discussion continues, violence will be suspended in favor of a common search for meaning and direction (*Politique*, 257–260). Through its integration of the structures of community life and tradition with a technically proficient society, the state can provide ACCESS to *sens* for its citizens. Weil views the state as beginning not with a clean slate of individuals without a past but rather with the idea that the matter of politics in the state is the evolving beliefs and practices that people bring to political life. Weil's political philosophy is concerned with how politics has preserved and modified these traditions and how the state has made a clearing in which discussion and not violence can guide our lives, opening a space in which the question of *sens* can be posed.

Weil's political philosophy, though it accepts some of the presuppositions of French Hegelianism—especially in its Kojèvian form— differs from that mainstream in important respects. History is for Weil, as it is for Kojève, the becoming of truth, and the fully developed (i.e., universal) state will be the highest historical expression of this truth. Kojève, however, says that this state is good because it is the last;[15] he rejects even the thought that the final stage of history can be distinct from "the good." Weil does not differ from Kojève on basic, philosophical grounds; that is, he accepts the Hegelian model of progress. He recognizes, however, that in fact progress has not satisfied, indeed, that it has created the conditions for a new and fundamental despair which can lead to radical, senseless violence. To call that violence posthistorical, and hence meaningless, is perverse, because the twentieth-century forms of that violence have shaped our lives as much as any creative negations could have done. Weil does not simply present another End to the Big Story of Hegelianism but tries instead to see within this emplotment of history how people might recover the meaning and direction lost in the course of the march of World Spirit. He does not, though, think of this recovery in suprahistorical terms. Redemption has nothing to do with the interventions of a god, nor is there a guarantee for *sens* in the essential sameness of Being. On the contrary, Weil tries to find in progress as realized in the modern state an opportunity for people to continue their search for their meaning and direction in history.

There is a reflexive, perhaps even allegorical, significance to Weil's political philosophy which should not be overlooked. He writes of the threat to, even the destruction of, the possibility of *sens* in a modern society that values only efficiency and success. He wrote, moreover, in an intellectual context that had little concern for finding "meaning and direction." In 1956—the year in which *Philosophie*

---

15. Kojève to Leo Strauss, 19 September 1950.

politique was published—both Hyppolite and Kojève had already started to retreat from questions of historical significance in favor of a conservation/repetition of the Same and of an analysis of how philosophic discourse is put together, respectively. More generally, the mid-1950s saw the development within the human sciences of a conceptually well-tooled interest in the synchronic in contradistinction to the diachronic. "Meaning and direction" or, more accurately, making meaning out of historical directionality was quickly pushed to the margins by the combined weight of advancing structuralism, rehabilitated Heideggerian philosophy, and—perhaps most important—the failure of contemporary historical events to follow the happy direction that Hegelian Marxism had mapped out for them.[16]

Weil's vision of the task of politics and philosophy as the preservation of the question of *sens* acquires for us a special force in this context. He was no less concerned than his intellectual contemporaries that the possibility of historical unification would become the organized death of human action; indeed, he devoted considerable energy to showing that the "totalization of peace" could be a nightmare of technological totalitarianism.[17] Yet he refused to renounce this technē and the idea of scientific progress that legitimated it. He refused, in other words, to adopt the position of sociopolitical marginality that a veneer of intellectual radicalism often conceals and instead struggled to find and preserve the opening in historical reality through which meaning and direction could still be pursued. For Weil the pursuit of *sens* presupposed the continuation of discussion and of some forms of tradition and community, which also set him apart from many of his intellectual contemporaries whose valorizations of the other, of difference, of marginality, and of discourse (not communication) betrayed at best an indifference to community.[18] This

16. As noted above, the great—but by no means the only—exception to this trend is Sartre, who from *L'être et le néant* to *La critique de la raison dialectique* became more concerned with change over time and historical thinking. An analysis of his intellectual development, readily available elsewhere, lies beyond the scope chosen for this work.

17. Weil, "Christianisme et politique," *Critique* 9, no. 75–76 (1953), 748–776; *E.C.*, 2:45–79.

18. On this indifference see Richard Rorty, "Le cosmopolitisme sans émancipation: En reponse à Jean-François Lyotard," *Critique* 41, no. 456 (1985), 467–480, and "Method, Social Science and Social Hope," in *Consequences of Pragmatism: Essays, 1972–1980* (Minneapolis, Minn., 1982).

pursuit could fail—perhaps even as a result of intellectual marginality—and philosophy itself could disappear. Even in such a case, however, Weil had faith that the "science of *sens*" would not die. As long as meaning and direction were absent, violence present, the possibility existed of philosophy and of a history that could be made meaningful (*Politique*, 121). Contemporary events and intellectual fashions both seemed to testify that the human was not—or was no longer—the subject of history, yet Weil's political philosophy maintained that people could find a way to make this history their own by giving it meaning and direction.

Between Hope and Nostalgia

If Weil's political philosophy is an inquiry into the possibilities of *sens* given the results of historical action, his moral philosophy is the attempt to give a content to this *sens*, to provide a steady perspective from which to judge the flux of historical change. We have noted Weil's early concern with the diversity of histories which resulted from our search for meaning and direction in our pasts. The *Philosophie morale* articulated a way of discriminating among these histories as it redeveloped the Kantian demand that the maxim of an action be in principle universalizable.

Weil considers moral action's ties to self-consciousness. Only after the members of a community become aware of the particularlity of their own beliefs and practices, only after they become aware that viable traditions exist other than their own, does the moral, properly so-called, exist. As Weil says, "In the beginning there is moral certainty: one knows what it is necessary to do and avoid, what is desirable or not, good or bad. The conflict of morals (visible only after such conflicts) leads to reflection on morality. More exactly, it is the loss of certainty, or its refusal, which leads to it."[19] Again we see certainty as a lost object at the birth of self-consciousness. In the *Morale*, however, Weil underlines another facet of the origin of reflection: the possibility of nihilism, the refusal of all meaningful action, the withdrawal of the individual in silence or cynicism. Moral

19. Weil, *Morale*, 13.

philosophy is therefore marked by the loss of certainty and by its continual choice against nihilism.

In the *Politique* the loss of certainty led to an openness to history, to the effort to reconcile reason and rationality within a historical community. History does not offer in the *Morale* the same basis for reflection. From the point of view of individuals who seek the pure moral law to guide their lives, history offers only a "domain of violence" or a reservoir of excuses for failing to act in accordance with the universal. The moral person looks at history as the domain of the senseless, which in itself has no real interest. Only when organized in relation to moral progress, individual or social, can the burnt ground of history be transformed for the moral person into fertile soil.[20] To be useful for him or her, this ground has to be carefully cultivated, the weeds removed that typically contaminate change over time. If not properly prepared, the soil of history will prove a quicksand for the moral person looking for firm ground on which to stand.

If as moral individuals we do not take our bearings directly from history, however, we do not want to be completely divorced from it. In the search for the moral we choose a meaning for our individual histories; we structure them as a progression toward the good.[21] In this way we separate the accidental from the essential, that which is merely particular from that which can be integrated into the universal. Our "interest," as moral individuals, in telling the story this way is that it gives us reason to hope.[22] It puts us into a story at the end of which we can find reasonable happiness. The lack of such a story—the loss of certainty which begins reflection on the moral—is not only a cognitive problem; reflection on the moral stems more importantly from a sentiment of unhappiness, and it continues in order to find meaningful, reasonable happiness.[23]

Happiness in reason should not be confused with satisfaction. Satisfaction, for Weil, entails our dependence on things that are not really our own, hence on things that can be taken away. The happiness of the moral person, on the other hand, is essentially a self-contentment, morally sensible insofar as it is in principle universalizable.

Here again a comparison with Kojève is helpful. For Kojève "sat-

20. Ibid., 55.
21. Ibid., 74. See also *Problèmes kantiens* (Paris, 1963), 115.
22. *Philosophie morale*, 75. See also *Problèmes kantiens*, 115, 139.
23. *Philosophie morale*, 101.

isfaction" is a key term, and when people are essentially satisfied—when recognition has become universal—there is nothing left to be done. Weil's rejection of the primacy of satisfaction is a facet of his revolt against Kojève's idea of the End of history. Kojève understands satisfaction as the death of desire, for the structure of the desire for recognition results in the progressive displacement of satisfaction, thus keeping desire alive. The final satisfaction of desire in the End-state, however, leaves only emptiness, the acceptance of what Strauss calls "definitive mediocrity." Satisfaction for Kojève means the end of action and therefore the end of humanity, properly so-called.

Weil recognizes the force in Kojève's conception of history and its end. His description of the human triumph over need fits well into this conception:

> The true content of life was material concern; more accurately, need hid the emptiness of existence. It is natural that the problem of need has been attacked first. The absence of a positive content in life is shown after the triumph over need, however, and the sacred that replaced this content is revealed as a consolation for a suffering one no longer accepts, and, in principle, no longer has to accept. Men who lived in a condition of need have become free; but since they do not know what to do with their freedom, the new form of life is senseless in their eyes. A certain universal is realized: its realization confronts us with emptiness.[24]

In his moral philosophy Weil tends to conceive of the problem revealed by the triumph over need as postpolitical. Freedom from need, he now seems to say, might mean the end of history, but neither history nor politics is coextensive with the human. "It is not by accident," he tells us, "that every political theory aims at the end of politics."[25] We are political—we try to act reasonably and make history—when we live in need in an immoral world. We try to change this world not for the sake of action itself, and not simply to be satisfied, but to live in meaningful peace. In his moral philosophy "meaningful peace" is beyond politics, beyond uncertainty and history.

Weil no longer privileged action as Kojève had done. Action in the *Morale* is symptomatic of a discontent that aims beyond the domain

---

24. "Le particulier et l'universel en politique," *P.R.*, 236.
25. "Philosophie politique, théorie politique," *E.C.*, 2:418.

of history and need, that has as its target a reasonable happiness and peace.[26] Weil thinks that moral philosophy can point to a content of this peace or at least can show us which roads to avoid in our search for a reasonable happiness, a happiness in reason.[27] The object of this quest is not satisfaction in an absence of desire and action but meaningful contentment in the presence of shareable *sens*.

Weil devotes a large amount of the *Morale* to defending his views against charges of idealism and of formalism. These charges, he says, mistake moral philosophy for political philosophy and so are almost always off the mark. That is, they mistake the vision of the moral person for a program of political action and then show either how "peace with oneself" is politically irresponsible or how it is a new version of the old condescension toward material things in favor of "higher values." Weil responds that moral philosophy is at the origin and end of political philosophy but that it is not in any sense a replacement for political philosophy. He does not pretend to give a "higher" value to those who are still struggling for the "lower" ones; he is well aware that the self-repose of the moral person usually requires the achievement of basic satisfactions. These fundamentals—which are called the satisfactions of society in the *Politique*—do not, however, provide us with a path to *sens*:

> Survival has no *sens* in itself, and in order for it to become meaningful there must be a non-arbitrary concept of the good life. What one condemns as "aristocratism" is, on the contrary, the need for equal chances for all and for each. Indeed, all philosophic thought on politics is born of this need, which becomes a problem for it to resolve. This solution, however, is not the responsibility of the moral; it would forget its nature and goal if it wanted to take up this task, and it would inevitably fall into moral historicism. The concern of the moral is the possibility for each individual to find dignity and *sens* in his finite existence.[28]

We must avoid confusing moral and political philosophy, but Weil chooses the former as the goal and base of the latter. This choice was

26. Weil, "La fin de l'histoire," *Revue de métaphysique et de morale* 75, no. 4 (1970); *P.R.*, 174.

27. Weil, "Souci pour la philosophie, souci de la philosophie," *Die Zukunft der Philosophie* (Olten and Freiburg, 1968), in *P.R.*, 21.

28. *Morale*, 200. See also Weil, "Histoire et politique," in *Problèmes kantiens*, 109–142.

part of Weil's option for the *conscience kantienne* against the *pré-tention hégélienne*.[29] Weil's "interest" in Kant—which became progressively stronger after the *Politique*—and in moral philosophy generally expressed his effort to find "a reason to hope." A major facet of the pretension of Hegelianism for Weil was the idea that such a reason could be found in, or was identical with, history. This idea came to seem pretentious as the confidence that persons brought to history diminished, as the struggle to make meaning and direction out of change over time came to appear a Sisyphean task. Weil's pronounced Kantian turn was an attempt to uncover the point of this labor or at least to find in the storm of history a shelter that was more than a retreat to isolated particularity.

Weil's Kantian turn in the *Morale* relates to his early article on the human interest in history. In that essay he had posed the question of how one could justify the story one constructed out of a reading of the past.[30] Even if the story claimed universality, how, he asked, did one judge between competing universals? Weil's answer, repeated in various forms in the *Logique* and the *Politique*, was that as long as the story was open to discussion, it was open to reason. The possibility of agreement following discussion was the promise of a rediscovery of certainty in the story. One could learn to live with a meaning and direction to one's history through an openness to reason in the form of discourse.

In the *Morale*, Weil sought to provide both a foundation for this openness to reason and a form of protection against the possibility that even the best of discussions could lead to false conclusions. He wanted to show that the choice of and the effort at discussion were good in principle but also that the individual could justifiably reject its conclusions if they failed to meet positive moral standards.[31] The crucial subject in Weil's understanding of discussion was history, and like Kojève, Weil at one time accepted history as the court of judgment. Whereas Kojève finally adopted an ironic posture in the face

29. Weil, "Philosophie et réalité," *Bulletin de la Société française de philosophie* 57, no. 4 (1963); *P.R.*, 52.

30. See above, 151–154.

31. Note the difference from Kojève, for whom "justification" meant nothing more than success. Weil's turn to a moral philosophy was a turn away from a philosophy of history in which successfulness was a dominant criterion for evaluating action. He emphasized that failure was not a moral error: *Morale*, 126.

of what he saw as history's final verdict, however, Weil appeals to moral philosophy for a guarantee that happiness in reason can be attained despite history. If the *Politique* emphasized that discussion can preserve the question of *sens* in the domain of history and uncertainty, the *Morale* stressed that there is a happiness in reason beyond the domain of the historical.

Thus in the *Morale*, Weil no longer underlined the historical as that field in which the question of *sens* could be posed. He could not do so, because he wanted to emphasize that it is the moral which invested history with meaning and direction. In the *Morale* he searched for something to guarantee this investment, to diminish the threat of nihilism for the person who would be moral by legitimating an escape from the realm of uncertainty.

It is beyond uncertainty and history that the person who would be moral must look. The search is always conditioned by the history in which one lives, but the will to be beyond the merely historical for Weil defines the moral sphere. This "beyond," he tells us at the end of the book, is the *présence préhistorique*, that which allows us to make sense of history and our actions in it. As moral persons we aim to discover this presence in our happiness: a fullness of *sens* that directs our being in the world, an End to the question of and the longing for definitive meaning and direction.

More accurately, Weil's moral person seeks to *re*-discover this foundation in a happiness and self-repose that are universalizable. The presence his moral philosophy points to is another form of the certainty that philosophy always experiences as lost. In the *Politique* the absence of certainty is accepted in the recognition that history is the field in which *sens* can be made. In the *Morale*, however, we see what Weil calls a self-conscious "nostalgia for certainty,"[32] a longing for that wholeness or presence thought to lie just beyond the hysterical misery of history.

Weil's notion of a presence beyond the temporal may recall Hyppolite's "hopeful Heideggerian" position discussed in Chapter 1. Despite a parallel redirection vis-à-vis history, though, the two philosophers differ in fundamental ways. Hyppolite's embrace of Heidegger was part of his divorce from philosophical humanism and anthropocentrism. Weil's return to Kant and moral philosophy, on

32. *Morale*, 68.

the other hand, did not call for the displacement of the human from the center of things. The attempt to find a moral rudder with which to maintain a certain direction through the shifting tides of history never conflicted with the basic humanist voyage. If there was a moral order to be revealed by philosophy, its revelation was for us; more accurately, the search for an order, for *sens* was essentially linked to human action. For the individual living with the possibility of violence and the reality of a dominating society, the idea of a moral order gave reason to hope or, as Weil might have put it, hope in reason.

Weil's turn to moral philosophy was not, then, an attempt to retreat from anthropocentrism but instead an effort to preserve the human capacity to search for meaning and direction. Moral philosophy could do so by preserving a firm notion of the End of the human, despite the apparent senselessness of historical events.[33] But this does not mean that moral philosophy abandoned the historical. On the contrary, Weil insisted, following Kant, that faith in a *sens de l'histoire* was a necessity for the individual who would be moral: "All his doubts about the empirical value of humanity, as long as they are not transformed into scientific certitude . . . do not authorize the individual to deny the reality, morally necessary, of a progress, not only material and intellectual . . . but moral: without this conviction, the finite being, falling into despair, would cease to work for the realization of the reign of ends. Faith in a *sens* of history, in moral progress, is a duty."[34] This faith in a *sens* of history should be a comfort and inspiration in times when historical events do not lend themselves to a configuration of any meaning and direction, and, we can add, when intellectual activity simply ignores the question of historical significance.

Weil's understanding of discussion in his political philosophy points toward nonviolent and nondogmatic forms of participation as vehicles for posing the question of *sens* at the collective level. Historical change and uncertainty are the conditions in which the search for meaning and direction occurs. Living with uncertainty and with history demands much, at the least the presence of significant change that can be configured as progress. When Weil talks about faith in progress as a moral duty, he betrays his own lack of confidence in history and, I think, in participation. He plays down the working out

---

33. *Problèmes kantiens*, 85.
34. Ibid., 115.

of meaning and direction as a political task only always tentatively achieved and instead underlines it as an article of moral necessity. Weil calls the search for *sens* a duty because it ceases to inspire confidence as a project. It becomes an obligation in a historical context that holds inadequate promise of a reasonable happiness.

In contrast to Kojève, and in opposition to what is frequently called postmodern thought in France, Weil rejected the shift away from questions of significance in favor of questions of use or function. His opposition to this shift was not confined to a conception of political action but embraced a vision of how we make meaning out of change over time. The contrast of this vision with that of postmodernism could not be more extreme, as Gilles Deleuze and Felix Guattari make clear in this passage from *The Anti-Oedipus*: "The unconscious poses no problem of meaning, solely problems of use. The question posed by desire is not 'What does it mean?' but rather *'How does it work?'* . . . Desire makes its entry with the general collapse of the question 'What does it mean?' No one has been able to pose the problem of language except to the extent that linguists and logicians have first eliminated meaning; and the greatest force of language was only discovered once a *work* was viewed as a machine, producing certain effects, amenable to a certain use."[35] The theoretical and critical climate in France during the 1960s and 1970s thrived on suspending the questions of meaning and interpretation. This suspension, and a new reading of Nietzsche that goes along with it, creates new ways of understanding historical change. Weil's entire philosophic project was to combat what Deleuze and Guattari praised as the elimination of meaning. Weil, however, sought to locate significance even in this repudiation of significance, in a final effort to preserve the question of *sens*.

Apology for Meaningful History

The "Valeur et dignité du récit historiographique" was published in 1977, the year of Weil's death. Like the early article on history,

---

35. Gilles Deleuze and Felix Guattari, *The Anti-Oedipus*, trans. Robert Hurley, Mark Seem, and Helen R. Lane (New York, 1977), 109. The passage is quoted from Fredric Jameson, *The Political Unconscious* (Ithaca, N.Y., 1981), 22. Jameson makes a handy list—one that could easily be extended—of the major anti-interpretation texts in contemporary French criticism and philosophy, 21n.

this late work takes up the problem of conflicting historical narratives. The problematic of the later essay is quite different, however, insofar as it is concerned not so much with the proliferation of narratives as with their replacement by an apparently scientific or law-bound historiography.[36]

Weil does not have arguments to show that scientific historiography is doing something wrong. Instead, against the study by the social sciences of people as objects in a field of interrelations, he raises the question of the person as subject *and* object of history. He still thinks of the interest in history as fundamentally linked to the desire to piece together identity, although in the later essay he refers to a social or shared identity rather than to a personal one.[37] He emphasizes a person as the subject of history and historiography not as an alternative to the objective study of the past but as the reason for turning to the human sciences in the first place. In defending historical narrative, Weil is once again trying to show the primacy of the question of *sens* in relation to the discovery of laws that govern a field of facts. In response to the mounting popularity of the analysis of structures, Weil presses the claims of memory, the claims of history as that aspect of our lives in which we make meaning out of shared experience.[38] For him, it is a grave mistake to attempt to comprehend the past by repressing the question of its significance for us. By decentering the human and unsettling the subject, we may be only reiterating the status quo minus the possibilities, the projects, it contains.

His apology for historical narrative is tied to a conception of the person as subject, and thus again we find Weil embracing a much-despised idea. He does not, however, have in mind here the notion of a unified subject as an anchor beneath the multiplicity of events. Weil is linking narrative to the open question of the subject, recognizing that the conflict of narratives is a facet of the differences among—even within—persons. A unified subject and an agreed upon

36. On the connection between contemporary French historiography and narrative theory, see Paul Ricoeur, *Temps et récit*, vol. 1 (Paris, 1983), 138–158, 247–320. Ricoeur's own thinking shows important affinities with Weil's. See Ricoeur's review of *Philosophie politique* in *Esprit* 25, no. 254 (1957), 412–429.

37. That is, in the early essay Weil saw the fundamental question that brought one to history as "Who am I?" while in the late essay he spoke of the question "Who are we?"

38. Weil, "Valeur et dignité du récit historiographique," *Archives de la philosophie* 40, no. 4 (1977); *P.R.*, 187.

narrative have become not an actual project but a regulative ideal for Weil; they point to an unfinished task rather than to an origin. The will to unify narratives is the will to share meaning, which for Weil is prior to any development of scientific historiography.[39] The latter loses sight of its goal, and of the desire out of which it emerges, by concentrating solely on techniques or methodologies that can consider people as objects. The "value and dignity" of historical narrative is its implicit recognition that history has to be made sensible *for us.* It is through the conflict of histories that we piece together meaning and direction, or—given the moral weight that Weil attaches to this construction—that we should piece together a *sens* we can share if we choose not to live in a world dominated by arbitrary violence.

Thus in this late article Weil returned to the interest we have in history. In the later essay, however, he was forced to defend this interest as part of our effort to give meaning and direction to our lives, whereas earlier he had concentrated on how to maintain in discussion the multiplicity of these efforts. He made discussion into a central principle of his political philosophy because it provided for the possibility that people would find a shareable *sens* in and through history. If the end of history was in sight, as Weil had maintained in his early work, if indeed it had been revealed by Hegel, then one could show that the search for *sens* was going in the right direction.[40]

By making the faith in a *sens* of history a duty, Weil's late moral philosophy attempts to provide a transcendental ground for the search for meaning and direction. This ground destroys—or at least renders nugatory—our doubts as moral individuals about "the empirical value of humanity," giving us the capacity to look beyond our immediate history and toward the ultimate "realization of the reign of ends." In other words, from the moral ground we can look beyond politics and history. Weil did not seem to consider that to do so also might point us "beyond discussion," thereby devaluing our participation in this immoral world. Indeed, by helping us avoid nihilistic despair through a faith in meaning and direction for human existence, Weil might also be legitimating an avoidance of politics and history. Ironically, the effort to guarantee that the quest for *sens* will not be in vain may

---

39. *P.R.*, 191.
40. *Hegel et l'état* (Paris, 1950), 101–102; *Logique de la philosophie* (Paris, 1950), 54–55.

undermine the collective form of this quest, politics, which always takes place within conditions of uncertainty and of history.

The various criticisms of Hegelianism repeated by structuralism, poststructuralism, and the *nouveaux philosophes* can be directed at Weil without too much difficulty. To develop these criticisms systematically and in detail requires a full intellectual history of contemporary French culture. Instead, I have devoted the next chapter to the major alternative to Hegelianism which develops by the early 1960s, that for which Nietzsche is the locus of philosophic authority.

Still, if Weil's work helps close a period of Hegelian philosophy in France, it is at best premature to conclude that it evinces—along with the work of Hyppolite and Kojève—the failure of the Hegelian understanding of the connection between knowing and history. Such a conclusion requires one to have grasped the Protean forms of the major reactions against French Hegelianism, forms whose history still remains open. In at least Deleuze's interpretation of Nietzsche, and in the work of Michel Foucault, reactions against Hegelianism can run aground on basic questions about the legitimation of positive historical change and of criteria for political judgment.

The contemporary celebration of marginality and heterogeneity can be, as Fredric Jameson has argued,[41] an initial moment in the effort to think through the interrelatedness of dispersed practices. Such an effort can appropriate the struggle of Hegelians in France to work through the connection between knowing and history in an effort to think about how positive political change can legitimately be connected to a sense of history. On the other hand, the apparently successful criticisms of the Hegelian conception of history (usually discussed as "historicism") can become simply an excuse for forgetting how to think at all about change over time. Incapacity to think about historical change serves only those who already have the power to control historical change. Such a forgetting satisfies only one's sense of Kojèvian irony, in being truly the end of history, properly so-called.

41. Jameson, "On Interpretation," in *The Political Unconscious*, 17–102.

Afterword

Chapter Nine

Styles of Delegitimation: Nietzsche, Deleuze, and Foucault

> In the eternal return, precisely as the desire of potential, *no memory*. The *voyage* is a passage without trace, a forgetting.
> What can a politics without memory be, ahistorical, and from this fact, non-representative.
>
> —*Jean-François Lyotard, 1972*

French philosophy from the 1930s through the postwar period was marked by confrontation with Hegel. Hegelian philosophers such as Jean Hyppolite, Alexandre Kojève, and Eric Weil turned to history as the source of truths and criteria of judgment. In contrast to their neo-Kantian predecessors, these thinkers and many of their students and colleagues were concerned less with the "conditions of possibility" (transcendental or epistemological) of science and ethics than with coming to terms with, and having an influence on, the rapidly changing world around them. Hegel provided them with a vehicle for making meaning out of, or finding knowledge in, this world. The connection they made between history and knowing they forged as a means of engaging their contemporary intellectual and political concerns. At least through the mid–1940s their Hegel was not the systematizer of the *Logic* but the narrator of the *Phenomenology*. He was a thinker who had marked out a path from the personal to the political and who could now be read as providing a link between existentialism and Marxism. In showing how historical action could be reasonable, Hegel also showed how certain political programs could be legitimated by philosophers. Not only did he unveil the drama of the "unhappy consciousness," he also defined the progressive within historical change.[1]

By the 1950s, however, history was not only that in which philosophy found knowing, it was a burden from which many thinkers sought an escape. By the middle of the decade they had withdrawn from the historical in search of a more secure, or hopeful, subject for philosophical reflection. Hyppolite made his own turn from a heroic Hegelianism to a hopeful Heideggerianism. Kojève left behind his militant Hegel by the end of the 1940s, adopting an ironic attachment to the idea of the End of history as a critical perspective on his own present and the possibilities for change contained therein. Weil's work from the 1950s until his death in 1977 is a re-turn to Kant and a concern with the possibilities of a knowing not plagued by the ruses of reason and the uncertainties of history. Weil turned to Kant to find some ground for morals (and hence for politics) which would not quake under the weight of events.

In this shift away from Hegelianism we witness one of the crucial transformations in modern intellectual history: the change from a concern with questions of significance to a concern with questions of use or function. Hegelian historical narrative focused on the meaning of History. In the retreat from Hegelian history is a shift from "What does our history mean?" or "How can we make sense of our past?" to "How does this history work?" or "How is this past put together?" This shift was, as one might expect, overdetermined. Certainly the freezing of historical possibilities in the 1950s had much to do with it. In addition, the apparent explanatory successes of analytic non- or antihistorical social sciences—especially structuralist anthropology—provided great support for a synchronic or systemic approach to social phenomena. In this chapter, however, I concentrate on the major philosophical alternative to Hegelian historicism available in France by the end of the 1950s: Nietzsche. I examine briefly how Nietzsche, and it is often a Nietzsche mediated by Heidegger, replaces Hegel as the locus of philosophical authority in France and evaluate the significance of this shift for our understanding of how

1. Jean Hyppolite often focused on the figure of the unhappy consciousness in Hegel. See, for example, *Genèse et structure dans la Phénoménologie de Hegel* (Paris, 1946), 184–208. See also Jean Wahl, *Le malheur de la conscience dans la philosophie de Hegel* (Paris, 1929), passim. On Hegel's legitimation of political action see Kojève, "Hegel, Marx et le christianisme," *Critique* 3–4 (1946), 339–366.

we make meaning and direction out of change over time. The attempt to avoid some of the problematics of Hegelianism by turning to Nietzsche did remove the questions of progress and historical significance from the central place they had for Hyppolite, Kojève, and Weil, but it also resulted in a serious inability to connect philosophical reflection with political judgment.

To say that Nietzsche replaces Hegel is greatly to oversimplify. Nietzsche had already attracted considerable attention in France before the 1950s, and thinkers like the surrealists and Bataille (to take just two examples) had long thought about Hegel and Nietzsche together.[2] That said, there seems to have been a shift in attention during this decade, and by the 1960s, Hegelian historicism (often linked, of course, with Marxism) was the object of a new sort of critique, one waged under the banner of Nietzsche.[3] The great exception to this trend was Sartre, who in the 1960s was still working on political problems within a paradigm of historicism. Indeed, for Foucault the *Critique of Dialectical Reason* was "the last work of the 19th century," a "magnificent and pathetic effort of a 19th century man to think the 20th century."[4] It is clear that for Foucault the Hegelian (and Marxist) approach to contemporary problems was worse than false, it was *passé*.

2. On Nietzsche in France see Pierre Boudot, *Nietzsche et l'au-delà de la liberté: Nietzsche et les écrivains français de 1930 à 1960* (Paris, 1960). On the ways in which Nietzsche provides tools against Hegelian historicism, see Luc Ferry and Alain Renault, *La pensée 68: Essai sur l'anti-humanisme contemporaine* (Paris, 1985), 30–37; Allan Megill, *Prophets of Extremity: Nietzsche, Heidegger, Foucault, Derrida* (Berkeley, Calif., 1985), 267–280, 294–298; and Pierre Klossowski, *Nietzsche et le cercle vicieux* (Paris, 1969), 32. On Kojève's appeal to the early French Nietzscheans see Vincent Descombes, *Le même et l'autre* (Paris, 1979), 26–28, and a very interesting article by Jean-Michel Besnier, "Bataille: Le système (de l')impossible," *Esprit* 38 (February 1980), 148–164.

3. In this book I will not discuss Jacques Derrida's complex use of Nietzsche, which, I think, would have to be understood in connection with his treatment of Hegel in a great number of texts. In this regard see the various versions of *The Question of Style* (Venice, 1976) and *Glas* (Paris, 1981). John H. Smith has provided insight into Derrida's reception of Hegel in his "U-topian Hegel: Dialectic and Its Other in Poststructuralism," *German Quarterly*, Spring 1987. If this subject (still changing with Derrida's shifts) deserves more extensive treatment—and I confess to uncertainty in this regard—it requires more space than I can provide in this Afterword.

4. Remo Bodel, "Foucault: Pouvoir, politique et maîtrise de soi," *Critique*, January 1976, in Foucault, *Power/Knowledge: Selected Interviews and Other Writings, 1972–1977*, ed. Colin Gordon (New York, 1980), 78–92, and Foucault, "L'homme est-il mort?" *Arts et loisirs* 38 (1966), 15–21.

I focus here on Gilles Deleuze's interpretation of Nietzsche (who has had an important impact on Deleuze's oeuvre as a whole) and on the work of Michel Foucault.[5] The criticisms of Deleuze contained in this chapter apply to the rest of Deleuze's work only insofar as his view of Nietzsche affects those writings. Deleuze's reading of Nietzsche as a supremely antidialectical thinker attempts to make the nineteenth-century philosopher's idea of the Eternal Return accomplish many of the tasks that Hegel had thought to be the goals of human (historical) action. I then assess Foucault's general contribution in light of his Nietzscheanism. His genealogy finds both ruptures and possibilities in the past, and his refusal of mediation led to an uneasy connection between these findings and action in the present.

Both Deleuze and Foucault adopt Nietzsche's legacy of the intellectual as a delegitimator; however, they have enormous difficulty in legitimating this adoption and more important, in validating the political style that animates their writings. This is a crucial difficulty insofar as a political style, even if it extols marginality, must be a public, shareable way of thinking and being. In the absence of a legitimation of the critical tradition of which they are a part, it is hard to see how personal commitments, important though they may have been and, in the case of Deleuze, may still be, can be connected to a political community.[6] Of course, if—for bureaucratic or for postmodern reasons—one wants to deny the value and possibility of connecting politics to any kind of community, the presentation in this chapter will seem beside the point. Neither Deleuze nor Foucault, however, would share in this denial.

Deleuze's *Nietzsche et la philosophie* (1962) is the most thoughtful and interesting reading of Nietzsche as an anti-Hegelian. For Deleuze,

5. Although the literature on Deleuze is growing at a less rapid pace than material on other French thinkers, it is already substantial. See, for example, Theodore Mills Norton, "Line of Flight: Gilles Deleuze, or Political Science Fiction," *New Political Science* 15 (Summer 1986), 77–93; and the special issues of *SubStance* 13, nos. 3/4 (1984), of *Semiotext(e)* 2, no. 3 (1977), and of *L'arc* 49, new ed. (1980). As an introduction, see also his discussions with Claire Parnet in *Dialogues* (Paris, 1977), and the very helpful remarks in chap. 5 of Descombes, *Le même et l'autre*.

6. In this regard see Richard Rorty, "Le cosmopolitisme sans émancipation: En réponse à Jean-François Lyotard," *Critique* 41, no. 456 (1985), 467–480. See also his "Method, Social Science and Social Hope," in *Consequences of Pragmatism: Essays, 1972–1980* (Minneapolis, Minn., 1982).

the opposition between Hegel and Nietzsche is total and radical: "There is no possible compromise between Hegel and Nietzsche. Nietzsche's philosophy has a great polemical range; it forms an absolute anti-dialectics and sets out to denounce all mystifications that find a last refuge in the dialectic."[7] Deleuze's reading guides us to a Nietzsche who is quintessentially anti-Hegelian. Deleuze constructs the opposition (not as contradiction but as difference) between the two thinkers and underlines the *difference this opposition makes* for understanding the connection between our actions in the present and our sense of the past.

Deleuze sets up what he himself thought of as a paradigm shift between Hegel and Nietzsche. Michel Foucault illuminates both the powers and the limitations involved in rejecting the dialectical emplotment of history in favor of the construction of a genealogical history of the present. Foucault's work is a sustained attempt to find a modern style in which a Nietzschean approach to the past can be coherently and persuasively maintained. And this Nietzschean approach is in large part charged by anti-Hegelianism: "In order to liberate difference, we need a thought without contradiction, without dialectic, without negation: a thought which says yes to divergence; an affirmative thought the instrument of which is disjunction; a thought of the multiple—of dispersed and nomadic multiplicity that is not limited or confined by constraints of similarity; . . . We must think problematically rather than question and answer dialectically."[8] Foucault's Nietzscheanism altered as it was confronted with

7. Gilles Deleuze, *Nietzsche et la philosophie* (Paris, 1962), 223. I have used here the translation by Hugh Tomlinson, *Nietzsche and Philosophy* (New York, 1983), 195, hereafter *NP*. Mina Koenigson praised Deleuze's emphasis on Nietzsche as an anti-dialectical thinker in the review in *Les études philosophiques* 21, no. 1 (1966), 61–77; Jean Granier's review in *Revue philosophique de la France et de l'étranger* 159, no. 1 (1969), 91–100, criticized this same emphasis. Jean Wahl rather timidly suggested that Deleuze "donne libre cour à une certaine mauvaise humeur . . . contre hégélianisme," *Revue de métaphysique et de morale* 68, no. 3 (1963), 352–379. See also his remarks following Henri Birault's Deleuzian reading of Nietzsche in *Nietzsche* (Paris, 1967), 39. Daniel Breazeale provides a more straightforward critique of Deleuze and argues that Hegel and Nietzsche are allies in the struggle against metaphysics in "The Hegel-Nietzsche Problem," in *Nietzsche Studien* 4 (1975), 146–164. Stephen Houlgate extends and deepens this argument in his *Hegel, Nietzsche and the Criticism of Metaphysics* (Cambridge, 1986).

8. Foucault, "Theatrum philosophicum," *Critique* 282 (1970), 899. Modified translation in *Language, Counter-Memory, Practice*, ed. Donald F. Bouchard (Ithaca, N.Y., 1977), 185, 186.

different methodological possibilities and changing political choices. What Deleuze said of Nietzsche, however, he might also have said of Foucault: *"L'anti-hégélianisme traverse l'oeuvre comme le fil de l'agressivité."*[9]

Deleuze's Nietzsche and the Return of Progress

As early as 1954 Deleuze made clear the importance of the abandonment of Hegelianism. In a review of Hyppolite's *Logique et existence*, he applauded the author for breaking with a merely anthropological philosophy (as in Hegel's *Phenomenology*) and choosing instead an *ontologie du sens*.[10] Hyppolite should leave behind not only essences and foundations but also the human as the measure of all things—leave behind, that is, the Hegelian approach to history and knowing. In *Logique et existence* Deleuze rightly recognized Hyppolite's most important break with the Hegelian tradition that had nourished a generation's philosophizing, but for the younger philosopher the *coupure* was not clean enough.

Deleuze pointed out that Hyppolite's choice for ontology still left open the possibility of a return to anthropologism. The problem may stem from Hyppolite's fidelity to a Hegelian conception of contradiction. Why not go all the way to embrace an ontology of pure difference?[11] "Can one make an ontology of difference which would not have to go as far as contradiction, because contradiction would be less than difference and not more? Is contradiction not only the phenomenal and anthropological aspect of difference?"[12] Nietzsche was the thinker who provided Deleuze with a vehicle both for abandoning anthropologism—a code word for the Hegelian idea of creative change through negation—and for thinking instead the primacy of difference and the free play of affirmative possibilities.

Deleuze finds in Nietzsche the insurance against the return to anthropologism which he fears might be possible for Hyppolite. An-

9. Deleuze, *Nietzsche et la philosophie*, 9.

10. Deleuze, "Analyse de *Logique et existence*," *Revue philosophique de la France et de l'étranger* 94 (1954), 457–458.

11. Ibid., 460. This would become the theme of Deleuze's *Difference et répétition* (Paris, 1968).

12. Deleuze, "Analyse de *Logique*," 460.

thropologism is identified with a Hegelian vision of History. In this vision the past is seen in its multiplicity and diversity, but these factors are subordinated to a guiding principle, or Reason. Thus History, in the Hegelian mode, tends to become One (or, in the case of Kojève's reading, "tended to become One") as its *sens*, meaning and direction, becomes (or became) clearer. The history of the world is the progress in the consciousness of freedom, Hegel says. The *histories* of the world become a History through the totalizing, retrospective vision of the philosopher.

Over the past twenty-five years we have tended to lose sight of the reasons for the insistence of Hegelian philosophy on the potential or final unity of history. Instead, criticisms of the totalizing thrust— suggesting "totalitarian"—of Hegelian philosophy of history have passed for both political and philosophical counterarguments. We have seen how for the French Hegelians, history becomes that by which one can legitimate judgments about politics, morality, and aesthetics. The final unity and reasonableness of history was thought to be necessary for using it as a source of criteria for legitimate judgment. History provided protection from nihilism and relativism for thinkers who had abandoned nature as a transhistorical standard and God or religion as a suprahistorical guarantee, and who did not want to identify political, moral, and aesthetic choices with capriciousness. Although by the 1950s Hyppolite and Weil no longer saw in history the values they had hoped it would legitimate, they still sought the protection they at one time had thought such legitimation would provide.

It is this protection which Deleuze wants to give up, but he does not, of course, return to either the standard or the guarantee. Instead, he invokes Nietzsche's essential pluralism: "The history of a thing, in general, is the succession of forces which take possession of it and the co-existence of forces which struggle for possession. The same object, the same phenomenon changes meaning according to the force which appropriates it. History is the variation of meaning.... Nietzsche's philosophy is not understood unless one takes account of its essential pluralism."[13] Pluralism is made to stand against unity,

13. Deleuze, *Nietzsche et la philosophie*, 4; modified translation, *NP*, 3–4. For a discussion of Nietzsche's pluralism and fragmentary thinking connected with Deleuze's interpretation, see Maurice Blanchot, "Réflexions sur le nihilisme," in his *L'entretien infini* (Paris, 1969), 201–255.

the genealogy that separates and compares discrete elements is opposed to the dialectic that ties these elements together in a coherent whole.

Deleuze does not merely want to distinguish these two ways of looking at the past. He wants, of course, to show the superiority of the Nietzschean perspective. His mode of argument is instructive. A Hegelian would typically show the *primitiveness* of a less-than-Hegelian position. As Deleuze rightly notes, the Hegelian criticism of pluralism takes this form: pluralism is one of the stages that one must pass through (and leave behind) in order to get at the truth.[14] The Nietzschean or genealogical method is to ask who is served by an idea: "What does he want, *this person* who says this, who thinks or proves that?"[15] And so Deleuze asks, what is the will that is willing the dialectic? "A spent force which has not the strength to affirm its difference, a force which no longer acts but reacts to forces which dominate it: only such a force brings to the foreground the negative element in its relation with the other. Such a force negates all that it is not, and makes of this negation its own essence and the principle of its existence."[16] The dialectical point of view is the point of view of the slave (in both the Nietzschean and the Hegelian sense), and the will to negate is the expression of the slaves' fundamental resentment against those who express their strength, their difference.[17]

Thus Deleuze makes dialectical thinking an expression of weakness and, more important, weakness disguised within a specific form of power. Within this form of power the Hegelian talks about the necessity of conflict and the creativity of bloody battles. Dialectical thinking leads, according to Deleuze, to a thirst for vengeance disguised as justice and finally not to freedom but to a philosophical nihilism as an achievement of the search for truth.[18] Nietzschean pluralistic empiricism, on the other hand, rejects this whole paradigm of progress through negation leading to the End of History. "That

14. Deleuze, *Nietzsche et la philosophie*, 4–5.

15. Ibid., 88. This focus on the "who" is left in quite general terms, so that a specific person ("subject") is never at the origin of an idea. That is, genealogy will concentrate not on the biography of an individual thinker but on the social or discursive position that might be tied to an idea. My thanks to William Pietz for helping me to think about this point.

16. Ibid., 10–11. Translation, slightly modified, *NP*, 9.

17. On the dialectic as the ideology of resentment, ibid., 139.

18. Ibid., 186.

dialectic is a job, and empiricism a *jouissance,*" Deleuze says, "is to characterize them sufficiently."[19]

It is curious to note the repetitiousness and vehemence of the dismissal of "contradiction" and "negation" in a book claiming that the negation of a position does not successfully lead to a new position. The reason for it becomes clear when we recall why these concepts are important in Hegelian philosophy in the first place. The Nietzschean alternatives are seen to dissolve the problems to which they are addressed.

Negation is the motor of Hegelian History. The process of contradiction and conflict configured the story of change as progress by giving meaning and direction to suffering. There is a reason why slavery existed and had to be abolished through a painful and costly process: in this way we learn a lesson about human freedom. The Reign of Terror becomes comprehensible for the Hegelian as a necessary moment through which we can grasp the limits of absolute freedom. History is not merely a slaughterbench, it is the birth of the Truth through the labor of the negative.

Deleuze's attack on negativity goes to the heart of the Hegelian notion of history. Without the idea of the "work of the negative," history for the Hegelian is a merely random series of occurrences. The suffering of the past makes no sense, and the present holds no reasonable hope. Human action, properly so-called, ceases to exist, because nothing significant exists to differentiate action from motion. Without the work of negativity the wounds of history will never heal, and without this healing there will be nothing but sickly or cynical nihilism.

We have already seen, however, that Deleuze's Nietzsche lays nihilism at the door of the Hegelian view of history. But Deleuze also rejects the affirmation of history *tout court,* that is, the mere acceptance of the Real as given: "Affirmation conceived as acceptance, as affirmation of that which is, as veracity of the true or positivity of the real, is a false affirmation. It is the yes of the ass."[20] Dialectical thinking underlines change, and Deleuze does not want the rejection of this way of thinking to be taken for a form of resignation in the face of the impossibility of change. On the contrary, he underlines

19. Ibid., 10.
20. Ibid., 211. Modified translation, *NP,* 184.

that the *jouissance de l'affirmation* is seeing the world as living, as the will to power. And to will is to differentiate, to set apart, or, as Deleuze stresses near the end of the book, "to live is to evaluate. There is no truth of the world as thought, no reality of the sensible world. All is evaluation, even and above all the sensible and the real. ... To affirm is still to evaluate, but to evaluate from the perspective of a will which takes joy [*jouit*] in its own difference in life, instead of suffering the pains of opposition which itself it inspires in this life. *To affirm is not to take responsibility for, to accept that which is, but to release, to set free what lives.*"[21] The affirmation of the will to power is, then, an evaluation that "knows how to say no" and creates values rather than merely accepting them.[22] In a continual cycle of affirmation, Deleuze sees a multiplication of pleasures, a superfluity of differences celebrating their distinctiveness without negation. The will to power is creative rather than reactive; instead of fostering a mere acceptance of the given, it forces the world to change by helping release that which is living—differentiating—within it.[23] The desire for recognition is satisfied through negation; the will to power is stimulated/satisfied by an affirmation of difference.

How does this notion of a differential affirmation affect our understanding of the past? If the Hegelian notion of the work of negativity provided us with a meaningful narrative of History's progress, what kind of story are we likely to get from Deleuze's Nietzsche? First, for Deleuze the whole effort to come up with a unified, narrative history is a symptom of dialectical, reactive thinking. It is a product of the slave mentality that always seeks to justify itself. No grand history can arise from a Nietzschean vision, because such an outlook would always be splitting off into other perspectives, other stories. The affirmation of difference leads not to an integrative narrative that represents a "meaningful" Real but to a discontinuous series of interpretations, of useful and partial acts of will.

Nietzsche's approach to the past is not confined to a critique of integrative, narrative history. Deleuze's Nietzsche rejects the encapsulation of difference in totality and, through the idea of the will to

21. Ibid., 212. The emphasis is in the text.
22. Ibid., 212–213.
23. See especially ibid., 216–217.

power, affirms plurality and diversity instead. But Nietzsche is not only the thinker of the "will to power"; he is also the thinker of the "eternal return." And, as Heidegger had already pointed out by the time Deleuze wrote his *Nietzsche et la philosophie*, all interpretations of the philosopher had to come to terms with the combination of these two ideas.[24]

As one might expect, Deleuze puts less weight on the eternal return than he does on the will to power's creation and affirmation of difference. After all, the eternal return might be (correctly) understood as the *return of the same*, and, though surely appropriate for a philosophy of radical affirmation and *amor fati*, such a notion poses many problems for the thinker who delights in ever greater differentiation. Nietzsche says the will's great gnashing of teeth is that it cannot will backward, and, for Zarathustra, acceptance of the necessity of eternal return is the most difficult of affirmations. To dance to the music of the eternal return is the will's greatest accomplishment, because to do so is to will one's destiny, again and again. In perhaps the greatest departure from the Hegelian understanding of history as progress, Nietzsche's will must celebrate its own inability to change the world.

We have departed from Deleuze's reading of Nietzsche which, despite its rhetoric, is much closer to Hegel's goals for history than it is to Nietzsche's nongoal. The negative for Hegel was the concept through which change was thought. And change meant progress. Deleuze understands the eternal return not as the will's great hurdle but as the culmination of its progressive historical struggle. He refuses, as we saw above, to think of affirmation as a form of complacency. If he accepts the idea of *amor fati*, it is only because for Deleuze the idea of fate already has built into it a happy (re)turn. The eternal return is our fate, perhaps even our history, but it is only a partial return. Just as the Hegelian story of change depends on the elimination of the unreasonable and of unfreedom, so the Deleuzean/Nietzschean story depends on the elimination of the negative. The two stories may have different enemies, but both want to make history something we can live with—want to make our fate lovable— by cleaning it up. As Deleuze says: "Nietzsche's speculative teaching

---

24. See Vincent Pecora's incisive critique of Deleuze's reading of Nietzsche on the "will," in "Deleuze's Nietzsche and Post-Structuralist Thought," *SubStance* 48 (1986), 34–50.

is the following: becoming, multiplicity and chance contain no negation; difference is pure affirmation; return is the being of difference excluding the whole of the negative."[25] A return that excludes that which is most detested is surely not so difficult to accept. The idea of the eternal return, which Nietzsche announced with such ominous effort and foreboding, becomes in Deleuze's account very Good News indeed: "The lesson of the eternal return is that there is no return of the negative."[26]

The Hegelian philosophy of history in France makes meaning and direction out of the past in order to legitimate changes desired in the present. Those changes cannot be grasped as necessary until they have been integrated into the story of the past. The responsibility for initiating changes, which take place through struggle or bloody battle, falls on people as historical actors. Deleuze's Nietzschean philosophy, although it rejects the building of significance through negation, also makes meaning and direction out of the past in order to legitimate a way of being in the present. But the responsibility for making history meaningful no longer falls on people. Persons are no longer considered subjects of their history—actions, that is, are no longer seen in relation to the intentions of their "authors" and resistances to these intentions or projects, actions no longer represent projects or people.[27] Although Deleuze gives up on persons *qua* historical actors, however, he does not give up on the idea of a history given meaning by its directionality. As long as work, pain, and negativity reign in history, the will is denied; history cannot, then, be given a sense. But the "secret" of the eternal return is that "being is selective."[28] How is history to be made meaningful? *Being* will do it for us!

> The eternal return must be compared to a wheel; but the movement of the wheel is gifted with a centrifugal power which eliminates all the negative. Because Being affirms itself as becoming, it expels from itself all which contradicts affirmation, all forms of nihilism and all forms of reaction:[29]

25. Deleuze, *Nietzsche et la philosophie*, 218. Modified translation, *NP*, 190.
26. Ibid., 217. Cf. Klossowski's interpretation in *Nietzsche et le cercle vicieux* (Paris, 1969).
27. See especially Deleuze, *Différence et répétition* (Paris, 1968), 3–4, 18–19.
28. Ibid.
29. Deleuze, *Nietzsche* (Paris, 1965), 38.

The eternal return is Repetition; but it is Repetition which selects, Repetition which saves. Prodigious secret of a liberating and selective repetition.[30]

The responsibility of struggle is replaced by the celebration of irresponsibility.[31] Under the guise of giving up on the idea of the *sens de l'histoire* as a vestige of Hegelianism, our history, which also means our future, is simply *affirmed* to have a meaning and direction. The threat of nihilism which motivates political action—action that can be legitimated discursively in a community—is replaced by a joyful confidence in a clean, happy, exciting selectivity, which makes it unnecessary to give action meaning and direction.

The point is not that Deleuze's Nietzsche fails a Hegelian test for legitimating political action (he does, but the failure is trivial insofar as Deleuze rejects the assumptions that make the Hegelian test significant). Instead, within his reading of the power of Nietzsche's notions of affirmation and differentiation lies a commitment to evaluation and historical selection which returns a concept of progress to the configuration of history. There is a political point to reintroducing progress: the selectivity of the eternal return saves affirmation from being mere resignation in the face of the status quo.

By making the directionality of history a virtue of the Eternal Return, however, Deleuze's Nietzsche makes it impossible to legitimate any particular historical aims. The point is relevant to Deleuze's reading because he does not abandon the notion of historical aims; he does not abandon progress, although the problematic of progress was supposedly left behind as a vestige of dialectical thinking. He gives up instead the need for the difficult process of legitimating *particular* historical aims. He does so in *Nietzsche et la philosophie* insofar as the removal of "all the negative" is the result of neither bloody battle nor joyful play; rather it is the "gift" of a centrifugal power that is not our own, that we do not need to defend, and for which we take no responsibility.

30. Ibid., 40. See also "Conclusions: Sur la volonté de puissance et l'Eternel Retour," in *Nietzsche* (Paris, 1967), 284; in *Nietzsche et la philosophie* he says that "negativity expires at the gates of Being" (190). "Natural selection" takes on a new meaning in the preface to the English edition, where Deleuze underlines the same point, saying that only action and affirmation are "fit to return" (*NP*, xi).

31. *Nietzsche et la philosophie*, 25.

Afterword

Foucault: Genealogy and the Possibilities of Change

Michel Foucault's writings on the past and his other political interventions display a sustained attempt to think and apply the lessons
of Nietzsche. Although Foucault's Nietzsche differs from Deleuze's,
they do share some crucial features. Perhaps the differences are due
to the fact that, as Foucault emphasized again at the end of his life,
he came to Nietzsche through Heidegger: "Heidegger was always for
me the essential philosopher. I began by reading Hegel then Marx and
I started to read Heidegger in 1951 or 1952; and in 1953 or 1952, I no
longer remember, I read Nietzsche.... All my philosophic becoming
was determined by my reading of Heidegger. But I recognize that it
is Nietzsche who took it over.... I tried to read Nietzsche in the 50s,
Nietzsche alone meant nothing to me! Whereas Nietzsche and Heidegger, that was *le choc philosophique!*"[32] If Heidegger remains an
absent target of Foucault's writing, Nietzsche figures prominently
and directly in two important texts. Both deal with making sense of
the past and thus show the distance we have traveled (and that Foucault had traveled) from French Hegelianism. By examining them in
some detail, we can assess how helpful it is to think of Foucault's
oeuvre as an example of a French Nietzscheanism and how that
oeuvre refigures the connection between history and knowing.

In the Royaumont Colloquium of the summer of 1964 Foucault
delivered a lecture on Nietzsche, Marx, and Freud. In this talk he
examines what he elsewhere calls a new episteme, a new way of
knowing and thinking about the world. This way is the path of interpretation. Of course, interpretation existed well before the nineteenth
century, but then it aimed at the discovery of resemblances. In the
nineteenth century, and in particular in the work of Marx, Nietzsche,
and Freud, there arises again "the possibility of a hermeneutic."[33]
This possibility is based on an awareness of the reflexivity of interpretation and an increased attention to the meanings of the surface
of signs (their interconnections) rather than a probe into their depths
(their references).

It is particularly the reflexivity of interpretation—the idea that an

32. Foucault, "Le retour de la morale," *Les nouvelles*, 28 June–5 July 1984, p. 40.
33. Foucault, "Nietzsche, Marx et Freud," in *Cahiers de Royaumont* (Paris, 1967),
185.

interpretation can best be understood by turning interpretive strategies back on the interpretation itself—which leads Foucault to the second major characteristic of nineteenth-century hermeneutics: "Interpretation finally became an infinite task."[34] For these thinkers, the task is infinite because no secure origin or goal acts as a standard for judging meanings.

Foucault notes that for Nietzsche, there is no origin of meaning. As interpretation tries to get beneath signs to something more fundamental, it discovers only more interpretations. Meaning comes through the imposition of interpretations.[35] Signs, then, are not prior to interpretations; instead, signs are always already the product of interpretations: "Beginning in the 19th century, beginning from Freud, Marx and Nietzsche, it seems to me that the sign is going to become malevolent; I mean that there is in the sign an ambiguous and even suspect means of willing evil, and of *'malveiller.'* That is insofar as the sign is already an interpretation which does not present itself as such. Signs are interpretations which try to justify themselves, and not the inverse."[36] In a world without beginnings, without a secure meaning to search out, the goal of interpretation becomes mysterious also. Interpretation for Nietzsche—as for Freud and Marx—is always incomplete, and a total hermeneutic is closer to *"experience de la folie"* than it is to "absolute knowledge."[37] Dialectical thinking had erred in trying to attribute positive meaning and direction to the play of meaning.[38] In contrast to this appropriation of interpretation for something more secure, and in contrast to the semiologist's faith in the *existence absolue des signes*—and thus a possible systematization of their relationships—Nietzsche, Marx, and Freud leave us with an *hermeneutique qui s'enveloppe sur elle-même,*

34. Ibid., 187.
35. Ibid., 190.
36. Ibid., 191.
37. Ibid., 188–189. In 1964 Foucault still held fast to the notion of a pure *expérience de la folie*. For a critical appraisal, see Jacques Derrida, "Cogito et histoire de la folie," in *L'écriture et la différence* (Paris, 1967), coll. "Points," 51–97. Derrida's critique was originally made in a lecture given in 1963. For a historical treatment of Foucault's early views on madness, see Pierre Macherey, "Aux sources de l'*Histoire de la folie*: Une rectification et ses limites," in *Critique* 42, nos. 471–472 (1986), 753–774.
38. *Nietzsche, Marx et Freud*, 191. See also Foucault's resistance to adding Hegel to the trilogy in the discussion following the article, p. 194.

an endless interpretation without foundation and without goal. For Foucault, this legacy defines the current period and, of course, his own interpretation of it:

> The problem of the plurality of interpretations, of the war of interpretations, is, I believe, made strictly possible by the very definition of the interpretation, which goes on to infinity, without there being an absolute point beginning from which it is judged and is decided upon. Thus, the following: the fact that we are destined to be interpreted at the very moment where we interpret; all interpreters must know it. This plethora of interpretations is certainly a trait which profoundly characterizes Western culture now."[39]

Seven years after the lecture at Royaumont, Foucault returned to Nietzsche in an essay that defined his historical practice for the rest of his life. In "Nietzsche, la généalogie, l'histoire," Foucault showed what was at stake in adopting a Nietzschean perspective, if not method, on the past instead of either the traditional historiographical or the "metaphysical" mode of comprehending historical change.

Foucault begins his description of genealogy where his previous discussion of interpretation left off. Genealogy is an examination of the minutiae of history, not of great deeds. It rejects the "metahistorical deployment of ideal significance and of indefinite ideologies" and instead concentrates on the play of interpretations, on primal disparity and not bedrock essence.[40] In fact, Foucault tries to steer genealogy between two dangerous points: Hegelian philosophy of history and conventional historiography.

The Hegelian philosophy of history—"metaphysics" in Foucault's essay—looks for an essence beneath historical events. Rather than seek out the meaning that links all events in a coherent whole, the genealogist recognizes irremediable diversity and discontinuity. Genealogy thus depends on a notion of hermeneutics, because it presupposes the primacy of interpretation over the sign. That is, the genealogist expects that the past will contain only more interpretations, and he or she does not seek out a basic truth or essence to serve as a standard of transhistorical judgment: "If interpretation were the

39. Ibid., 195–196.
40. Foucault, "Nietzsche, généalogie et l'histoire," in *Hommage à Jean Hyppolite* (Paris, 1971), 146.

bringing slowly to light of meaning buried in the origin, then only metaphysics could intepret the becoming of humanity. But if interpretation is the violent or surreptitious appropriation of a system of rules (which in itself has no essential meaning) in order to impose a direction, to bend it to a new will, to force its participation in a different game, and to subject it to secondary rules, then the development of humanity is a series of interpretations."[41] Whereas the metaphysical (Hegelian) historian searches for a *sens de l'histoire*, the Nietzschean genealogist makes use of a *sens historique*. The division between these two terms is the chasm that for Foucault separates traditional historiography or philosophy and his own work.

The search for a *sens de l'histoire* has been animated by a desire to give meaning and direction to the present by finding its development in the past. In a crucial sense this practice is always one of legitimation. To know the direction of history is to validate a certain contemporary practice, to make it "realistic," or "reasonable," or "progressive." The point becomes clear when those in power justify the exercise of their power through an appeal to history, and Hegel himself gave the best example in the *Philosophy of Right*. When the State is the highest product of the final stage of history, the appearance of the divine on earth, criticism of it becomes, quite literally, a form of non-sense.

But the legitimating function of a *sens de l'histoire* is relevant not only to those in power. The same function is operative for those who use history to criticize those in power, of whom Marx is the most obvious example. The theory of history does not so much predict future historical change as justify a certain kind of political action aimed at bringing about these changes. We examined this point in detail in Chapter 2, with regard to Merleau-Ponty's justification of the purge trials in *Humanisme et terreur*, and in Chapter 5, with regard to Kojève's use of the idea of the End of history as a form of propaganda for Marxist political action.[42]

The effort to find a *sens de l'histoire* connects present to past in order to ground judgments and actions. History becomes the place to which one turns for continuity, stability, and the possibility of acting

41. Ibid., 158. Modified English translation from *Language, Counter-Memory, Practice*, 151–152, hereafter *NGH*.

42. See also Michael S. Roth, review of Barry Cooper's *The End of History*, in *Political Theory* 13, no. 1 (1985), 148–152.

in a meaningful—that is, nonarbitrary—way. Without nature or a god to guide us, a *sens de l'histoire* can legitimate an identity as well as a program for change.[43]

Foucault rejects legitimation through history as metaphysical. The *sens historique* is counterhistorical when compared with the Hegelian approach to the past. Rather than providing stability or continuity, it disconnects the present and its pasts: "The search for descent [*provenance*] is not the erecting of foundations: on the contrary, it disturbs what was previously considered immobile; it fragments what was thought unified; it shows the heterogeneity of what was imagined consistent with itself."[44] Nietzschean genealogy sees the "becoming of humanity as a series of interpretations."[45] Foucault uses genealogy to uncover the appearance of these interpretations and their eclipse. And the question "Interpretations of what?" is no longer admissible, because of his view of language. Interpretations are primary; there is nothing beneath or behind an interpretation except another interpretation, and the same holds true for the work of the genealogist. The reflexive dimension remains crucial for Foucault. Genealogy cannot take itself for a science that regards the interpretations of the past from some suprahistorical point of view. Genealogy affirms itself as another in a series of interpretations. The *sens historique* is nonmetaphysical to the extent that it rejects all absolutes.[46]

In "Nietzsche, la généalogie, l'histoire," Foucault follows Nietzsche in calling history without absolutes "effective history." At least since Ranke, historians have taken metaphysicians as easy targets for their empirical wrath, but Foucault is not linking genealogy with traditional historiography:

> "Effective" history differs from that of the historians in that it does not stand on any constant; nothing in man—not even his body—is stable enough for recognizing other men and being recognized by them. . . . It is

43. Thus Dewey can be rightly seen as legitimating hope and solidarity, even if he was a critic of his time. The contrast with Foucault is powerfully drawn by Richard Rorty in "Method, Social Science and Social Hope," 203–208.

44. Foucault, "Nietzsche, généalogie et l'histoire," 153; translation, *NGH*, 147.

45. "Nietzsche, généalogie et l'histoire," 158.

46. Ibid., 159. The rejection of absolutes is clearly aimed at what Foucault calls the Platonic tradition (nature as absolute) and the Hegelian tradition (end, or *sens*, of history as absolute). It is also aimed at semiotics to the extent that it strives for a systematic, that is, more than interpretive, understanding of past interpretations.

necessary to destroy that which permits the consoling play of recognitions. To know, even in the historical order, does not signify to "re-find," and above all not to "re-find ourselves." History will be "effective" to the extent that it introduces discontinuity into our very being...Knowledge is not made for comprehension, it is made for cutting.[47]

Effective history will be a "countermemory" that teaches us that we live without foundations, that the events of our past do not contain the anticipation of meanings fully realized in the present or the future.[48] Effective history knows itself to be a partial interpretation in the service of particular interests in the present; its inquiry includes a genealogy of itself.[49]

If effective history knows itself to be an interpretation of still other interpretations that never lead to stable identity or to comprehension, why should anyone do this kind of history? Foucault notes that its reflexive dimension makes genealogy a *carnaval concerté*,[50] and that its first function is to parody those elements in the present which find their legitimation in a proud lineage. The second use of effective history is the "systematic disassociation of our identity":[51] "The purpose of history, directed by genealogy, is not to discover the roots of our identity, but to commit itself, on the contrary, to its dissipation."[52] By dissolving the bases of our identity, effective history undermines the very foundation of our attempts to know ourselves. The genealogist not only asks about the difficulties of knowing a certain object but also undercuts the subject who would know. This is the third usage of effective history: to destroy the knowing subject by uncovering the hidden vicissitudes of the will to truth. And it is here that Foucault ends his essay, pointing out the way in which a genealogical, Nietzschean history can undermine the security of foun-

---

47. Ibid., 160. Translation, slightly modified, *NGH*, 153, 154. For a critique of "continuous history," see Foucault, *The Archaeology of Knowledge*, trans. A. M. Sheridan Smith (New York, 1972), 216.

48. "Nietzsche, généalogie et l'histoire," 167, 162. Hayden White has talked about Foucault's project as a "disremembrance of things past," in "Foucault Decoded: Notes from the Underground," *History and Theory* 12 (1973), 23–54, reprinted in *Tropics of Discourse: Essays in Cultural Criticism* (Baltimore, Md., 1978), 233.

49. "Nietzsche, généalogie et l'histoire," 163.

50. Ibid., 168.

51. Ibid.

52. Ibid., 169; *NGH*, 162.

dations, continuity, and identity, and place our will to know within the fabric of our desire to interpret.

Although "Nietzsche, la généalogie, l'histoire" marks an important step in Foucault's account of his own work, it is no less a description of what he had already written than a program for what he intended to do. In L'histoire de la folie and La naissance de la clinique, Foucault had already privileged the discontinuous and the destabilizing. It has been rightly pointed out that in the former he retained an essentialist notion of the "experience of madness" which remained pure and stable over time, but the work as a whole surely aims to undermine our faith in categories of both mental illness and reason.[53] In La naissance de la clinique, Foucault describes his project as both historical and critical insofar as it is concerned "with determining the conditions of possibility of medical experience in modern times."[54] But the entire point of determining these possibilities is to bring to mind the opportunities for change. In all of his historical works Foucault situates himself at the beginning of a contemporary shift in the way we interact with the world (episteme, discourse formations, a prioris, paradigms). His histories are effective insofar as they contribute to hasten this shift by exposing the limits of the present structures of experience.[55]

Les mots et les choses can be situated in this nascent shift. The book was written when structuralism's critique of historicism and humanism was fashionable, and it contributed to this critique by providing an account of how the notion of "man" became the center of our thinking. Foucault not only contributed to the polemic against the "anthropologization" of knowledge, he also pointed to signs of the disappearance of "man" from our thinking and tried to show the transitory nature of "man" so as to hasten that disappearance.[56]

53. See Derrida's critique of Foucault cited above, and Foucault's response, Histoire de la folie (Paris, 1972), 583–603. See also the critical commentary on the "nondebate" by Alain Renault and Luc Ferry in La pensée 68 (Paris, 1985), 120–129, and Macherey, "Aux sources." Georges Canguilhem has underlined the centrality of Histoire de la folie in Foucault's work as a whole in "Sur l'Histoire de la folie en tant qu'événement," débat 41 (1986), 37–40.

54. Foucault, The Birth of the Clinic: An Archaeology of Medical Perception, trans. A. M. Sheridan Smith (New York, 1973), xix.

55. I draw here on the first part of my "Foucault's 'History of the Present,' " History and Theory 20, no. 1 (1981), 32–46.

56. Foucault, The Order of Things: An Archaeology of the Human Sciences (New York, 1970), 384.

The book argues that a culture speaks and thinks through different epistemes, and that these epistemes limit the possibilities of perception, cognition, and expression. These limitations are unconscious, because they are the very conditions of our discourse. Although Foucault says we are imprisoned within our own language and cannot describe our own episteme, his project is centered on the belief that a new beam of light is beginning to shine into our prison. As a perceiver of this new dawn, as an archaeologist who can place this light in relation to the past and present structures of experience, Foucault appears to have one foot in the modern world and one in whatever world will follow.[57]

The genealogist's act of interpretation is an act of will to foster change. The notion of *effective* history becomes more concrete when we see that the desired effect of interpretation is (at least in part) the disintegration of our contemporary conditions of experience and knowing. Foucault says nothing about the content of change, because for him any future episteme is unknowable. It is perhaps the question why one would choose to foster change about which one knows nothing that leads him to examine in detail the mechanisms by which change takes place. How are different forms of power exercised in various movements for change and in various resistances to these movements? This examination, although it does not directly answer the question "why one should," does provide a "thicker" interpretation, one that may make action in the present more open to discursive legitimation than it otherwise would be.

Foucault's work always had something to do with power, but only with *Discipline and Punish* did this concern come to the fore. Whereas previously he had examined the constellation of power/knowledge beginning from the side of the possibilities of knowing, with this book he began to examine it from the side of the exercise of power.[58] In a sentence that fits perfectly into his view of Nietzsche's *Genealogy of Morals*, Foucault stresses the connection of knowledge

57. Ibid., 207. See Roth, "Foucault's 'History of the Present,' " 39.

58. Because I am interested here in Foucault as a Nietzschean thinker, I have stressed the role genealogy has played throughout his work rather than divide his work into archaeological and genealogical phases. For a subtle, nuanced discussion using this division, see Hubert L. Dreyfus and Paul Rabinow, *Michel Foucault: Beyond Structuralism and Hermeneutics*, 2d ed. (Chicago, 1983), esp. 104–125. Dreyfus and Rabinow see a clear shift away from discourse in Foucault's interests after May 1968.

and power: "We must admit that power produces knowledge... that power and knowledge directly imply one another; that there is no power relation without the correlative constitution of a field of knowledge, nor any knowledge that does not presuppose and constitute at the same time power relations."[59] *Discipline and Punish* not only describes the birth of the prison, it explores the knowledge/power constellation that makes systematic normalization possible.

Foucault's understanding of power has been discussed in great detail elsewhere; here we need note only that he is attaching himself to an interpretation of Nietzsche which underlines the interconnection of the will to power and the will to truth. Most important, power is viewed not as something that inhibits truth but as something that produces truth. Thus power is not only repressive, it is creative. And the ability of a strategy for the exercise of power to create truths, or a regime of truth, is the secret to the self-legitimation of the strategy.[60]

Foucault describes *Discipline and Punish* as a history of the present, and here he means more than just "the history of a paradigm that is about to become outmoded." In this work the development of prisons—of penal "reform"—is linked to mechanisms of power which he clearly thinks need to be resisted now. Resistance to normalization means resistance to the network of power in which the prison has existed. Practical political work for prisoners and against a specific exercise of power has replaced more distant, if still vaguely apocalyptic, references to shifts in the structures of discourse: "The meaning which bears and determines us has the form of a war rather than that of a language: relations of power, not relations of meaning. History has no 'meaning,' though this is not to say it is absurd or incoherent. On the contrary it is intelligible and should be susceptible to analysis down to the smallest detail—but this in accordance with the intelligibility of struggles, of strategies and tactics."[61] The contrast between relations of power and relations of meaning recalls that between *sens historique* and *sens de l'histoire*. The problem with the

---

59. Foucault, *Surveiller et punir: Naissance de la prison* (Paris, 1975), trans. by Alan Sheridan as *Discipline and Punish: The Birth of the Prison* (New York, 1977), 27.
60. On Foucault's truth/power connection see, for example, Rabinow and Dreyfus, *Michel Foucault*, 126–142, and Larry Shiner, "Reading Foucault: Anti-Method and the Genealogy of Power-Knowledge," *History and Theory* 21 (1982), 382–398.
61. Foucault, "Truth and Power," in *Power/Knowledge*, 114.

latter terms in each opposition is that they assume a generalizable or transcendent function that allows for judgment among particulars. In other words, considerations of meaning and considerations of the *sens de l'histoire* are totalizable. This conclusion is problematic for Foucault because genealogy assumes (and shows) the fragmentation and discontinuity of the past. When Foucault criticizes the search for meaning in History, he is criticizing the notion that there is a uniform meaning or a uniform History, and he aims both at Hegelianism and at semiology: "Neither the dialectic, as logic of contradictions, nor semiotics, as the structure of communication, can account for the intrinsic intelligibility of conflicts. 'Dialectic' is a way of evading the always open and hazardous reality of conflict by reducing it to a Hegelian skeleton, and 'semiology' is a way of avoiding its violent, bloody and lethal character by reducing it to the calm Platonic form of language and dialogue."[62] Semiology is abandoned along with dialectics because both have a pretension to nonlocal knowledge. Foucault sees this pretension as an evasion of the *specific* connections of knowledge and power.[63]

That changes in the past have been fragmentary and discontinuous also shows us something about how our *sens historique* should foster change in the present. Analysis of history, if it is to be "effective" (that is, genealogical), must not only examine how power and knowledge are related but also situate itself in the present in accordance with specific strategies and tactics of resistance, in accordance with another exercise of power. In the 1977 interview from which I have been quoting, Foucault makes clear that the emphasis on specific struggles, strategies, and tactics is a post-1968 phenomenon. One of the lessons of those *événements* is that the state is everywhere but that in order to combat it without imitating its structure, one has to organize resistance at the micro or local level.[64] In this environment the role of the intellec-

---

62. Ibid., 114–115.
63. See Remo Bodei, "Foucault: Pouvoir, politique et maitrise de soi," *Critique* 41, nos. 471–472 (1986), 908.
64. Note Deleuze's remark that "we have no need to totalize that which is invariably totalized on the side of power"; "Intellectuals and Power," in *Language, Counter-Memory, Practice*, 212. In an interview not long before his death, Foucault commented on how the ties between the events of 1968 and Marxism broke the latter's grip on political thinking in France; *The Foucault Reader*, ed. Paul Rabinow (New York, 1984), 385–386.

tual also changes. Whereas intellectuals had once spoken in the name of universal values and Truth, they now speak "within specific sectors, at the precise points where their own conditions of life situate them."[65] The valorization of the specific as opposed to the universal intellectual is connected to the dismissal of all attempts at universal history and to an antirepresentational politics that underlines the "indignity of speaking for others."[66]

The problem with this view of the intellectual—and of everyone who speaks—is that it effaces, or accepts the effacement of, public life. According to this view, I cannot speak for you because I do not share the "conditions of life that situate you." The inability to share these conditions undermines one's ability to speak for or to anybody at all. Foucault has not only dissolved the possibilities for representation, he has also dissolved the possibilities of communication as a form of political participation. Such participation, certainly the heart of any democratic politics, requires that some conditions—Weil called them traditions, or parts of the community that go without saying— be shared. However, the emphasis Foucault puts on discontinuity, fragmentation, and division makes clear that our ability to share such conditions with others is, at best, limited. Politics is thereby reduced to the pursuit of small, special interests (although as all interests are now "special," the word loses much of its force). There is no General Will to which the intellectual can attach him or herself because there is no longer a public sphere that transcends our specific situations, struggles, and strategies; there is, in sum, no longer the possibility of community. Even more strongly, there never has been such a possibility; there has been only the exercise of a specific kind of power in whose interest the illusion of such a possibility functioned. Such at least seems to be Foucault's view.[67]

Even in the 1977 interview, however, some doubts emerge. The

65. Foucault, "Truth and Power," 126.

66. Deleuze says that Foucault's fundamental lesson was the "indignity of speaking for others," and "the theoretical fact that only those directly concerned can speak in a practical way on their own behalf"; "Intellectuals and Power," 209. See in this regard Mark Poster, *Foucault, Marxism and History: Mode of Production vs. Mode of Information* (Cambridge, 1984), 153–157.

67. At the end of his life, Foucault spoke about the rights of persons being "immanent in the discussion." It is important to note, though, that Foucault was talking about discussion at least partly in contradistinction to politics, rather than linking discussion and participation. *Foucault Reader*, 381–382.

view of the specificity of intellectuals can become a form of skepticism. We cannot speak for anybody because we can never know what anybody really thinks or wants. Such a skepticism might be theoretically amusing if joined to verbal and textual play, but in political terms it is surely impotent. The specific intellectual has renounced the universal, but what then can the basis be for his or her ability to join with other people, or to teach, learn from, or persuade other people, to work together for change? What, in other words, can serve as the bases of commonality essential for politics? Or does this skepticism entail an anemic view of politics as essentially the pursuit of private interest? Foucault's answer seems to be that our commonality is that we share in the regime of truth production. We are parts of a technology of producing truth; we are enmeshed in "the ensemble of rules according to which the true and the false are separated and specific effects of power attached to the true."[68] The critical intellectual's general task, then, is "that of ascertaining the possibility of constituting a new politics of truth." The point is not to change what people think but to change the way the regime produces truth.[69]

Here we return to the equivalent of the references to the vague shifts in our archive or episteme that animated Foucault's earlier works. The specific intellectual is supposed to work within his or her own situation for change. A university professor, for example, might argue for a democratization of the university or for equality in hiring— at least these seem to be the kinds of things for which Foucault hoped the intellectual would argue. Of course, there are no transcendent or even general criteria for evaluating arguments for change, and so an intellectual with opposed arguments could be just as specific. "Foucault," Paul Veyne tells us, "admits to being incapable of justifying his own preferences; he can appeal to neither a human nature, nor an equivalence to an object....Because knowledge is power: it is imposed and one imposes it."[70] Perhaps this is why Foucault was not satisfied with specificity as a positive political value. In any case, the intellectual is also on a more general level insofar as he or she supports

68. Foucault, "Truth and Power," 132.
69. Ibid., 133.
70. Veyne admires greatly his friend's "warrior ethic," which includes an understanding that the enemy has good reasons for fighting, too. "Le dernier Foucault et sa morale," *Critique* 42, nos. 471–472 (1986), 937–938.

or undermines the regime of truth. There is no way to "emancipate truth from every system of power," just as there was no way to think without language or without epistemes or archives. The political task (for those who share Foucault's sympathies) is to "detach the power of truth from the forms of hegemony . . . within which it operates at the present time."[71]

Because we know that truth will always be attached to a system of power, we want to know not only that we are detaching the power of truth but to what new regime we are attaching it. This is the crucial political dilemma of the specific intellectual, but Foucault has nothing specific to say about it. The position recalls his earlier apocalyptic rhetoric, where nothing can be said of the next archive because we can think only within our own archive. The epistemology seems to get in the way of the politics, although one might argue that the failure in political thinking is justified through an epistemology. In any case, it seems that in shifting from large-scale talk about discursive possibilities to more specific local accounts of power, Foucault better positions himself to provide an account of the mechanisms of power and the possibilities for *specific* forms of desirable change. But this is not the case. Instead, the gap separating the present and any goals for change remains supreme. It is a gap of theoretical silence, and it is the gap of politics.[72]

In Deleuze's Nietzsche, as we have seen, the affirmation of diversity and change for its own sake is complemented, not to say vitiated, by the idea that all difference eventually returns again without negativity. Thus for Deleuze, there was selection without pain, progress without action made meaningful. Foucault's understanding of change starts from some of the same Nietzschean premises used by Deleuze, although Foucault does not display the same faith in the selectivity of Being. Both thinkers embrace a Nietzsche who endorses the flux

71. Foucault, "Truth and Power," 133.

72. Ian Hacking points to this same "gap" but does not view it as a weakness in Foucault's work. Hacking claims that Foucault, like Kant, disconnected freedom (and politics) from knowledge precisely because there are no truths to know about the good life. It is not clear, though, that the fact that there are no truths to know about the good life requires that we undermine our capacity to discuss our projects to construct a better life; that is, that we undermine our capacity for political participation. "Self-improvement," in *Foucault: A Critical Reader*, ed. David C. Hoy (New York, 1986), 235–240. I called attention to Foucault's Kant-like position in "Foucault's 'History of the Present,' " 38.

of things, who destroys the stable, continuous narrative that legitimates an identity and instead celebrates the blooming, buzzing confusion that might replace it. But Foucault knows that there is no possibility of thinking or living in direct contact with this world of raw Power, Being, or Truth. These forces are always already interpreted, always already within the context of a regime. When Foucault talks of change, he is not talking of a liberation from certain constraints; he is talking about the creation of a new regime.

The problem is that there is no indication of what this regime will look like, because of the epistemological point that one cannot describe future paradigms, only the present one and those of the past. To call attention to this epistemological point is not enough, however, because it also holds true for the Hegelian philosophy of history. Recall the flight at dusk of Hegel's owl of Minerva, or Kojève's notion that we have only dialectical knowledge of the human past. But neither Hegel nor Kojève left politics as simply a gap in theory.

They did not leave such a gap because within the Hegelian model, all human change is mediated. Apprehending mediation within this model is equivalent to comprehending the meaning and direction of history. Thus for Kojève an understanding of the master/slave dialectic is the key for configuring history in such a way as to understand what kind of action is progressive. For Foucault, as we have seen, history has no meaning, and it certainly has no direction. There is no possibility of mediation in Foucault, and this is perhaps the most important aspect of his Nietzscheanism *qua* reaction against Hegelianism. For Nietzsche, as for Foucault, there are events, but these are great irruptions into history. Change is not what we desire, work toward, and achieve only out of something that resists our purposeful labor, it is that which happens *between* archives; however, we can understand only that which occurs *within* an archive. Change is not something we intend, it is at best something we can one day (genealogically) map.[73] To borrow a phrase from Charles Taylor, Foucault leaves us with "strategies without projects."[74]

Foucault was sensitive to this criticism of his work. He did not merely mouth the evasion that the ideas of community and the pos-

73. See Deleuze, "Ecrivain non: Un nouveau cartographe," *Critique* 31, no. 343 (1975), 1207–1227, and *Foucault* (Paris, 1986), 31–51.

74. Charles Taylor, "Foucault on Freedom and Truth," *Political Theory* 12, no. 2 (1984), 168.

sibility of nonarbitrary, nonprivate action had somehow been deconstructed with the deferral of metanarratives. Instead, he pointed to his political action as that which indicated the direction in which he thought change should occur, and what he was willing to do to further such change.[75] His action was in principle nontotalizable, that is, one could not derive from it the foundation for a theory of progress or progressive action in general. The struggles he wrote about and supported were, in other words, "anarchistic."[76] Perhaps the key issues tying them together were: Who are we? How is it that a form of power "categorizes the individual, marks him by his own individuality, attaches him to his own identity, imposes a law of truth on him which he must recognize and which others have to recognize in him. It is a form of power which makes individuals subjects."[77] If Foucault's work did not indicate the direction of desired change, perhaps it could indicate how we have become subjects who desire to know this direction. Perhaps it could indicate how the connections have been formed between our ways of knowing and our ways of desiring. A critical understanding of these connections might help us to construct not a foundation but a framework for our action in the present. Foucault turned to the history of sexuality for this understanding because this history revealed how we are constituted as subjects.

The three volumes of the *Histoire de la sexualité* have more than one agenda, but the project clearly aims at an understanding of the

---

75. Foucault, private communication, 1981. Rabinow and Dreyfus seem to accept this defense; see "Habermas et Foucault: Qu'est-ce que l'âge d'homme?" *Critique* 42, nos. 471–472 (1986), 857–872, in English as "What is Maturity? Habermas and Foucault on 'What is Enlightenment?' " in *Foucault: A Critical Reader*, 109–122. The defense is repeated in the interviews in *The Foucault Reader*, where Foucault goes so far as to say that he "never tried to analyze anything whatsoever from the point of view of politics," 385.

76. Foucault, "The Subject and Power," in Rabinow and Dreyfus, *Michel Foucault*, 211. Even if he refused to thematize his various political gestures, his appeal to them is an appeal to what he thought was "progressive" at any particular moment. Foucault has been taken to task for his inability to provide a ground for positive action or for his own critique. See, for example, Michael Walzer, "The Politics of Michel Foucault," in *Foucault: A Critical Reader*, 51–68; Nancy Frazer, "Michel Foucault: A 'Young Conservative'?" *Ethics* 96 (1985), 165–184; and Habermas, *Der philosophische Diskurs der Moderne* (Frankfurt am Main, 1985), chaps. 9–10. David Hoy puts these criticisms into an intellectual context in the Introduction to *Foucault: A Critical Reader*, 1–25. Foucault "responds" to some of those criticisms in the interviews in the *Foucault Reader* by saying he belongs to no political group.

77. Foucault, "The Subject and Power," 212.

history of how the subject has been constituted.[78] That is, Foucault wants to show how various "technologies of the self" have created a specific notion of the individual in relation to his or her conduct, desires, and experience. These relations eventually situated sexuality in a moral domain rather than in a "style of life."[79] The configuration placed sexuality within a network of power and truth which, in its Christian form, made desire not only something to be managed or molded but something to be condemned as inherently evil.

Foucault situates his work in relation to other histories. He does not stress the difference between genealogy and history but instead notes that his essay is a philosophic exercise. At stake, he says, is "knowing to what extent the work of thinking one's own history can liberate thought from what it thinks silently, and to permit it to think otherwise."[80] The idea of thinking in another way he had already raised in the Introduction to volume 2: "There are moments in life where the question of knowing if one can think otherwise than one thinks and see otherwise than one sees is indispensable for continuing to look and to reflect."[81] How does a study of sexuality among the Greeks and Romans constitute a philosophic exercise? How should it help us to "think otherwise"?

The study of ancient sexuality can be seen as a part of a genealogy of morals. That is, Foucault finds that morality has little to do with with following a rule, everything to do with how the self is understood. The difference between pagan and Christian morality is the difference in their strategies for forming an independent and free self: "The evolution . . . from paganism to Christianity does not consist in a progressive interiorization of rule, of act and of responsibility; instead it produces a restructuration of forms of the relation to self and a transformation of practices and techniques on which this relation

---

78. This part of the agenda becomes clear only in volumes 2 and 3. Volume 1 is more concerned with showing how the idea of "repression" is inadequate for making sense of sexuality, in part because power is creative and not just repressive. See, for example, the interview with Foucault, "On the Genealogy of Ethics: An Overview of Work in Progress," in Rabinow and Dreyfus, Michel Foucault, 229–252.

79. Hayden White has written provocatively on the importance of rhetoric and style in Foucault's work before that work had an explicit concern with style. See "Foucault's Discourse," in Structuralism and Since: From Lévi-Strauss to Derrida, ed. John Sturrock (Oxford 1979), 81–115.

80. Foucault, Histoire de la sexualité, 2: L'usage des plaisirs (Paris, 1984), 15.

81. Ibid., 14.

was based."[82] Thus for Foucault, the study of ancient sexuality is a philosophic exercise because it shows how we first constitute ourselves as subjects who need rules by which to live. It helps us to think otherwise by calling attention to a way of life not determined or even conditioned by the attempt to follow a rule, one that instead can be described as the cultivation of a style: "Among the Greeks, the same themes of restlessness . . . took form in a reflection which aims neither at a codification of acts, nor at a constitution of an erotic art, but in the establishment of a technique of living. . . . The physical rule [régime] of pleasures and the economy it imposes are part of a whole art of the self."[83] If Foucault's historical studies offered no criteria for evaluating change, they could explore possibilities in the past which might allow us to begin to think, and live, otherwise. They uncover neither models we are to imitate nor rules we are to try to follow, but innovations that might allow us to create other ways of being. These innovations provide not criteria for prediction—or even production—but material for aesthetic inspiration. The possibilities are not substitutes for lost foundations, nor are they only objects of nostalgia. Instead, they are meant as contradictions to the historical givens that we take as natural or necessary.

If Foucault's work in the 1970s is clearly connected to Nietzsche's *Genealogy of Morals*, the last two volumes of the *History of Sexuality* are more closely tied to Nietzsche's *Birth of Tragedy*. There Nietzsche found in pre-Socratic Greece a time when life was justified as an aesthetic phenomenon, when the cruel bite of scientific Socratic irony had not yet corrupted an aesthetic balance between the Appolonian and the Dionysian. Foucault likewise finds in the Greeks a moment before the constitution of the subject as a moral problem. Here we can perhaps see how Foucault's reading of Nietzsche was mediated by Heidegger, the *philosophe essentiel*.[84] Heidegger's search for a point before the fall is part of a long German fascination with the Greeks. Foucault does not adhere to this tradition completely; he does not search for a romantic origin that must be lamented, or recaptured, or

---

82. Ibid., 74.

83. Ibid., 155–156. See also, for example, 30, 106, 107, 111, 133, 224, 248, 275–278; vol. 2:49, 58, 85, 116, 117, 272–273.

84. Deleuze points out that Foucault's "heraclitism" is more profound than Heidegger's, because he goes on to say—with a discretion that gives a content to his notion of irresponsibility— "phénoménologie est trop pacifiante, elle a béni trop des choses." *Foucault* (Paris, 1986), 120.

reiterated.[85] But he does find in the Greeks the notion of morality as a style that might allow us to escape the exigencies involved in establishing universal values through the creation of philosophical criteria legitimated by a notion of the subject. "A moral experience essentially centered on the subject no longer appears to me to be satisfactory.... The search for styles of existence as different as possible from one another appears to me one of the points on which contemporary research within particular groups can start. The search for a form of morality which would be acceptable to everyone—in the sense that everyone must submit to it—appears catastrophic to me."[86]

Foucault's failure to provide a criterion for judging change should be understood as a refusal. As Habermas has pointed out, Foucault's critique of power depends on criteria from the "analytic of the true" (the Enlightenment tradition) that his criticism undermines.[87] In the terms we have been using, not only does Foucault offer his readers an alternative style, he provides them with a detailed criticism of their values and their limitations. Yet the criticism is attached only to a desire for change, not to an argument for legitimate change.

Deleuze defends this style of criticism as a Nietzschean mode of the history of the present. He sees Foucault as having written a series of historical ontologies that examine the diverse conditions of power, of truth, and of the self. But these conditions are never apodictic, they are problematic:[88] "No solution is transferable from one epoch to another, but there can be encroachments where the penetration of problematic fields which form the 'data' of an old problem are reactivated in another."[89] However, Deleuze recognizes here the same problem that concerns Habermas: How is one to connect the various

85. As Deleuze nicely puts it, for Foucault there is no Greek miracle, as there is for Heidegger. *Foucault*, 121.

86. Foucault, "Le retour de la morale," 41.

87. Habermas, "Une flèche dans le coeur du temps présent," *Critique* 42, no. 471–472 (1986), 799. See also the article by Dreyfus and Rabinow in the same issue, "Habermas et Foucault: Qu'est-ce que l'âge d'homme," 857–872. English versions of both of these articles are in Hoy's collection. Foucault, with Habermas in mind, talks of a "consensus model" as a critical principle, but not a "regulatory principle," in *The Foucault Reader*, 379.

88. Deleuze, *Foucault*, 122.

89. Ibid.

historical ontologies? How are concerns for change in the present to be connected to historical ontologies? Finally, Deleuze writes, "it is practice which constitutes the only continuity from past to present, or inversely, the manner in which the present explicates the past."[90]

Once again the absence of a transhistorical criterion to connect the various epochs (clearly what Habermas thinks he can provide) with one another and with the present is filled by appeal to a practice. For Foucault's Greeks, who did not *feel* the absent criterion because they were not looking for it, "style" was the equivalent of "practice." For Deleuze's Nietzsche, the connection was made by a happy reading of the eternal return. The selectivity of the eternal return insured a form of progress that was not dependent on negativity; real (nonreactive) practice presumably gets selected. Present and past are linked by a cycle that forces out those (reactive) elements most deserving of criticism.

At the end of his recent essay Deleuze rightly brings together his Nietzsche and his Foucault. With regard to the future they can "indicate only germs [*ébauches*], in the embryological sense, not yet functional."[91] And in pages that will be either frightening or invigorating, depending on one's appreciation of science fiction, he speaks of both the difficulty of knowing the future and the importance of imagining a future in which new forces will be liberated. The liberation of these new forces includes what Foucault called the "death of man" and what Nietzsche named the "superman." In the final sentence of the work, which may recall Heidegger's remark that only a god can save us now, Deleuze adds: "As Foucault would say, the death of man is much less then the disappearance of existing men, and much more than the change of a concept; it is the advent of a new form, neither God nor man, of which one can hope that it will not be worse than its two predecessors."[92] By now, of course, we know there can be no foundation for this hope. Foucault might have added that what is possible is a style of life in which it could be manifest, but we must recall that his focus on style of life, or on the construction of the subject, is apolitical—or at least a politics reduced

90. Ibid.
91. Ibid., 139.
92. Ibid., 141.

to the private. Foucault's earlier work not only dismantled the notion of progress but also undermined the notion of social hope upon which his own cultural criticism fed.[93] In his later turn toward the subject, Foucault finds perhaps a personal hope, an ethos that provides a possibility of individual freedom. The distance between individual freedom through the construction of a style of life and political freedom may, however, be as great as the distance between epistemes. In any case, it is a distance, according to Foucault, about which we are reduced to silence.

Conclusion

The replacement of a Hegelian approach to the past with a Nietzschean one insures that politics will occur in a realm that cannot be legitimated, because this realm either is that about which nothing can be said or is itself pointed to as the practical connection between ways of thinking and experiencing. A politics based on a Hegelian approach to the past is legitimated by a reading of history. Foucault's gloss on Nietzsche's idea that a "truth is an error that cannot be refuted,"[94] or his general point that truth is a product of power, is easily accepted by the Hegelian. *Weltgeschichte ist das Weltgericht* means precisely this.

My point here is not that the Hegelian approach to the past legitimates whereas the Nietzschean approach critiques. As we have seen throughout this book, the Hegelian connection between history and knowing is an important way of legitimating a critique or validating a form of delegitimation. Perhaps we can conclude that the turn in French thought represented by Deleuze and Foucault is a radicalized strategy of delegitimation, because it makes no attempt to save itself from those things which are undermined. But this would be a strange use of the word radical, for the result of the practice can be a return, dizzying but a return nonetheless, to the status quo. I do not question the personal commitments of Deleuze and Foucault to certain styles of politics. However, their inability or refusal to justify that politics

93. See Rorty, "Method, Social Science and Social Hope," 206–208. Habermas's criticism of Foucault, cited above, is also relevant here, although social hope need not be founded on criteria acceptable to the Enlightenment tradition.

94. Foucault, "Nietzsche, généalogie et l'histoire," 149–150.

makes it a *personal* commitment rather than a commitment that is in principle open to discussion, that is, a political one. As such, it is an option, a style, perhaps, soon to be outmoded.

Perhaps it will be objected that what counts as political here is foreign to the redefinition of the political for which Deleuze and Foucault deserve partial credit. For Deleuze, however, progress remains a problem to be avoided, not merely an irrelevant legacy of an outmoded, nineteenth-century thinking. And Foucault's effort to think through how we have become subjects who desire certain forms of legitimation indicates that he took seriously the political problem of legitimation even as he tried to historicize it.

Foucault runs into many of the same difficulties that troubled his teacher, Hyppolite. In the latter's heroic Hegelian phase he saw the great problem in philosophy as the connection between historicity and history, between existentialism and Marxism. Foucault's late work evinces this same problematic: How to connect the construction of a style of life with an effort at political change? How are the microstruggles in which specific individuals are engaged interrelated? The rejection of the Hegelian connection between history and knowing, and the detour through structuralism and archaeology, did little to answer these questions.

Foucault's last books are an extraordinary attempt to escape these questions. Genuinely bothered by them, and unable to speak to them in a satisfactory way (even for himself), Foucault turned to genealogy for an understanding of their perhaps limited significance. Maybe our search for connections and criteria is as culture-specific as our sexual practices and our diets. To imagine and reflect on a culture that did not desire these connections and criteria might help us abandon our own search for them.

The abandonment of the search for criteria leaves us with the condition of uncertainty so important for Weil's understanding of politics. Uncertainty and community were for Weil the conditions in which one engaged in politics, that is, in the construction of meaning and direction. Deleuze's rejection of this kind of engagement left him with a simplistic, wishful reading of Nietzsche which guaranteed "selection" as an alternative to action that could be *given* meaning. Foucault's critique of any possibility of a *sens de l'histoire* has enriched our thinking about history and challenged our assumptions about continuities in our culture and in ourselves as subjects. However, his critique also confined him to an aestheticized view of the Greeks as an (impossible) alternative to our political culture. As he surely realized, to imagine another culture may not alter the possibilities for changing one's own.

Kojève would surely have seen the French Nietzscheanism that replaced Hegelianism as posthistorical. For him, historical action, properly so-called, always was motivated by the desire for recognition and attempted to change the world by negating it. Although both Deleuze and Foucault have received much recognition, in most of their writings neither seems to believe that mutual recognition is possible or desirable. Rather than attempt to seize the direction of history, they place any directionality beyond our grasp. For Kojève, they would certainly have been like Queneau's posthistorical ironic heroes: radical political thinkers whose radicalism was impotent because for them, politics beyond the private was impossible. For Kojève, politics without the possibility of recognition was impossible, thus confining his own stance, once he no longer saw this possibility, to evocative irony.

But to criticize the radical delegitimation in the Nietzschean approach to history is not, of course, to defend the Hegelian approach. In this book I have not argued for a return to Hegelianism. I have aimed instead to explicate some of the most important texts and issues of French Hegelianism and to claim that a reconsideration of these texts and issues enriches our current thinking about historical change.

The criticisms of Hegelian historicism by philosophers and by the victims of those who claimed to believe in it are powerful and important, and I do not pretend to have dealt with them in this chapter. Instead, I have shown how the emergence of a Nietzschean approach to the past avoids the hard choices of a philosophy that takes seriously the problematics of progress. "Progress" is not ignored by either Deleuze or Foucault; it is relevant to their political/theoretical concerns. But their Nietzschean approaches to the past do not enable them to think through how to legitimate any particular historical actions as progressive. Thus we may question whether the substitution of style for criteria creates increasing difficulties not only for making sense of change in the past but for struggling in common for change in the present.

Such struggles will depend in some measure on how we think about our pasts and how we connect that thinking to our desires for the future. The problematics of French Hegelianism are no longer our own, but the reactions against it—or the efforts to displace it—are not adequate for making sense out of the connection of our thinking about the past and our desires for the future. The task still open is to find, through action that can be made meaningful, a way of connecting knowing and history which will allow us to create a politics that will not ignore our historicity—a politics that will make possible a shared search for and construction of meaning and direction.

Appendix

Participants in Kojève's seminar at the Ecole Pratique des Hautes Etudes, Section des Sciences Religieuses, 1933–1939

1933–1934

Number of students registered: 19
  Elèves diplômés: Corbin
  Elèves titulaires: Adler
  Auditeurs assidus: Gordin, Gottlieb, Queneau, Ralli, Spire, Mme. Carlos, Mlle. Lattes, Mlle. Ostermann
  Others: André Chaslet, Miguel de Urrela, Marie-Claude Pfenninger, Simone Bouka, Azary Weber, Passweg, Gerrit Haendordaal

1934–1935

Number of students registered: 11
  Elèves diplômés: Corbin
  Elèves titulaires: Adler, Queneau
  Auditeurs assidus: Fessard, Bataille, Lacan, Poplavski, Stearn, Weil, Mme. Tatarinoff
  Others: Julien Verplaete, Jacques Aurchuski, Jean-Claude Coulon, Aron Gurvitsch

Appendix

1935–1936

Number of students registered: 9
Elèves titulaires: Adler, Fessard, Queneau
Auditeurs assidus: Bataille, Gardine, Lacan, Stern, Weil
Others: Aron Gurvitsch, (?) Gastambide, (?) Tarr, Margarita Vieef
de Massa, (?) Terroux jubes, (?) Ferraasi

1936–1937

Number of students registered: 10
Elève diplômé: Corbin
Elèves titulaires: Adler, Fessard, Queneau, Weil
Auditeurs assidus: Gordin, Lacan, Polin, Stephanopoli, Terraux,
Mme. Gastembes
Others: Gérard de Vignoux, Marthe Nicholas, Arcade Monnette,
Cécile Firle, Nina Ivanoff, Henri Jouet, Olivier Picard, Jean-
Marie Autret, Pierre Moujet (?).

1937–1938

Number of students registered: 11
(No details are given)
Others: Marie J. Duploye, Victor Weintraub, Eric Weil, Jean Martin,
Eméric Lorand, Auguste Raymond Confeneau, Gaston Fes-
sard, Georges Bataille, Maurice Jacques Merleau-Ponty,
Denise Mosseri, Alexandre Adler, Arno Natanson, Claude
Valéry, Jean-Henri Jolliers, Pierre Julien Golliet, Boris
Babtchenco

1939–1940

No reference to seminar as independent course in *Annuaire*. Students
signed for Kojève as instructor.
Others: A. Patrick Waldberg, Marie, Oriol-Crel, Jean-Claude Ver-
dun, Hélène Nicolaou, Jean de Jolliers, Denise Mosseri, Jose

(?) Valerstinas, France Keim, Taoo Okamot, Gaston Fessard, André Fernand Deblois, Pierre Kauffmann, Alexandre Adler, Pierre Julien Golbiet, François Cuzin, Jean Desanti.

Source. This Appendix has been compiled from the *Annuaire* and the *Registre des Inscriptions* of the Ecole Pratique des Hautes Etudes.

Bibliography

As primary sources, this bibliography lists only the texts of Hyppolite, Kojève, and Weil. Bibliographies of Foucault and Deleuze are readily available elsewhere. The texts listed as interpretive material are those that proved helpful in the completion of this book. Most of the literature on French Hegelianism is listed therein, but not all of it.

The following abbreviations are used:

R.M.M.	Revue de métaphysique et de morale
R.P.F.E.	Revue philosophique de la France et de l'étranger
B.S.F.P.	Bulletin de la societé française de philosophie
R.P.	Recherches philosophiques
T.M.	Les temps modernes

I. Primary Texts

Jean Hyppolite

1. "L'esthétique de Paul Claudel." Lecture (1931), in *Figures* (see no. 89).
2. "Les travaux de jeunesse de Hegel d'après des ouvrages récents." *R.M.M.* 42, nos. 3 and 4 (July and October 1935), 399–426, 547–577.
3. "Vie et prise de conscience de la vie dans la philosophie hégélienne d'Iéna." *R.M.M.* 45, no. 1 (January 1938), 45–61.
4. "La signification de la révolution française dans la *Phénoménologie* de Hegel." *R.P.F.E.* 9–12 (1939).
5. Preface for Hegel's *Principes de la philosophie du droit*. Paris, 1940.
6. "L'aliénation hégélienne et la critique" (1945). In *Atti del Congresso internazionale di filosofia*, 53–55. Milan, 1947.
7. "Jaspers." *Dieu vivant* 3 (1945).
8. "Note sur Paul Valéry et la crise de la conscience." *La vie intellectuelle* 14, no. 3 (March 1946), 120–126.

9. "L'existence dans la *Phénoménologie* de Hegel." *Revue des études germaniques* 2 (April–June 1946).

10. "Marxisme et philosophie." *La revue socialiste* 5 (November 1946), 540–549.

11. Review of P. Burgelin, *L'homme et le temps. Dieu vivant* 5 (1946), 137–140.

12. Review of H. Niel, *De la médiation dans la philosophie de Hegel. Dieu vivant* 6 (1946).

13. "La conception hégélienne de l'état et sa critique par Karl Marx." *Cahiers internationaux de sociologie* 2 (1946), 142–161.

14. *Genèse et structure de la Phénoménologie de l'esprit de Hegel*. Paris, 1946.

15. "Situation de l'homme dans la 'Phénoménologie' hégélienne." *T.M.* 19 (March 1947).

16. "Situation de Jaspers." *Esprit* 1 (January 1948).

17. "De la structure du Capital et quelque présuppositions philosophiques de l'oeuvre de Marx." *B.S.F.P.* 6 (1948).

18. Introduction to Hegel's *L'esprit du christianisme et son destin*. Paris, 1948.

19. *Introduction à la Philosophie de l'histoire de Hegel*. Paris, 1948.

20. "Humanisme et hégélianisme" (1949). In *Umanesimo e scienza politica: Atti del congresso internazionale di studi umanisti*, 217–228. Milan, 1951.

21. Preface to Marcel Deschoux's *La philosophie de Léon Brunschvicg*. Paris, 1949.

22. "Vie et philosophie de l'histoire chez Bergson." *Actes du premier international de philosophie*. Mendoza, 1949.

23. "Du bergsonisme à l'existentialisme." *Mercure de France* 1031 (July 1949).

24. "L'existence, l'imaginaire, et la valeur chez Alain." *Mercure de France* 1034 (October 1949).

25. "Aspects divers de la mémoire chez Bergson." *Revue internationale de philosophie* 3, no. 10 (October 1949).

26. Review of H. J. Marrou, "Histoire de l'éducation dans l'antiquité." *Esprit* 1 (1949), 147–149.

27. "Note sur Amos." *Dieu vivant* 13 (1949).

28. Review of J. Danielou, *Le mystère de l'Avent. Dieu vivant* 13 (1949), 139–141.

29. "Le peintre et le philosophe." *Mercure de France* 1042 (1950).

30. "Vie et existence d'après Bergson (faiblesse et grandeur de l'intelligence)" (1950). In *Figures*.

31. "Aliénation et objectivation: A propos du livre de Lukács sur 'La jeunesse de Hegel.'" *Etudes germaniques* 6, no. 2 (April–June 1951).

32. "Paul Valéry et la conscience de la vie." *Anhembi* 3, no. 2 (June 1951).

33. "La liberté chez Jean-Paul Sartre." *Mercure de France* 1055 (July 1951).

34. "Alain et les dieux." *Mercure de France* 1060 (December 1951).
35. "Essai sur la *Logique* de Hegel." *Revue internationale de philosophie* 19 (1952).
36. "Ruse de la raison et histoire chez Hegel." In *Congresso internazionale di studi umanistici.* Rome, 1952.
37. "Note en manière d'introduction à *Que signifie penser?*" *Mercure de France* 1075 (March 1953).
38. *Logique et existence: Essai sur la "Logique" de Hegel,* Paris, 1953.
39. "La critique hégélienne de la réflexion kantienne." *Kant-Studien* 45, nos. 1–4 (1953–1954).
40. "Gaston Bachelard ou le romantisme de l'intelligence." *Revue philosophique* 144 (January–March 1954).
41. "Ontologie et phénoménologie chez Martin Heidegger." *Etudes philosophiques* 3 (July–September 1954).
42. Preface to Robert Lapoujade, *Les mécanismes de la fascination.* Paris, 1955.
43. *Etudes sur Marx et Hegel.* Paris, 1955. Includes numbers 3, 4, 9, 10, 13, 15, 17, 31, and 35.
44. "Pathologie mentale et organisation" (1955). In *Figures.*
45. "Hegel et Kierkegaard dans la pensée française contemporaine" (1955). In *Figures.*
46. "Histoire et existence" (1955). In *Figures.*
47. "Commentaire parlé sur la 'Verneinung' de Freud" (1955). In Jacques Lacan. *Ecrits.* Paris, 1966.
48. "Psychanalyse et philosophie" (1955?). In *Figures.*
49. "A Chronology of French Existentialism." *Yale French Studies* 16 (1955–1956), 100–102.
50. "Dialectique et dialogue dans la 'Phénoménologie de l'esprit' " (1955 or 1956). In *Figures.*
51. "Du sens de la géométrie de Descartes dans son oeuvre." *Cahiers de Royaumont* 2 (1957).
52. "La 'Phénoménologie' de Hegel et la pensée française contemporaine" (1957). In *Figures.*
53. " 'Phénoménologie' de Hegel et psychanalyse." *La psychanalyse* 2 (1957).
54. "Le 'Coup de dés' de Stéphane Mallarmé et le message." *Etudes philosophiques* 4 (October–December 1958).
55. "L'idée fichtéenne de la doctrine de la science et le projet husserlien." In *Husserl et la pensée moderne.* The Hague, 1959.
56. "Philosophie et psychanalyse" (1959). In *Figures.*
57. "L'existence humaine et la psychanalyse" (1959). In *Figures.*
58. "Nécessité et liberté dans l'histoire et la connaissance historique" (1960). In *Figures.*
59. "La machine et la pensée" (1961). In *Figures.*
60. "Existence et dialectique dans la philosophie de Merleau-Ponty." *T.M.* 184–185 (October 1961).

Bibliography

61. "L'évolution de la pensée de Merleau-Ponty" (1961). In *Figures.*
62. "L'épistémologie de Gaston Bachelard." *Revue d'histoire des sciences* 6 (December 1962).
63. "Projet d'enseignement d'histoire de la pensée philosophique" (1962). In *Figures.*
64. "L'imaginaire et la science chez Gaston Bachelard" (1963). In *Figures.*
65. *Marxisme et existentialisme, controverse sur la dialectique.* Paris, 1962.
66. "Sens et existence dans la philosophie de Maurice Merleau-Ponty." The Zaharoff Lecture. Oxford, 1963.
67. "Leçon inaugurale" (19 December 1963). *Collège de France: Leçons inaugurales,* 31–40. Paris, 1960–1964.
68. "Sur *Les mots* de Jean-Paul Sartre" (1964?). In *Figures.*
69. "L'idée de la doctrine de la science et le sens de son évolution chez Fichte." In *Etudes sur l'histoire de la philosophie.* Paris, 1964.
70. "La phénomène de la 'Reconnaissance Universelle' dans l'experience humaine" (1964). In *Figures.*
71. "Le tragique et le rationnel dans la philosophie de Hegel." *Hegel-Jahrbuch.* Meinsenheim am Glan, 1964.
72. "L'état du droit (la condition juridique)" (1964). *Hegel-Studien* 3 (1966).
73. "Discours d'introduction" at the "Hegel-Tage Royaumont" (1964). *Hegel-Studien* 3 (1966).
74. Summaries of seminars. *Annuaire du Collège de France.* Paris, 1966, 1967, 1968, 1969.
75. "Le mythe et l'origine. A propos d'un texte de Platon." *Archivio di filosofig.* Padua, Italy, 1965.
76. "La situation de la philosophie dans le monde contemporain" (1965). In *Figures.*
77. Preface to Fichte's *La destination de l'homme.* Paris, 1965.
78. "Langage et être, langage et pensée." *Actes du XIIIe congrés des Societés de philosophie de langue française.* Geneva, 1966.
79. "Essai d'interprétation de la préface de la *Phénoménologie*" (1966). In *Figures.*
80. "Hegel à l'ouest" (1966). In *Figures.*
81. "La première philosophie de l'esprit de Hegel" (1967). In *Figures.*
82. "Information et communication" (1967). In *Figures.*
83. "Note sur la préface de la *Phénoménologie de l'esprit* et le thème: L'absolu est sujet" (1967?). In *Figures.*
84. "Structure du langage philosophique d'après la préface de la Phénoménologie de l'esprit" (1967). In *Figures.*
85. "Le 'scientifique' et l' 'idéologie' dans une perspective marxiste." *Diogène* 64 (October–December 1968).
86. "Une perspective nouvelle sur Marx et le marxisme." *La philosophie contemporaine* 4:339–357. Florence, 1971.
87. "La psychanalyse existentielle chez Jean-Paul Sartre" (n.d.). In *Figures.*
88. "L'intersubjectivité chez Husserl" (n.d.). In *Figures.*
89. *Figures de la pensée philosophique.* 2 vols. Paris 1971. A collection of

previously published and unpublished texts, numbers 1, 5, 7, 9, 15, 16,
20, 22, 23, 24, 25, 29, 30, 13, 32, 33, 34, 35, 36, 37, 38, 39, 40, 41, 42,
43, 44, 45, 46, 47, 48, 49, 50, 51, 52, 53, 54, 55, 56, 57, 58, 59, 60, 61,
62, 63, 64, 65, 66, 67, 68, 69, 70, 71, 72, 73, 74, 75, 76, 77, 78, 79, 80,
81, 82, 83, 84, 85, 86, 87, and 88.

Alexandre Kojève

I list Kojève's published writings, as well as some of the longer, more
important manuscripts to which I have had access. The list is by no means
a complete inventory of his unpublished work but gives an idea of the important texts that exist among his personal papers. Until 1936 Kojève's texts
appeared under the name of Koschewnikoff or Kojevnikoff.

a. Published Writings

1. "Religionsphilosophie Wladimir Solowjews." Philosophy diss. Heidelberg, 1920, 1921.
2. Review of K. Ambrozaitis, "Die Staastslehre Wladimir Solowjews." *Archive für Sozialwissenschaft und Sozialpolitik* 1, no. 1 (February 1929),
   199.
3. "Die Geschichtsphilosophie Wladimir Solowjews: Sonderabdruck." *Der
   russische Gedanke: Internationale Zeitschrift für russische Philosophie, Literaturwissenschaft und Kultur* 1, no. 3. Bonn, 1930.
4. Review of R. Grousset, "Les philosophies indiennes." *Revue d'histoire
   de la philosophie* 5 (July–December 1931), 416–418.
5. Review of H. Gouhier, "La vie d'Auguste Comte." *Zeitschrift für So-
   cialforschung* 1, nos. 1–2 (1932).
6. Review of J. Kraft, "Von Husserl zu Heidegger." *RP* 2 (1932–1933), 475–
   477.
7. Review of N. Hartman, "Zum Problem der Realitätsgegebenheit." *RP* 2
   (1932–1933).
8. Review of G. Misch, "Lebensphilosophie und Phänomenologie." *RP* 2
   (1932–1933), 470–475.
9. Review of R. Zocher, "Husserls Phänomenologie und Schuppes Logik."
   RP 2 (1932–1933), 477–480.
10. Review of R. Ingarden, "Das literarische Kunstwerk." *RP* 2 (1932–1933),
    480–486.
11. Review of R. Poirier, "Essai sur quelques caractères des notions d'espace
    et de temps." *Deutsche Literaturzeitung* 1 (January 1933), 12–17.
12. Review of R. Poirier, "Remarques sur la probabilité des inductions."
    Deutsche Literaturzeitung 16 (April 1933), 726–729.
13. Review of W. Illemann, "Husserls vor-phänomenologische Philosophie";
    Fr. Weidauer, "Kritik der Transzcendental-Phänomenologie Husserls";
    and "La phénoménologie: Journées d'études de la société thomiste."
    RP 3 (1933–1934), 428–431.
14. Review of A. Eddington, "The Expanding Universe"; J. Jeans, "The New
    Background of Science"; and H. Weyl, "The Open World: Three Lec-

Bibliography

tures on the Metaphysical Implications of Science." *RP* 3 (1933–1934), 464–466.

15. "Les philosophies des sciences de M. Bavink." *Revue de synthèse* 8, no. 2 (October 1934), 17.

16. Review of G. Kraenzlin, "Max Schelers phänomenologische Systematik." *RP* 4 (1934–1935), 398–400.

17. Review of A. Sternberger, "Der verstandene Tod: Eine Untersuchung zu Martin Heideggers Existentialontologie." *RP* 4 (1934–1935), 400–402.

18. Review of H. Dingler, "Philosophie der Logik und Arithmetik." *RP* 4 (1934–1935), 430–433.

19. Review of M. Granet, "La pensée chinoise." *RP* 4 (1934–1935), 446–448.

20. Review of W. Sesemann, "Die logischen Gesetze und das Sein." *RP* 4 (1934–1935), 402–403.

21. Review of Fr. Weidauer, "Objectivität, voraussetzungslose Wissenschaft und wissenschaftliche Wahrheit." *RP* 5 (1935–1936), 419–420.

22. "La métaphysique religieuse de Vladmir Soloviev." *Revue d'histoire et de philosophie religieuses* 14, no. 6 (1934), 534–544, and 15, nos. 1–2 (1935), 110–152.

23. Review of A. Delp, "Tragische Existenz. Zur Philosophie Martin Heideggers." *RP* 5 (1935–1936), 415–419. I consulted a more detailed manuscript that was the basis for this review.

24. Review of Flitz Kluge, "Aloys Mullers Philosophie der Mathematik und der Naturwissenschaft." *RP* 5 (1935–1936).

25. Review of E. Tomomatsu, "Le bouddhisme." *RP* 5 (1935–1936), 400.

26. Review of "Archives d'histoire des sciences et des techniques." *Thales* 2 (1936), 237–253.

27. "Les peintures concrètes de Kandinsky." Unpublished ms, Vanves, July 23–25, 1936. This was the basis for an article on Kandinsky in *XXe siècle* (1966).

28. Review of M. Gueroult, "Dynamique et métaphysique leibnizienne." *Archiv für Sozialforschung* (1936).

29. Review of A. Fischer, "Die Existenzphilosophie Martins Heideggers." *RP* 6 (1936–1937), 396–397.

30. Review of J. Hessing, "Das Selbstbewusstwerden des Geistes." *RP* 6 (1936–1937), 395–396.

31. Review of D. Stremoonkhoff, "Vladimir Soloviev et son oeuvre messianique." *Revue de philosophie*, n.s., 8 (1939).

32. Co-author, *Aussenpolitische Blätter*, Neue Folge, 1 (October 1944).

33. *Esquisse d'une phénoménologie du droit*. Written in Marseille, 1943. Published Paris, 1981.

34. "Hegel, Marx et le christianisme." *Critique* 3–4 (1946), 339–366.

35. "Christianisme et communisme." *Critique* 3–4 (1946), 308–312.

36. *Introduction à la lecture de Hegel*. Ed. Raymond Queneau. Paris, 1947.

37. "Difficultés et espoirs de l'O.E.C.E.." *France illustration* 206 (September 24, 1949), 310. Published article is unsigned, but manuscript is among Kojève's personal papers.

38. "Préface à l'oeuvre de Georges Bataille." Manuscript dated May 1950. Published in *L'arc* 44 (May 1971).
39. "L'action politique des philosophes." *Critique* 41, 42 (1950), 46–55, 138–155. Later published in Leo Strauss, *On Tyranny*. Glencoe, Ill., 1963.
40. Review of G. R. G. Mure, "A Study of Hegel's *Logic*." *Critique* 54 (1951), 1003–1007.
41. "Les romans de la sagesse." *Critique* 60 (1952), 387–397.
42. *Essai d'une histoire raisonnée de la philosophie païenne.* Written in 1955. 3 vols. Paris, 1968, 1972, 1973.
43. *Kant.* Written in the 1950s. Paris, 1973.
44. "Le concept et le temps." *Deucalion* 5 (October 1955), 11–20.
45. "Le dernier monde nouveau." *Critique* 111–112 (1956), 702–708.
46. "L'empereur Julien et son art d'écrire," 1958. Published in English in *Ancients and Moderns: Essays on the Tradition of Political Philosophy in Honor of Leo Strauss*, ed. J. Cropsey. New York, 1964.
47. "Nécessité d'une révision systématique des principes fondamentaux du commerce actuel." *Développement et civilisations* 19 (September 1964), 44.
48. "L'origine chrétienne de la science moderne." *Mélanges Alexandre Koyré*, 2. Paris, 1964. Also in *Sciences* 31 (May–June 1964).
49. "Entretien avec Gilles Lapouge." *La quinzaine littéraire* 53 (1–15 July 1968), 18–19.
50. "Lettres à Georges Bataille." *Textures* 6 (Brussels, 1970), 61–71.
51. "La spécificité et l'autonomie du droit." *Commentaire* 9 (Spring, 1980), 122–130. An extract from number 33.
52. "Préface à mise à jour du système hégelien du savoir." *Commentaire* 9 (Spring 1980), 135–137. Extract from unpublished number 12.
53. "Marx est Dieu, Ford est son prophèt." *Commentaire* 9 (Spring 1980), 135–137. Extract from unpublished number 12.
54. "Una lettera di Kojève su Platone." *Quaderni di storia* 12 (July–December 1980), 223–237.
55. "Deux lettres inédites d'Alexandre Kojève à Vassily Kandinsky." *Kandinsky: Album de l'exposition*, 64–74. Paris, 1984.
56. "Les peintures concrètes de Kandinsky." *RMM* 90, no. 2 (1985), 149–171. See number 27.
57. "Correspondence with Leo Strauss (1934–1962)." Forthcoming.

b. *Unpublished Writings*
1. Review of Leang k'I-tch' Ao, "La conception de la loi et les théories des légistes à la veille des Ts'in." Peking, 1926. Written in Russian, 1927.
2. Review of S. Radhanrishnan, "Indian Philosophy." Vol. 1. London, 1927. Written in Russian, 1927.
3. Review of M. Walleser, "Die Sekten des alten Budhismus." Heidelberg, 1927. Written in German and French, 1927.
4. Review of J. Perrin et al., "L'orientation actuelle des sciences" (1931). Written in French.

Bibliography

5. "L'idée du déterminisme dans la physique classique et dans la physique moderne." Book-length manuscript, Vanves 1932.
6. Review of K. Jaspers, "Die geistige Situation der Zeit," 1931. Written in 1932.
7. Review of M. Granet, "La civilisation chinoise." Paris, 1929. Written in German, 1932.
8. Review of N. Sakurazawa, "Principe unique de la philosophie et de la science d'Extrême-Orient." Paris, 1931. Written in French and German, 1932.
9. Review of G. Fessard, "Pax nostra: Examen de conscience international," and "La main tendue? Le dialogue communiste-catholique est-il possible?" Written at Vanves, June 1936–1937.
10. Review of A. Gregoire, "Immanence et transcendance: Questions de Théodicée." Written at Vanves, 1939.
11. "Esquisse d'une doctrine de la politique française." Dated 27 August 1945.
12. "Le concept, le temps et le discours: Essai d'une mise à jour du 'Système du savoir hégélien.'" Vol. 1: "Introduction du Système du savoir." unpublished manuscript of 182 pages, Vanves 1952– .
13. Deuxième introduction du "Système du savoir"—Introduction logique du temps (d'après Platon). Manuscript of 178 pages, Vanves 1952– .
14. "Kolonialismus in europäischer Sicht." Lecture, 16 June 1957.
15. "Qu'est-ce que la dialectique?" Lecture, 14 March 1962.
16. "Note pour Monsieur Clappier: Essai d'une solution du problème anglais pour les dix années à venir." Manuscript, Paris, 8 February 1963.
17. "Structure et histoire de la philosophie." Lecture, 6 February 1965.

Eric Weil

A complete bibliography of Weil's published work is contained in a collection of his articles, *Philosophie et réalité* (Paris, 1982), and the Italian translation of *Problèmes kantiens* (Urbino, 1980) concludes with a bibliography of Weil's work and articles on it. Here I list only his book-length publications and collections of his articles.
1. "Des Pietro Pomponazzi Lehre von dem Menschen und der Welt." Berlin, 1932. Hamburg Philosophy diss. French translation in preparation.
2. *Hegel et l'état.* Paris, 1950.
3. *Logique de la philosophie.* Paris, 1950, 1967.
4. *Philosophie politique.* Paris, 1956.
5. *Philosophie morale.* Paris, 1961.
6. *Problèmes kantiens.* Paris, 1963, 1970.
7. *Essais et conférences.* 2 vols. Paris, 1970, 1971.
8. *Philosophie et réalité: Derniers essais et conférences.* Paris, 1982.
9. "Lettres à Georges Bataille." Bibliothèque Nationale, Nouvelles acquisitions françaises, file no. 1584.

II. Secondary Texts

Evidential Material

Abensour, Miguel. "Les procès des maîtres rêveurs." *Libre* 4 (1978), 207–230.

Alquié, Ferdinand. "Humanisme surréaliste et humanisme existentialiste." In *L'homme, le monde et l'histoire: Cahiers du Collège philosophique.* Paris, 1948.

——. "Une philosophie de l'ambiguïté: L'existentialisme de Maurice Merleau-Ponty." *Fontaine* 11 (1947), 47–70.

Andler, Charles. "Le fondement du savoir dans la "Phénoménologie de l'esprit" de Hegel." *RMM* 38, no. 3 (1931), 317–340.

Aron, Raymond. "Entrevue." *L'Express* no. 1136 (16–22 April 1973), 152–155.

——. *Essai sur la théorie de l'histoire dans l'Allemagne contemporaine: La philosophie critique de l'histoire.* Paris, 1938.

——. *L'opium des intellectuels.* Paris, 1955, 1968.

Asaad-Mikhail, Fawsia. "Heidegger interprète de Nietzsche." *RMM* 73, 1 (1968), 16–55.

Bataille, Georges. "Hegel, l'homme et l'histoire." *Monde Nouveau* 11, nos. 96–97 (January–February 1956), 20–33, 1–14.

——. *La haine de la poésie.* Paris, 1947.

——. "Nietzsche et Jésus selon Gide et Jaspers." *Critique* 6 (1950), 42, 99–114.

Beauvoir, Simone de. *Force of Circumstance.* Trans. R. Howard. New York, 1964.

——. *Memoirs of a Dutiful Daughter.* Trans. J. Kirkup. New York, 1959.

——. *The Prime of Life.* Trans. P. Green. London, 1963.

Benoist, Jean-Marie. *La révolution structurale.* Paris, 1975.

Birault, Henri. "De la béatitude chez Nietzsche." In *Nietzsche.* Paris, 1967.

Blin, Georges. "La 'non-philosophie' de Jean Wahl." *Fontaine* 9, nos. 51, 52 (April, May 1946), 632–648, 808–826.

Bonnel, Pierre. "Hegel et Marx à la lumière de quelques travaux contemporains." *Critique* 34 (March 1949), 221–232.

——. "Lukács contre Sartre." *Critique* 27 (August 1948), 678–707.

Bourricaud, F. "Sociologie économique—philosophie de l'histoire." *Philosophie (Chronique des années d'après guerre), Actualités scientifiques et industrielles* no. 1104, 225–230. Paris, 1950.

Brehier, Emile. "Compte rendu de *Hegel et l'état.*" *RPFE* 144 (1954).

——. "Compte rendu de l'*Introduction à la philosophie de l'histoire.*" *RPFE* 140 (1950).

——. *Histoire de la philosophie, le XIXe siècle: Période des systèmes (1800–1850).* Vol. 2. Paris, 1932.

——. *Les thèmes actuels de la philosophie.* Paris, 1951, 1967.

——. *Transformation de la philosophie française.* Paris, 1950.

Breton, André. *Manifestes du surréalisme.* Paris, 1972.

Caillois, Roland. "Attitudes et catégories selon Eric Weil." *RMM* 583 (1953), 273–291.

Bibliography

——. "Destin de l'humanisme marxiste." *Critique* 22 (March 1948), 242–251.
——. "Etudes sur Marx." *Critique* 30 (November 1948), 1011–1016.
——. "Le monde vécu et l'histoire." *L'homme, le monde, l'histoire: Cahiers du Collège philosophique*. Paris, 1948.
——. "Note sur *Genèse et structure de la Phénoménologie de l'esprit de Hegel*." *TM* 31 (1948), 1898–1904.
Calvez, Jean-Yves. "Marxisme, idéologie et philosophie." *Critique* 111–112 (1956), 777–796.
Canguilhem, Georges. "Hegel en France." *Revue d'histoire et de philosophie religieuses* 28–29, no. 4 (1948–1949), 282–297.
Cassirer, Ernst. "Kant und das Problem der Metaphysik." *Kant-Studien* 36 (1931), 1–26.
Catesson, J. "A propos de la philosophie morale d'Eric Weil." *RMM* 67, 3 (1962), 362–375.
Chassard, Pierre. *Nietzsche: Finalisme et histoire*. Paris, 1977.
Commission de critique du cercle des philosophes communistes. "Le retour à Hegel: Dernier mot du révisionisme universitaire." *Nouvelle critique* 2, no. 20 (November 1950), 43–54.
Cranaki, Mimica. "Jean Hyppolite: *Logique et existence*." *RMM* 59 (1954), 202–205.
Croce, Benedetto. "Anti-historicisme." *RMM* 38 1 (1931), 1–12.
——. "Un cercle vicieux dans la critique de la philosophie hégélienne." *RMM* 38 3 (1931), 277–284.
——. "La naissance de l'historicisme." *RMM* 44, 3 (1937), 603–621.
Darbon, Michel. "Hégélianisme, marxisme, existentialisme." *Les études philosophiques* 4, nos. 3–4 (July–December 1949), 346–370.
Deleuze, Gilles. "Analyses de *Logique et existence*." *RPFE* 144 (1954), 457–460.
——. "Conclusions: Sur la volonté de puissance et l'Eternel Retour." In *Nietzsche*. Paris, 1967.
——. *Différence et répétition*. Paris, 1968.
——. "Ecrivain non: Un nouveau cartographe." *Critique* 31, no. 343 (1975), 1207–1227.
——. *Foucault*. Paris, 1986.
——. *Nietzsche*. Paris, 1965.
——. *Nietzsche et la philosophie*. Paris, 1962, 1973.
——, and Felix Guattari. *The Anti-Oedipus*. Trans. R. Hurley, M. Seem, and H. Lane. New York, 1977.
——, and Claire Parnet. *Dialogues*. Paris, 1977.
Derrida, Jacques. *Glas*. Paris, 1981.
——. *L'écriture et la différence*. Paris, 1967.
——. *De la grammatologie*. Paris, 1967.
——. *Marges de la philosophie*. Paris, 1972.
——. *Positions*. Paris, 1972.
——. "La question du style." In *Nietzsche aujourd'hui*, vol. 1: *Intensités*. Paris, 1973.

——. *Eperons: Les styles de Nietzsche.* Venice, 1976.

Desanti, Jean. "Hegel, est-il le père de l'existentialisme?" *La nouvelle critique* 6, no. 56 (June 1954), 91–109.

"Deux documents sur Heidegger." *TM* 1, no. 4 (June 1945), 713–724.

Domenach, J. M. "Le parti communiste français et les intellectuels." *Esprit* 17, no. 155 (May 1949), 729–739.

Dufrenne, Mikel. "Actualité de Hegel." *Esprit* 17, no. 9 (September 1948), 396–408.

——. "A propos de la thèse de Jean Hyppolite." *Fontaine* 11, no. 61 (1947), 461–470.

——. *Entretiens sur les notions de Genèse et structure.* Paris and The Hague, 1968.

——. "Histoire et historicité: Un aspect de la sociologie de Marx." *Cahiers internationaux de sociologie* 4, nos. 1–2 (1948), 92–118.

——. "Plaidoyer pour la liberté de l'enseignement philosophique." *Esprit* 15, no. 131 (1947), 414–427.

Erval, François. "Georges Lukács et l'autocritique." *TM* 52 (1949), 1109–1121.

Feraud, H. "Un commentaire de la *Phénoménologie de l'esprit* de Hegel." *La revue internationale* 3, no. 17 (1947).

Fessard, Gaston. "Attitude ambivalente de Hegel en face de l'histoire." *Archives de philosophie* 24, no. 2 (1961), 207–241.

——. *De l'actualité historique,* vol. 1: *A la recherche d'une méthode.* Paris, 1960.

——. "Image, symbole et historicité." *Archivo di filosofia* 1–2 (1962), 43–68.

Foucault, Michel, "Allocution à l'Ecole Normale Supérieure." *RMM* 2 (1969).

——. *The Archaeology of Knowlege and the Discourse on Language.* Trans. A. M. Sheridan Smith. New York, 1972.

——. *Birth of the Clinic: An Archaeology of Medical Perception.* Trans. A. M. Sheridan Smith. New York, 1973.

——. "Correspondance." In *Pour un temps/Pierre Klossowski.* Ed. Andreas Pfersmann. Paris, 1985.

——. *Discipline and Punish: The Birth of the Prison.* Trans. Alan Sheridan. New York, 1977.

——. *The Foucault Reader.* Ed. Paul Rabinow. New York, 1984.

——. *Language, Counter-Memory, Practice.* Ed. Donald Bouchard. Ithaca, N.Y., 1977.

——. "L'homme est-il mort?" *Arts et loisirs* 38 (1966), 15–21.

——. "Nietzsche, Marx et Freud." In *Cahiers de Royaumont.* Paris, 1967.

——. *The Order of Things.* New York, 1970.

——. *Power/Knowledge: Selected Interviews and Other Writings, 1972–1977.* Ed. Colin Gordon. New York, 1980.

——. "Le retour de la morale." *Les nouvelles,* 28 June–5 July 1984, p. 40.

Gandillac, Maurice de. "Ambiguïté hégélienne." *Dieu vivant* 11 (1948).

Goldmann, Lucien. "Matérialisme dialectique et histoire de la philosophie." *RPFE* 138 (1948), 160–179.

Granier, Jean. "Nietzsche et la philosophie." *RPFE* 159, no. 1 (1969), 91–100.

Bibliography

Groethuysen, Bernard. *Anthropologie philosophique*. Paris, 1952.
——. *Introduction à la pensée philosophique allemande depuis Nietzsche*. Paris, 1926.
Guibert, Bernard. "Hegelianism in France." *Modern Schoolman* 26, no. 2 (January 1949), 173–177.
Hartmann, Nicolai. "Hegel et le problème de la dialectique du réel." *RMM* 38 3 (1931), 285–316.
Heidegger, Martin. *Basic Writings*. Ed. D. F. Krell. New York, 1977.
——. *Being and Time*. Trans. J. Macquarrie and E. Robinson. New York, 1962.
——. "Hegels Begriff der Erfahrung." In *Holzwege*. Frankfurt am Main, 1950.
——, and Ernst Cassirer. *Débat sur le kantisme et la philosophie (Davos, mars 1929)*. Trans. P. Aubenque, J. M. Fataud, and P. Quillet. Paris, 1972.
Herr, Lucien. "Fragments manuscrits d'un ouvrage sur Hegel." In *Choix d'é-crits de Lucien Herr*. Paris, 1932.
——. "Hegel." In *La grande encyclopédie*, vol. 19. Paris, 1932.
Kanapa, Jean. "Chronique philosophique." *La pensée* 17 (April 1948), 117–121.
——. *L'existentialisme n'est pas un humanisme*. Paris, 1947.
——. "Les interprètes de Hegel." *La pensée* 16 (February 1948), 117–121.
Klossowski, Pierre, *Nietzsche et le cercle vicieux*. Paris, 1969.
Konigson, M.-J. Mina. "Nietzsche et la philosophie." *Les études philosophiques* 51, no. 1 (1966), 61–77.
Koyre, Alexandre. "L'évolution philosophique de Martin Heidegger." *Critique* (1946); rpt. in *Etudes d'histoire de la pensée philosophique*. Paris, 1961. Hereafter *EHPP*.
——. "Hegel à Iéna." *Revue d'histoire et de philosophie religieuses* (1934); rpt. in *EHPP*, 247–289.
——. "Note sur la langue et la terminologie hégéliennes." *Revue philosophique* (1931); rpt. in *EHPP*, 191–224.
——. "Rapport sur l'état des études hégéliennes en France." *Verhandlungen des ersten Hegel-Congresses, La Haye, 1930* (1931); rpt. in *EHPP*, 225–251.
——. "Compte rendu: Dilthey, *Gesammelte Schriften*, Vol. VIII." *RPFE* 113 (January–June, 1932), 487–491.
Lacan, Jacques, *The Language of the Self*. Trans. A. Wilden. Baltimore, Md., 1968.
Lacroix, Jean. "Hegel et Marx." *Le monde*, October 27, 1947, p. 3.
Lefebvre, Henri. "Le marxisme et la pensée française." *TM* 137–138 (July–August 1957), 104–137.
Lévi-Strauss, Claude. "Histoire et dialectique." In *La pensée sauvage*. Paris, 1962.
Madaule, Jacques. "De l'histoire universelle à la promotion ouvrière." *Esprit* 15, no. 132 (April 1947), 681–689.
Marrou, Henri Irénée. "La philosophie de l'histoire." In *La philosophie au milieu du vingtième siècle: Chroniques, III*. Florence, 1958.
Matteucci, Nicola. "La philosophie politique et sociale en France." *La philosophie au milieu du vingtième siècle: Chroniques, III*. Florence, 1958.

Merleau-Ponty, Maurice. *Les aventures de la dialectique*. Paris, 1955.
——. "Eloge de la philosophie: Leçon inaugurale faite au Collège de France, 15 Janvier, 1953." Paris, 1953.
——. "L'existentialisme chez Hegel." In *Sens et non-sens*. Paris, 1948.
——. *Humanisme et terreur: Essai sur le problème communiste*. Paris, 1947.
——. "Les idées autour du marxisme." *Fontaine* nos. 48/49 (1946), 309–331.
——. "Machiavélisme et histoire." *Umanesimo e scienza politica; Atti del Congresso internationale di studi umanisti*. Milan, 1951.
——. "Marxisme et philosophie." In *Sens et non-sens*. Paris, 1948.
——. "La querelle de l'existentialisme." In *Sens et non-sens*. Paris, 1948.
——. *Phénoménologie de la perception*. Paris, 1945.
——. "Philosophie et non-philosophie depuis Hegel." *Textures* 8–9, 10–11 (1974), 83–129, 145–173.
Niel, Henri. "L'interprétation de Hegel." *Critique* 18 (November 1947), 426–437.
——. "Jaspers et le problème de la vérité." *Critique* 31 (December 1948), 1080–1091.
——. "Le matérialisme dialectique." *Critique* 29 (October 1948), 889–896.
——. *De la médiation dans la philosophie de Hegel*. Paris, 1946.
——. "Philosophie et histoire." *Revue internationale de philosophie* 8, no. 20 (1954), 283–294.
——. "Le témoignage posthume de Léon Brunschvicg." *Critique* 36 (May 1949), 412–421.
Patri, Aimé. "Dialectique du maître et de l'esclave." *Le contrat social* 5, no. 4 (July–August 1961), 231–235.
——. "Compte rendu de Kojève, *Introduction à la lecture de Hegel*." *Paru* 34 (September 1947), 98–99.
Picon, Pierre. "Compte rendu de Kojève, *Introduction à la lecture de Hegel*." *Fontaine* 10, no. 62 (October 1947).
Queneau, Raymond. "Premières confrontations avec Hegel." *Critique* 195–196 (August–September 1963), 694–700.
Rappaport, Charles. "La méthode marxiste." *La revue marxiste* 1 (1929), no. 1, 54–63, no. 2, 154–163, no. 3, 317–324, no. 5, 552–561.
Riquet, Michel. *Le Chrétien face au pouvoir, 1: Le maître et l'esclave*. Paris, 1949.
Sartre, Jean-Paul. *Critique de la raison dialectique*. Paris, 1960.
——. "Merleau-Ponty." In *Situations*. Trans. B. Eisler. Greenwich, Conn., 1965.
——. *L'être et le néant*. Paris, 1943.
——. *L'existentialisme est un humanisme*. Paris, 1946.
Stern, Alfred. "Le problème de l'absolutisme et du relativisme axiologique et la philosophie allemande." *Revue internationale de philosophie* 1 (1938–1939), 703–742.
Strauss, Leo. *The City and the Man*. Chicago, 1964.
——. "Comments on 'Der Begriff des Politischen' by Carl Schmitt." In *Spinoza's Critique of Religion*. New York, 1965.

Bibliography

——. *Natural Right and History.* Chicago, 1950.

——. "Political Philosophy and History." *Journal of the History of Ideas* 10, no. 1 (January 1949), 30–50.

——. "Preface to the English Edition." In *Spinoza's Critique of Religion.* New York, 1965.

——. "Restatement on Xenophon's *Hiero.*" In *On Tyranny.* Rev. and enl. ed. Glencoe, Ill., 1963.

——. *Thoughts on Machiavelli.* Chicago, 1958.

——. "What Is Political Philosophy?" In *What Is Political Philosophy?* Glencoe, Ill., 1959.

Taubes, Jacob. "On the Symbolic Order of Modern Democracy." *Confluence* 4, no. 1 (April 1955), 57–71.

——. "Review of Paul Tillich, *Love, Power, and Justice.*" *Journal of Religion* 35, no. 2 (April 1955), 99–100.

——. "Theology and Political Theory." *Social Research* 22, no. 2 (Spring 1955), 57–68.

Tosel, André. "Eric Weil." *Extrait des annales de la faculté des lettres et sciences humaines de Nice* 32 (1977), 9–12.

——. "The Meaning of Existence and History in the Thought of Eric Weil." *Dialectics and Humanism* 4 (1980).

Vermeil, Edmund. "La pensée politique de Hegel." *RMM* 38, no. 3 (1931), 441–510.

von Aster, Ernst. "De la philosophie allemande contemporaine." *RMM* 38, no. 2 (1931), 259–275.

Vuillemin, Jules. "La mort dans la philosophie de Hegel." *RPFE* 137 (1947), 194–202.

——. "Compte rendu de Kojève, *Introduction à la lecture de Hegel.*" *RPFE* 140 (1950), 198–200.

Waelhens, Alphonse de. "Conclusion." In *Phénoménologie et verité.* Paris, 1953.

——. "De la phénoménologie à l'existentialisme." In *Le choix, le monde et l'existence: Cahiers du Collège philosophique.* Paris, 1947.

Wahl, Jean. "A propos de *L'introduction à la Phénoménologie de Hegel* par A. Kojève." *Deucalion* 5, (October 1940), 80–99.

——. "Le Collège philosophique." In *Le choix, le monde et l'existence: Cahiers du Collège philosophique.* Paris, 1947.

——. "Gesammelte Abhandlungen." *RMM* 68, no. 3 (1963).

——. "Heidegger et Kierkegaard: Recherche des éléments originaux de la philosophie de Heidegger." *Recherches philosophiques* 2 (1932–1933), 347–370.

——. "Une interprétation de la *Logique* de Hegel." *Critique* 79 (December 1953), 1050–1071.

——. "Karl Jaspers en France." *Critique* 4 (1948), 523–530.

——. "Lettre-Préface." In Karl Jaspers, *Nietzsche.* Paris, 1950.

——. *Le malheur de la conscience dans la philosophie de Hegel.* Paris, 1929.

——. "Nietzsche et la mort de Dieu." *Acéphale*, January 1937, pp. 22–23.

——. "Nietzsche et la philosophie." *RMM* 68, no. 3 (1963), 352–379.

——. "Philosophie existentielle." In *La philosophie au milieu du vingtième siècle*, 2. Ed. R. Klibansky. Florence, 1958.

——. "Le rôle de A. Koyré dans le développement des études hégéliennes en France." *Hegel-Studien*, Supplement 3 (1964).

——. *Tableau de la philosophie française*. Paris, 1946.

——. "Vers le concret." In *Etudes d'histoire de philosophie contemporaine*. Paris, 1932.

Interpretative Material

Adorno, Theodor. *Negative Dialectics*. Trans. E. B. Ashton. New York, 1973.

Aillet, G. "Histoire et politique." *RMM* 43, no. 4 (1936), 603–627.

Alexander, Ian W. "The Phenomenological Philosophy in France. An Analysis of Its Themes, Significance and Implications." In *Sartre: A Collection of Critical Essays*. Ed. M. Warnock. Garden City, N.Y., 1971.

Althusser, Louis. *For Marx*. Trans. B. Brewster. New York, 1970.

——. *Lenin and Philosophy and Other Essays*. Trans. B. Brewster. London, 1971.

Arendt, Hannah. *The Life of the Mind*, vol. 2: *Willing*. New York, 1978.

——. "Walter Benjamin: 1892–1940." Introduction to Benjamin, *Illuminations*. New York, 1968.

Armengaud, André. "La démographie française de XXᶜ siècle." In *Histoire économique et sociale de la France*, book 4, vol. 2. Paris, 1980.

Aronson, Ronald. *Jean-Paul Sartre: Philosophy in the World*. London, 1980.

Asveld, Paul. "Zum Referat von Walter Bimel über die Phänomenologie des Geistes und die Hegelrenaissance in Frankreich." *Hegel-Studien*, supplement 2 (1974), 657–664.

Avineri, Schlomo. "Hegel Revisited." In *Hegel: A Collection of Critical Essays*. New York, 1972.

——. *Hegel's Theory of the Modern State*. Cambridge, 1972.

Axelos, Kostas. "Y a-t-il une philosophie marxiste?" In *Vers la pensée planétaire*. Paris, 1964.

Balakian, Anna. *Literary Origins of Surrealism: A New Mysticism in French Poetry*. New York, 1947.

——. *Surrealism: The Road to the Absolute*. New York, 1959.

Beaufret, Jean. "Heidegger et la question de l'histoire." In *Dialogue avec Heidegger*, 3. Paris, 1974.

Besnier, Jean-Michel. "Bataille: Le système (de l')impossible." *Esprit* 38 (1980), 148–164.

Bimel, Walter. "Die Phänomenologie des Geistes und die Hegel-Renaissance in Frankreich." *Hegel-Studien*, Supplement 2 (1974), 643–655.

Blanchot, Maurice. *L'entretien infini*. Paris, 1969.

Bodel, Remo. "Foucault: Pouvoir, politique et maîtrise de soi." *Critique* nos. 471–472 (1986), 898–917.

Bibliography

Boirel, René. *Brunschvicg: Sa vie son oeuvre.* Paris, 1964.

Boudot, Pierre. *Nietzsche et l'au-delà de la liberté: Nietzsche et les écrivains français de 1930 à 1960.* Paris, 1960.

Bourdieu, Pierre. *Homo academicus.* Paris, 1984.

——. *Leçon sur la leçon.* Paris, 1982.

——, and Jean-Claude Passeron. "Sociology and Philosophy in France since 1945: Death and Resurrection of a Philosophy without Subject." *Social Research* 34, no. 1 (Spring 1967), 162–212.

Breazeale, Daniel. "The Hegel-Nietzsche Problem." In *Nietzsche Studien,* vol. 4 (1975), 146–164.

Burgelin, Pierre. "Existentialism and the Tradition of French Thought." *Yale French Studies* 16 (1955–1956), 103–105.

Butler, Judith. "Geist est Zeit: French Interpretations of Hegel's Absolute." *Berkshire Review* 21 (1985), 66–80.

Canguilhem, Georges. "Sur l'*Histoire de la folie* en tant qu'événement." *débat* 41 (1986), 37–40.

Caron, François, and Jean Bouvier, "Guerre, crise, guerre." In *Histoire économique et sociale de la France,* book 4, vol. 2. Paris 1980.

Caute, David. *Communism and the French Intellectuals.* New York, 1964.

Chartier, Roger. "Intellectual History, or Sociocultural History? The French Trajectories." In *Modern European Intellectual History: Reappraisals and New Perspectives.* Ed. D. LaCapra and S. Kaplan. Ithaca, N.Y., 1982.

Châtelet, François. *Chronique des idées perdues.* Paris, 1977.

——. "La question de l'histoire de la philosophie aujourd'hui." In *Politiques de la philosophie.* Paris, 1976.

Clarke, Simon. *The Foundations of Structuralism: A Critique of Lévi-Strauss and the Structuralist Movement.* Totowa, N.J., 1981.

Clemens, Eric. "L'histoire (comme) inachèvement." *RMM* 76, 2 (1971), 206–225.

Dagognet, François. "Vie et théorie de la vie selon Jean Hyppolite." In *Hommage à Jean Hyppolite.* Paris, 1971.

Daumard, Adeline. "La bourgeoisie française au temps des épreuves (1914–1950)." In *Histoire économique et sociale de la France,* book 4, vol. 2. Paris, 1980.

Delacampagne, Christian. "De la génération existentialiste à la génération structuraliste." *Le monde,* 4 May 1979, p. 22.

Descombes, Vincent. "Le besoin de philosophie." *Débats* 4 (1980), 22–24.

——. *Le même et l'autre: Quarante-cinq ans de philosophie française (1933–1978).* Paris, 1979.

——. "Le mots de la tribu." *Critique* 41, no. 456 (May 1985), 418–444.

Donzelot, Jacques. "L'appréhension du temps." *Critique* 38, 417 (February 1982), 97–119.

Doumit, Elie. "Etat et société moderne dans la *Philosophie politique.*" *Archives de philosophie* 33, no. 3 (1970), 511–526.

Dreyfus, Hubert L. "Holism and Hermeneutics." *Review of Metaphysics* 34, no. 1 (September 1980), 3–23.

——, and Paul Rabinow. *Michel Foucault: Beyond Structuralism and Hermeneutics.* 2d ed. Chicago, 1983.

Eskin, Jean-Claude. "Critique de l'humanisme vertueux." *Esprit* 66 (1982), 7–19.

Ferry, Luc, and Alain Renault. *La pensée 68: Essai sur l'anti-humanisme contemporain.* Paris, 1985.

——. *Système et critique: Essais sur la critique de la raison dans la philosophie contemporaine.* Brussels, 1984.

——, et al., "Y-at-il une pensée 68?" *débats* 39 (1986), 31–54.

Fetscher, Iring. "Hegel in Frankreich." *Antares: Französische Hefte für Kunst, Literatur und Wissenschaft* 3 (1953), 3–15.

——. "Individu et communauté dans la philosophie de Hegel." *Actes du XIeme Congrès international de philosophie*, vol. 13 (1953), 125–130.

——. "Vorwort des Herausgebers." In Alexandre Kojève, *Hegel: Eine Vergegenwartigung seines Denkens.* Stuttgart, 1958.

Fohlem, Claude. *La France de l'entre-deux-guerres.* Paris, 1972.

Fraser, Nancy. "Foucault on Modern Power: Empirical Insights and Normative Confusions." *Praxis International* 1 (1981), 272–287.

——. "Michel Foucault: A 'Young Conservative'?" *Ethics* 96, no. 1 (1985), 165–184.

Gans, Eric. "Méditation kojèvienne sur la critique littéraire." *Critique* no. 294 (November 1971), 1009–1017.

Gillespie, Michael Allen. *Hegel, Heidegger and the Ground of History.* Chicago, 1984.

Goldmann, Lucien. *Lukács et Heidegger.* Ed. M. Ishaghpour. Paris, 1973.

Goudsblom, Johan. *Nihilism and Culture.* Oxford, 1960, 1980.

Gourevitch, Victor. "Philosophy and Politics." *Review of Metaphysics* 22, nos. 1, 2 (September, December 1968), 58–84, 281–328.

Graham, Gordon. "Can There Be History of Philosophy?" *History and Theory* 21, no. 1 (1982), 37–52.

Greimas, A. J. "Structure et histoire." *TM* 22, no. 246 (November 1966), 815–827.

Habermas, Jürgen. *Der philosophische Diskurs der Moderne: Zwolfe Vorslesungen.* Frankfurt am Main, 1985.

Heckman, John. "Hyppolite and the Hegel Revival in France." *Telos* 16 (Summer 1973).

——. Introduction to English translation of *Genèse et structure de la Phénoménologie de l'esprit de Hegel.* Evanston, Ill., 1974.

Hegel, G. W. F. *Aesthetics: Lectures on Fine Art.* Trans. T. M. Knox. Oxford, 1975.

——. *Lectures on the History of Philosophy.* Trans. E. S. Haldans. New York, 1965.

——. *Lectures on the Philosophy of History.* Trans. J. Sibree. New York, 1956.

——. *Logic.* Trans. W. Wallace. Oxford, 1975.

——. *The Phenomenology of Spirit.* Trans. A. V. Miller. Oxford, 1977. Trans. into French Jean Hyppolite. Paris, 1939, 1941.

Bibliography

——. *Philosophy of Right.* Trans. T. M. Knox. Oxford, 1967.

Hondt, Jacques d'. "Hegel en France, aujourd'hui." Unpublished manuscript, 1981.

——. *Hegel et l'hégélianisme.* Paris, 1982.

——. "Hegel et l'idéologie française." *Dialogue* (Montreal, 1971), rpt. in the author's *De Hegel à Marx.* Paris, 1972.

——. "In memoriam—Jean Hyppolite." *Etudes philosophiques* 1 (1969), 87–92.

——. "Première vue française sur Hegel et Schelling (1804)." *Hegel-Studien,* supplement 20.

Houlgate, Stephen. *Hegel, Nietzsche and the Criticism of Metaphysics.* Cambridge 1986.

Hoy, David C., ed. *Foucault: A Critical Reader.* New York, 1986.

Hughes, H. Stuart. *The Obstructed Path: French Social Thought in the Years of Depression, 1930–1960.* New York, 1966.

Husserl, Edmund. *Cartesian Meditations: Introduction to Phenomenology.* Trans. D. Cairns. The Hague, 1969.

——. *The Crisis of the European Sciences and Transcendental Phenomenology.* Trans. D. Carr. Evanston, Ill., 1970.

Ilting, K. H. "The Structure of Hegel's *Philosophy of Right.*" In *Hegel's Political Philosophy.* Ed. Z. A. Pelcyzunski. Cambridge, 1971.

Jameson, Fredric. *Marxism and Form.* Princeton, N.J., 1971.

——. *The Political Unconscious: Narrative as a Socially Symbolic Act.* Ithaca, N.Y., 1981.

Jay, Martin. *Marxism and Totality: The Adventures of a Concept from Lukács to Habermas.* Berkeley, Calif., 1984.

——. "Should Intellectual History Take a Linguistic Turn? Reflections on the Habermas-Gademer Debate." In *Modern European Intellectual History: Reappraisals and New Perspectives.* Ed. D. LaCapra and S. Kaplan. Ithaca, N.Y., 1982.

Kainz, Howard. *Hegel's Phenomenology, Part I: Analysis and Commentary.* Montgomery, Ala., 1976.

Kelly, George Armstrong. *Idealism, Politics and History: Sources of Hegelian Thought.* Cambridge, 1969.

Kirschner, Gilbert. "Absolu et sens dans la *Logique de la philosophie.*" *Archives de philosophie* 33, no. 3 (1970), 373–400.

——. "Eric Weil: La philosophie comme logique de la philosophie." *Cahiers philosophiques* 8 (September 1981), 25–69.

Kline, George L. "The Existentialist Rediscovery of Hegel and Marx." In *Sartre: A Collection of Critical Essays.* Ed. M. Warnock. Garden City, N.Y., 1971.

Knox, T. M. "Hegel and Prussianism." *Philosophy* 15, no. 57 (January 1940).

Koestler, Arthur. *Darkness at Noon.* New York, 1941.

Kurzweil, Edith. *The Age of Structuralism: Lévi-Strauss to Foucault.* New York, 1980.

LaCapra, Dominick. "Rethinking Intellectual History and Reading Texts." *History and Theory* 19 (1980), 245–276.

——. "Review of Fredric Jameson, *The Political Unconscious.*" *History and Theory* 21 (1982), 83–106.

Lacoue-Labarthe, Philippe, and Jean-Luc Nancy, eds. *Retrait du politique.* Paris, 1981.

Lacroix, Jean. "Hyppolite et Hegel." *Le monde,* 21–22 May 1972, pp. 21–22.

——. "La mort d'Eric Weil. Une philosophie de la raison." *Le monde,* 4 February 1977, p. 12.

Lefebvre, Henri. *La fin de l'histoire: Epilégomènes.* Paris, 1970.

——. *La somme et le reste.* Paris, 1959.

——. *Les temps des méprises.* Paris, 1975.

Lefort, Claude. "Maurice Merleau-Ponty." *Institut international de philosophie,* vol. 3. Florence, 1969.

Lichtheim, George. *Marxism in Modern France.* New York, 1966.

——. "Review of *On Tyranny.*" *Commentary,* November 1963, pp. 412–416.

Lukács, Georg. *The Young Hegel: Studies in the Relations between Dialectics and Economics.* Trans. R. Livingstone. Cambridge, 1966.

Lyotard, Jean-François, *La condition postmoderne: Rapport sur le savoir.* Paris, 1979.

——. *Le différend.* Paris 1983.

——. "Réponse à la question: Qu'est-ce que le post-moderne?" *Critique* 419 (1982).

——. *Tombeau de l'intellectuel et autres papiers.* Paris, 1984.

Macherey, Pierre. "Aux sources de l'*Histoire de la folie:* Une rectification et ses limites." *Critique* nos. 471–472 (1986), 753–774.

Megill, Allan. *Prophets of Extremity: Nietzsche, Heidegger, Foucault, Derrida.* Berkeley, Calif., 1985.

Nadeau, Maurice. *Histoire du surréalisme.* Paris, 1964.

Norton, Theodore Mills. "Line of Flight: Gilles Deleuze, or Political Science Fiction." *New Political Science* 15 (1986), 77–93.

O'Brien, George Dennis. *Hegel on Reason and History: A Contemporary Interpretation.* Chicago, 1975.

Pecora, Vincent. "Deleuze's Nietzsche and Post-Structuralist Thought." *SubStance* 48 (1986), 34–50.

Pelcyznski, Z. A. "The Hegelian Conception of the State." In *Hegel's Political Philosophy: Problems and Perspectives.* Cambridge. 1971.

Pitkethly, Laurence. "Hegel in Modern France (1900–1950)." Diss., University of London, 1978.

Poster, Mark. *Existential Marxism in Postwar France: From Sartre to Althusser.* Princeton, N.J., 1975.

——. *Foucault, Marxism and History: Mode of Production vs. Mode of Information.* New York, 1985.

"Qu'est-ce qu'une critique de la raison?" Table Ronde. *Esprit* 64 (1982), 89–111.

Raynaud, Philippe. "Le destin de la philosophie kantienne." *Commentaire* 7, no. 26 (1984), 278–283.

Bibliography

Regnier, Marcel. "Hegelianism and Marxism." *Social Research* 34, no. 1 (Spring 1967), 31–46.

Rickert, Heinrich. *Die Grenzen der naturwissenschaftlichen Begriftsbildung.* Tübingen, 1929.

Richir, Marc. "La fin de l'histoire: Notes préliminaires sur la pensée politique de Georges Bataille." *Textures* 6 (1970), 41–47.

Ricoeur, Paul. "La 'philosophie politique' d'Eric Weil." *Esprit* 25, no. 10 (October 1957), 412–428.

——. "Le paradoxe politique." *Esprit* 25, no. 5 (May 1957), 721–745.

——. *Temps et récit,* vol. 1 Paris, 1983.

Riley, Patrick. "Introduction to the Reading of Alexandre Kojève." *Political Theory* 9, no. 1 (February 1981), 5–48.

Rorty, Richard. *Consequences of Pragmatism: Essays, 1972–1980.* Minneapolis, Minn., 1982.

——. "Le cosmopolitisme sans émancipation: En réponse à Jean-François Lyotard." *Critique* no. 456 (1985), 567–480.

——. "Habermas, Lyotard et la postmodernité." *Critique* no. 442 (1984), 181–197.

——. *Philosophy and the Mirror of Nature.* Princeton, N.J., 1980.

——. "A Reply to Dreyfus and Taylor." *Review of Metaphysics* 34, no. 1 (September 1980), 39–46.

Rosen, Stanley. *Nihilism: A Philosophical Essay.* New Haven, Conn., 1969.

——. "Review of Kojève, *Essai d'une histoire raisonnée de la philosophie païenne, I, Les présocratiques.*" *Man and World* 3, no. 1 (1970), 120–125.

Roth, Michael S. "Foucault's 'History of the Present.' " *History and Theory* 20, no. 1 (1981), 32–46.

——. "Note on Kojève's *Phénoménologie du droit.*" *Political Theory* 11, no. 3 (August 1983).

——. "A Problem of Recognition: Alexandre Kojève and the End of History." *History and Theory* 24, no. 3 (1985), 293–306.

Rubin, William S. *Dada, Surrealism and Their Heritage.* New York, 1968.

Salvadori, Roberto. *Hegel in Francia: Filosofia e politica nella cultura francese del novecento.* Paris, 1974.

Schact, Richard. "Hegel on Freedom." In *Hegel: A Collection of Critical Essays.* Ed. A. MacIntyre. New York, 1972.

Schalk, David. *The Spectrum of Political Engagement: Mournier, Benda, Nizan, Brasillach, Sartre.* Princeton, N.J., 1979.

——. "Hegel's *Phenomenology*: An Elegy for Hellas." In *Hegel's Political Writings.* Ed. Z. A. Pelcyznski. Cambridge, 1971.

Shiner, Larry. "Reading Foucault: Anti-Method and the Genealogy of Power-Knowledge." *History and Theory* 21 (1982), 382–298.

Shklar, Judith. *Freedom and Independence: A Study of the Political Ideas of Hegel's "Phenomenology of Mind."* Cambridge, 1976.

Short, Robert S. "The Politics of Surrealism, 1920–1936." *Journal of Contemporary History* 1, no. 2 (1966), 3–25.

Siegel, Martin. "Henri Berr's *Revue de synthèse historique.*" *History and Theory* 9, no. 3 (1970), 322–334.

Smith, John H. "U-topian Hegel: Dialectic and Its Other in Poststructuralism." *German Quarterly* 60, no. 2 (Spring 1987), 237–261.

Stoianovich, Traian. *French Historical Method: The Annales Paradigm.* Ithaca, N.Y., 1976.

Taylor, Charles. "Foucault on Freedom and Truth." *Political Theory* 12, no. 2 (1984), 152–183.

——. *Hegel.* Cambridge, 1975.

Tran-Duc-Thao. "La *Phénoménologie de l'esprit* et son contenu réel." *TM* 36 (1948), 493–519.

Thompson, E. P. *The Poverty of Theory.* London, 1978.

Veyne, Paul. "Le dernier Foucault et sa morale." *Critique* nos. 471–472 (1986), 933–941.

Vogt, W. Paul. "Identifying Scholarly and Intellectual Communities: A Note on French Philosophy, 1900–1939." *History and Theory* 21, no. 2 (November 1982), 266–278.

White, Hayden. *Metahistory.* Baltimore, Md., 1973.

——. "Method and Ideology in Intellectual History: The Case of Henry Adams." In *Modern European Intellectual History: Reappraisals and New Perspectives.* Ed. D. LaCapra and S. Kaplan. Ithaca, N.Y., 1982.

——. *Tropics of Discourse.* Baltimore, Md., 1978.

——. "The Value of Narrativity in the Representation of Reality." In *On Narrative.* Ed. W. J. T. Mitchell. Chicago, 1981.

Young, William. *Hegel's Dialectical Method.* New York, 1972.

Zeldin, Theodore. *France, 1848–1945: Intellect and Pride.* Oxford, 1977, 1980.

Index

Index

Index

Index

Index

Index

Index

Library of Congress Cataloging-in-Publication Data

Roth, Michael S., 1957–
  Knowing and history.

   Bibliography: p.
   Includes index.
    1. History—Philosophy. 2. Hegel, Georg Wilhelm Friedrich, 1770–
1831—Influence. 3. Hyppolite, Jean. 4. Kojève, Alexandre, 1902–
1968. 5. Weil, Eric. 6. Philosophy, French—20th century. I. Title.
D16.9.R68 1988   901   87–47870
ISBN 0–8014–2136–5 (alk. paper)